DOS® 6 *Running* Start

ALAN SIMPSON

toExcel
San Jose New York Lincoln Shanghai

DOS® 6 Running Start

This edition published by arrangement with toExcel,
a strategic unit of Kaleidoscope Software, Inc.

For information address:
iUniverse.com, Inc.
620 North 48th Street
Suite 201
Lincoln, NE 68504-3467
www.iuniverse.com

ISBN: 1- 58348 - 214 - 8

Library of Congress Catalog Card Number: 99-61425

To Susan, Ashley, and Alec Simpson

ACKNOWLEDGMENTS

My sincere thanks to the many people who helped create this book. On the authorial side, I'm grateful to Ellen Thro and Neweleen Trebnik who assembled and formatted my initial manuscript; to Elizabeth Olson, who updated the initial manuscript, wrote new material, and shaped everything into the final product you're reading now; and to Martha Mellor, who managed the entire project as it passed through many hands.

The SYBEX team included Sharon Crawford who helped develop the concept; Sarah Wadsworth, whose unerring editorial talents smoothed out all the rough edges; Kurt Hampe, whose scrupulous technical editing and suggestions kept me honest; Ann Dunn, who typeset the book; Cuong Le, who produced the screen graphics; Charlotte Carter, who fashioned text and graphics into this very presentable volume; and Carolina Montilla, who, with her sharp proofreader's eye, helped iron out the wrinkles.

And, as always, my thanks to all the gang at Waterside Productions for keeping my writing career moving ever forward.

TABLE *of* CONTENTS

PART II ALPHABETICAL REFERENCE

INTRODUCTION

DOS 6 Running Start shows you how to use the most important features of DOS 6, especially the new capabilities that make your computer easier to use and more efficient than ever. Several of these new features can save you considerable money—far more than the modest cost of upgrading to DOS 6.

You can use this book in two ways: First as a tutorial, to get you working productively in the DOS environment; and then as a concise reference guide to the most important DOS features. You'll get the most out of this book if you're new to DOS 6, but not an absolute beginner with personal computers.

Part I offers ten easy lessons:

Lesson 1: *Start the Engines* explains what DOS is, three ways to use it, how to start your computer, what's new in DOS 6, and why you should upgrade from older versions of DOS.

Lesson 2: *DOS Shell: The Easy Way to Use DOS* shows you how to use the DOS Shell to work with files, run programs, and issue DOS commands. The DOS Shell provides a graphical environment that's easier to use than the bare-bones commands for which DOS is infamous.

Lesson 3: *Using the DOS Command Prompt and Online Help* teaches you how to use the DOS command prompt, get online help from DOS, and understand the command syntax shown in DOS Help and in the reference entries in Part II of this book. You'll also learn how to look at files and redirect input and output of commands.

Lesson 4: *Managing Your Files and Directories* explains how to climb the DOS directory tree, use wildcards in file names, work with directories, and copy, move, rename, and delete files and directories using the DOS Shell or the DOS command line.

Lesson 5: *Keeping the Wolves at Bay: Avoiding Disaster* covers essential techniques for preventing data loss on your computer. You'll learn how to check disks for errors, use new DOS 6 Backup and Undelete features, format and unformat disks, and use Anti-Virus programs to protect your computer from potentially disastrous virus attacks.

Lesson 6: *Squeezing the Most from Your Hard Disk* shows you how to use two new DOS 6 programs, DoubleSpace and MS-DOS Defragmenter, to coax extra space from even the most cluttered hard disk. If you've ever been tempted to buy a new hard disk, check out this lesson first.

Lesson 7: *Thank You for the Memory* answers the questions you were afraid to ask about how DOS uses memory, shows you a quick and painless way to optimize memory with the new MemMaker program, and explains how to use the SMARTDrive program to speed up your hard disk.

Lesson 8: *Smarter Startup Configurations and Batch Programs* focuses on new features that let you customize your system's startup configuration and build "smart" batch programs that can make choices. This lesson also shows you how to use the DOS Editor to create, change, and print text files.

Lesson 9: *Transferring Files and Using a Laptop* explains how to connect two computers and share their files and printers. Lesson 9 also covers a new feature that conserves battery storage on laptop computers.

Lesson 10: *Staying out of Trouble* offers a practical guide to learning new programs quickly and easily and avoiding panic when things go wrong. Lesson 10 also presents an alphabetical listing of many DOS error messages and tells you what to do if they appear.

These lessons have been structured so that you can try out the examples on your own computer. However, you don't need to follow along at your computer in order to get the essential information from the lessons. New users will especially appreciate the strong foundation in DOS terminology and concepts provided in Lessons 1 through 4 and Lesson 10. Experienced users who are upgrading to DOS 6 can come up to speed with new features quickly by working through Lessons 5 through 9.

Part II of this book is a concise alphabetical reference to commands that you can type at the command prompt, place in batch programs, or use in the CONFIG.SYS startup file. In each entry you'll find detailed command syntax, a description of options, practical examples, and special tips. The goal is to give you a *running start* with DOS 6.

PART I

STEP-BY-STEP TUTORIAL

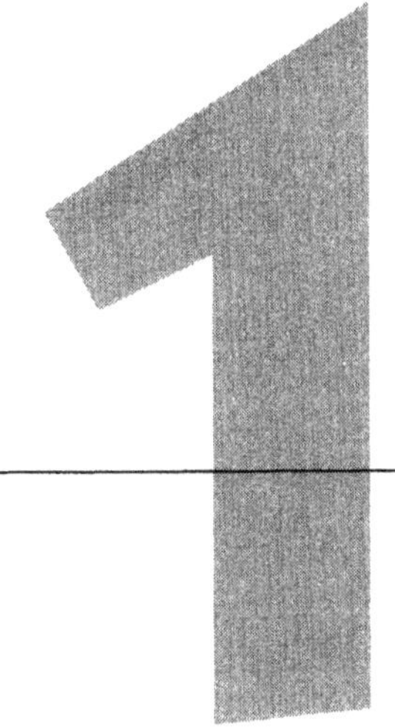

Start the Engines

INTRODUCING

What is DOS?

The DOS command prompt, DOS Shell, and Windows

Booting your computer

New features of DOS 6

Advantages of upgrading

In this lesson you'll learn what DOS is for, why you might want to upgrade to DOS 6 (the latest version of DOS), and how to boot (start up) your computer. You'll also learn about two important files—CONFIG.SYS and AUTOEXEC.BAT—that DOS uses to find out which hardware components are active on your system and to set up the initial "look and feel" of your computer.

WHAT IS DOS?

DOS is an acronym for Disk Operating System, the set of programs that manages the flow of information to and from the various parts of your computer system. When using an application program, such as WordPerfect, Microsoft Word, Lotus 1-2-3, Microsoft Excel, dBASE, or Paradox, you may be completely unaware of DOS and may never need to use it directly. Nevertheless, DOS is operating in the background, handling tasks such as managing files and directories, starting programs, maintaining disks, configuring and managing hardware, optimizing memory, speeding up programs, and customizing your computer. The lessons and reference section in this book explain how to use DOS to accomplish these tasks.

Many application programs offer file management capabilities that shield you from DOS to some extent. However, these programs still need DOS to run.

THE THREE FACES OF DOS

Once you install DOS (see Appendix A), you'll typically use it from the DOS command prompt, the DOS Shell, or Windows. In the sections that follow, I'll briefly introduce each of these alternatives.

THE DOS COMMAND PROMPT

The DOS command prompt provides a quick and powerful way to use DOS—although it's not the most user-friendly approach. Typically, it looks like this:

```
C>
```

or like this:

```
C:\>
```

Whenever the command prompt appears on your screen, you can type a DOS command and press the ↵ key (Enter). As soon as you press ↵, DOS attempts to carry out your request. Lesson 3 and the reference portion of this book focus on commands that you enter at the DOS command prompt.

Throughout this book, I'll use the symbol ↵ to represent the Enter key on your keyboard.

THE DOS SHELL

The DOS Shell provides an easy-to-use, visually-oriented way for you to work with many DOS commands, especially those that manage files and directories and run programs. DOS Shell commands are listed on menus, and you can select them easily using either the keyboard or a mouse. Lesson 2 explains how to use the DOS Shell.

WINDOWS

Windows is a powerful graphical environment that provides all the capabilities of the DOS Shell and much more. As with the Shell, commands are listed on menus and can be selected with the keyboard or a mouse. Figure 1.1 shows how your computer screen might look when you first open Windows. Although this book doesn't cover Windows specifically, I will mention it from time to time. For more information on Windows, please refer to the documentation that comes with your Windows package, my own *Windows 3.1 Running Start*, or any other introductory book on Windows.

If Windows is installed on your computer, you can usually start it by typing **win** *at the command prompt and pressing ↵.*

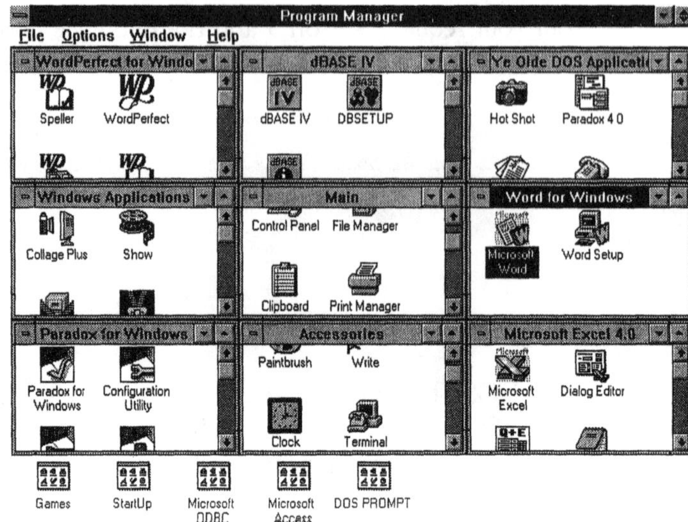

FIGURE 1.1: A typical Windows screen

GIVING YOUR COMPUTER THE BOOT

The process of starting your computer is called *booting*. Typically, you'll start your computer at the beginning of the day and leave it on until you're done at the day's end. At that time, you'll exit any programs you're running (the techniques you'll use to exit will vary from program to program), return to the DOS command prompt, and turn off the power.

TO BOOT OR NOT TO BOOT

Many users are tempted to restart or *reboot* the computer at the first sign of trouble. Generally, this is not a good idea, even if the system appears to be "locked up." Rebooting while a program is running can damage your data, especially if you're in the middle of updating a file or a group of files when you decide to reboot.

Frequently, you'll be tempted to reboot when your system isn't locked up at all. You're simply unsure of what to do next, or perhaps the operation you're performing is a bit slow. Before hitting the panic button, learn how to bail out of the program gracefully (often you'll need to press a function key or the Esc key). In fact, before doing any serious work with a new program, you should at least learn how to use the program's Help feature and find out how to exit the program properly. You should also get in the habit of watching the screen for any prompts or other clues about what to do next.

On rare occasions, your computer software really will lock up due to a "bug"—caused either by a programming error or a hardware problem. In these cases, your only alternative may be to reboot.

DOING A WARM BOOT

If you must reboot your system, you have two options: a warm boot or a cold boot. A warm boot is "gentler" and often quicker because the computer stays powered on during the procedure. To perform a warm boot, press the key combination Ctrl+Alt+Del. To use this key combination, hold down the Ctrl key, then hold down the Alt key, then hold down the Del key. Release all three keys after the screen clears and the computer restarts.

DOING A COLD BOOT

If a warm boot doesn't seem to clear up the problem completely, you can perform a cold boot. To do so, turn off the power, preferably using the switch on your computer's surge protector. Wait until the computer's hard disk has stopped rotating (counting to 30 slowly should do it), then turn the power on again.

Surge protectors provide inexpensive insurance against damage to your computer's electronic components and data in case of power fluctuations. To save wear and tear on your computer's power supply switch, use the switch on the surge protector to furnish power to the machine during a cold boot.

WHAT HAPPENS AT STARTUP?

When you start the computer (either with a cold or warm boot), the system performs a self-check, then loads certain DOS commands into memory from a file named COMMAND.COM. If you've compressed your disk drives with DoubleSpace, the hidden file named DBLSPACE.BIN (see Lesson 6), which provides access to your compressed drives, is loaded as well. Next, two special files, CONFIG.SYS and AUTOEXEC.BAT, are executed to determine the startup configuration and preferences for your computer.

Never modify, rename, or delete COMMAND.COM *or* DBLSPACE.BIN. *Also, avoid changing or deleting* CONFIG.SYS *or* AUTOEXEC.BAT *unless you thoroughly understand the effects of doing so.*

Many application programs also have their own startup or initialization files that contain commands specific to the application. When you open the application, its initialization files run automatically.

DOS commands that are in memory are called internal commands; *they are available at all times. Commands that are located on the disk and must be loaded into memory when you need them are called* external commands.

UNDERSTANDING CONFIG.SYS

The CONFIG.SYS file contains special commands that configure your computer's hardware components so that DOS and application programs can use them. It also defines how much memory is available and how it is to be managed. A typical CONFIG.SYS file looks like this:

```
device=c:\dos\himem.sys
device=c:\dos\emm386.exe noems highscan
buffers=30,0
files=40
```

In the example above, the first command loads the extended memory manager, HIMEM.SYS, which coordinates the use of your computer's extended memory. The next command loads the program EMM386.EXE, which uses the computer's extended memory to provide expanded memory support. The third command allocates memory for disk buffers, and the last command defines the number of files that DOS can access at one time.

Disk buffers hold data in memory temporarily while data is read from or written to disk. Extended and expanded memory are discussed in Lesson 7. CONFIG.SYS commands are discussed in Lesson 8.

Frequently used CONFIG.SYS commands include DEVICE, BUFFERS, and FILES. Though most commands can be located anywhere in the file, the order of the DEVICE commands is important, and it's a good idea to list them before any other commands (see Lesson 8).

You can change your CONFIG.SYS file by adding and defining any of its specialized commands. Simply load the file into the DOS Editor or another text editor, then enter the command, the = sign, and the value. Lesson 8 explains how to use the Editor and provides details about customizing CONFIG.SYS and AUTOEXEC.BAT.

The DOS MemMaker and DoubleSpace utilities and the setup programs for many application programs and hardware devices add commands to your CONFIG.SYS and AUTOEXEC.BAT files automatically, so you may never need to bother with this yourself.

UNDERSTANDING AUTOEXEC.BAT

The AUTOEXEC.BAT file, which is executed immediately after the CONFIG.SYS file, normally contains your own customized startup procedures to load programs automatically, display messages, and specify where DOS should search for commands that aren't already in memory. AUTOEXEC.BAT is a type of executable file called a *batch program*. A minimal (but useful) example of an AUTOEXEC.BAT file appears below:

```
@echo off
prompt $p$g
path c:\dos;c:\windows;c:\
doskey
```

The first command above, @ECHO OFF, hides the text of the AUTOEXEC.BAT batch program as it is running. Next, the PROMPT command defines the appearance of the DOS prompt. The PATH command tells DOS where to search for executable files and batch programs, and finally, the DOSKEY command invokes the DOSKEY program, which allows you to recall DOS commands typed recently, edit the command line, and define and run small programs called *macros*.

You'll learn how to create and maintain the AUTOEXEC.BAT batch program using the DOS Editor in Lesson 8.

WHAT'S NEW IN DOS 6?

DOS 6 retains the Shell (graphic interface) from DOS 5, as well as the traditional DOS directory and file organization, and the commands and utilities from earlier versions that are useful for today's computer systems. DOS 6 also provides new or improved features for systems that include hard disks, laptop computers, or Microsoft Windows. These features include

- More efficient use of your hard disk, including disk compression with DoubleSpace and defragmenting of hard disk files with MS-DOS Defragmenter (see Lesson 6).
- Improved memory use for 80386 or higher computers with MemMaker (described in Lesson 7).
- Expanded user control of system configuration. You can define multiple system configurations in the CONFIG.SYS file and select one when starting your computer. You also have better control of system startup commands. For example, the ability to bypass startup commands can help you pinpoint and solve system problems. Lessons 8 and 10 cover these capabilities.

- Support for laptop computers. Interlnk makes it easier to transfer files between a laptop and a desktop computer, while a new POWER program conserves laptop battery power (see Lesson 9).
- Virus protection. The new Microsoft Anti-Virus program can identify viruses, remove them, and protect your system from contracting viruses in the future. A version for Windows is also included (see Lesson 5).
- Improved file recovery. UNDELETE, UNFORMAT, and BACKUP (MSBACKUP) let you recover data from accidentally deleted files and formatted disks, and from floppy or hard disk backup volumes. UNDELETE and BACKUP are also available for Windows (see Lesson 5).
- More flexible batch programs. The new CHOICE command allows users to respond to questions and make choices while a batch program is running (see Lesson 8).
- Easier file management from the command prompt. Two new commands, MOVE and DELTREE, allow you to move files to new locations or disks, rename directories, and delete directories and subdirectories easily (see Lesson 4).
- Improved and expanded Help available from the command prompt (see Lesson 3).

SHOULD I UPGRADE?

If you're happy with your current version of DOS, particularly if your processor is an 80286 or earlier, you may not need to upgrade to DOS 6. This is also the case if you use DOS mainly for basic file management tasks, such as copying and deleting files, or if you use other programs, such as Microsoft Windows and WordPerfect's List Files, for file management.

However, there's a good chance you'll want to be able to configure your system to your own needs and make the system work as efficiently as possible—without having to tweak the configuration files manually or buy additional special-purpose programs. So if your hard disk always seems too small, if you'd like to have more memory available with your existing system, if you wish your computer would run faster, if you want to connect quickly to a laptop, or if you'd like protection against computer viruses, you would do well to upgrade to DOS 6. Its new features are designed to make it easy to configure and optimize your system, without having to increase your investment in hardware or software.

SUMMARY

In this lesson you've learned what DOS is, what it looks like, how to restart (boot) your computer, and what happens when you do so. You've also learned about four important files—COMMAND.COM, DBLSPACE.BIN, CONFIG.SYS, and AUTOEXEC.BAT—which are read when the computer is started. And, finally, you've seen what's new in DOS 6 and why you might want to upgrade.

REFERENCE ENTRIES

For additional information, see the following entries in the Alphabetical Reference:

- COMMAND
- DOSKEY
- EDIT
- PATH
- PROMPT

*D*OS SHELL: THE EASY WAY TO USE DOS

INTRODUCING

Using the DOS Shell windows and menus

Opening programs and files

Creating program items and program groups

Getting help from the Shell

Exiting the Shell

In this lesson you'll learn how to use the DOS Shell, which lets you work with files, run programs, and issue DOS commands in a graphical environment without exiting DOS.

STARTING THE SHELL

Starting DOS 6 couldn't be easier. If it's installed on a hard disk, you can start it up at any time simply by turning on the computer (and monitor, if it has a separate switch). DOS 6 will load automatically.

Depending on how you've installed DOS on your hard disk, either the *command prompt* (C:\> or something similar) or the *Shell* will appear when you start DOS 6. The Shell consists of a full screen of text and graphics. To get to the Shell from the command prompt (also called the command line), just type **dosshell** and press ↵.

Figure 2.1 shows how the Shell might look on your screen (your screen may display somewhat different information, but don't worry about that). The circled numbers in the figure refer to the descriptions in Table 2.1, and don't actually appear on the Shell screen. Take a moment now to identify these basic areas of the DOS Shell.

The appearance of the DOS Shell depends on the type of monitor you have and on selections you've made from the Options, View, and Tree menus.

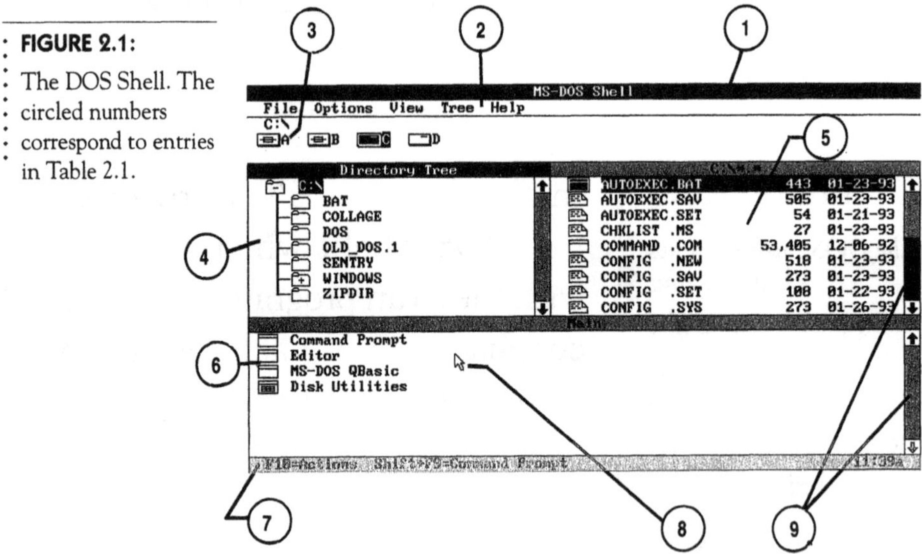

FIGURE 2.1:
The DOS Shell. The circled numbers correspond to entries in Table 2.1.

TABLE 2.1: Areas of the DOS 6 Shell

NUMBER	AREA/WINDOW	CONTENTS
1	Title bar	Name of current screen
2	Menu bar	Currently available options
3	Disk drives	Current and available disk drives. Drives A and B are floppy drives, while drives C and higher are hard disks and network drives.
4	Directory Tree window	Directories on the current disk drive
5	File List window	Files on the current directory
6	Program List window	Available programs and program groups
7	Status line	Available keystrokes and current time
8	Mouse pointer	
9	Scroll bar	Lets you access any information that does not fit in the window

SWITCHING BETWEEN THE COMMAND LINE AND THE SHELL

It's easy to move between the Shell and the command line. You can leave the Shell temporarily by pressing Shift+F9. DOS retains the current settings, but leaves a copy of the Shell in memory. To return to the Shell with your previous settings intact, just follow these steps:

1. Type **exit** and press ↵.
2. If prompted, press any key to get to the Shell.

Do not simply turn off or reboot your computer after you have exited temporarily to the command prompt. Instead, return to the Shell as described above, exit the Shell properly (as explained later in this chapter), and then turn off the power or reboot.

THE DOS SHELL MENU BAR

The second line from the top of the Shell screen is called the *menu bar*. Each item in the menu bar contains a *pull-down menu*, which comes into view when you click its name with your left mouse button. The menu bar includes five pull-down menus: File, Options, View, Tree, and Help.

If you choose to use the Shell from the keyboard, the keys or key combinations shown in Table 2.2 will let you perform any Shell operation.

TABLE 2.2: Keystrokes Used in the DOS 6 Shell

KEYSTROKE	MEANING
F10 or Alt	Select the menu bar at the top of the window
Page Up (PgUp)	Scroll to the previous page of information within a window
Page Down (PgDn)	Scroll to the next page of information within a window
Home	Move to the beginning of a line or list
Ctrl+Home	Move to the beginning of a list
End	Move to the end of a line or list
Ctrl+End	Move to the end of a list
Up Arrow ↑	Scroll up in a list, line by line
Down Arrow ↓	Scroll down in a list, line by line

TABLE 2.2: Keystrokes Used in the DOS 6 Shell (continued)

KEYSTROKE	MEANING
Left Arrow ←	Open the previous pull-down menu (if menu bar is active) or move to the previous drive letter in the disk drives area (if that area is active)
Right Arrow →	Open the next pull-down menu (if menu bar is active) or move to the next drive letter in the disk drives area (if that area is active)
Tab	Move to the next area of the Shell window or dialog box
Shift+Tab	Move to the previous area of the Shell window or dialog box
Letter	Move to the option with the highlighted letter or to the next item that begins with that letter in a list of items

USING THE MENUS

Commands on the pull-down menus follow certain conventions, which are summarized in Table 2.3. When DOS displays a keystroke combination, the + symbol means "hold down the first key, and then press the second one." Hence, Alt+F4 means "hold down the Alt key, press F4, and then release both keys."

Alt+F4 is a shortcut for exiting the Shell to the command prompt. To return to the Shell, type **dosshell** *and press* ↵.

Throughout this book, I'll represent a series of selections that you make from the menus in an abbreviated sequence, with a ➤ symbol separating each selection. For example, a sequence shown in this book as File ➤ Run means "Choose File from the menu bar, then choose Run from the pull-down menu that appears."

TABLE 2.3: Symbols Used in Pull-Down Menus

MENU SYMBOL	MEANING
Ellipsis (…)	Selecting an option that's followed by an ellipsis takes you to a dialog box.
Dimmed appearance	This command doesn't apply to the current situation, and therefore is not available.
Diamond (♦)	For on/off (or toggle) commands, this symbol appears when the option is on.
Shortcut key or combination	A key or keystroke combination, such as Alt+F4 next to Exit on the File menu, is available as a shortcut to this command.

The sections that follow illustrate the DOS Shell menus and explain what each menu can do for you.

THE FILE MENU

You'll use the File menu (Figure 2.2) to work with files, create directories, run programs, execute commands, and exit to the command line. You can use any DOS command in the Shell by selecting File ➤ Run (more on this later).

THE OPTIONS MENU

The Options menu (Figure 2.3) lets you control the warning prompts that appear when you copy, move, and delete files, or perform mouse operations; choose file display options; select files across several directories; enable Task Swapper; and customize the screen display.

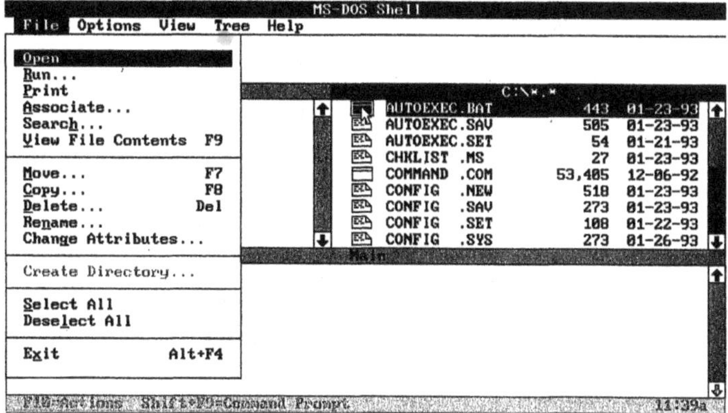

FIGURE 2.2:

The File pull-down menu

Task Swapper is a utility that allows you to have more than one program open at a time and to switch back and forth between programs.

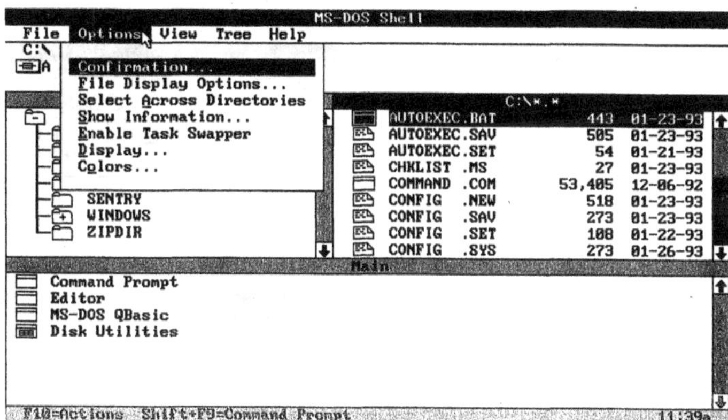

FIGURE 2.3:

The Options pull-down menu

THE VIEW MENU

The View menu (Figure 2.4) lets you customize the appearance of several areas of the Shell screen, including the Directory Tree window, the File List window, and the Program List. You can also use it to refresh or "repaint" the screen.

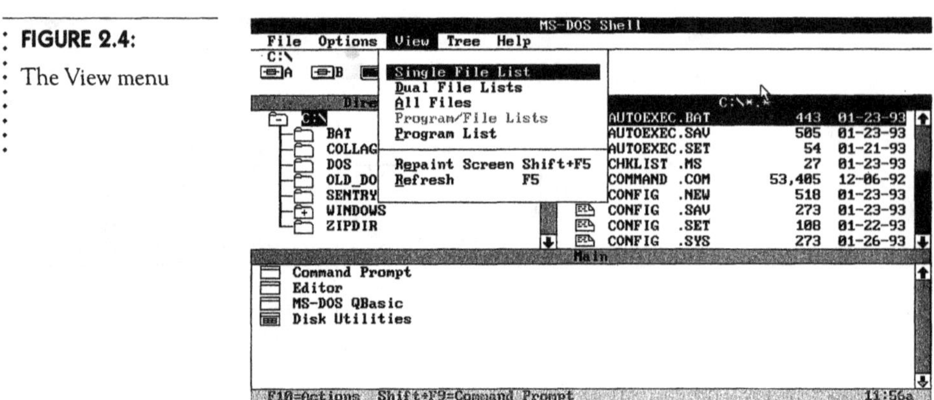

FIGURE 2.4:
The View menu

THE TREE MENU

The Tree menu (Figure 2.5) shows up in the menu bar only when you select the Directory Tree window, the File List window, or a drive icon. You can use its commands to choose the level of directory hierarchy displayed.

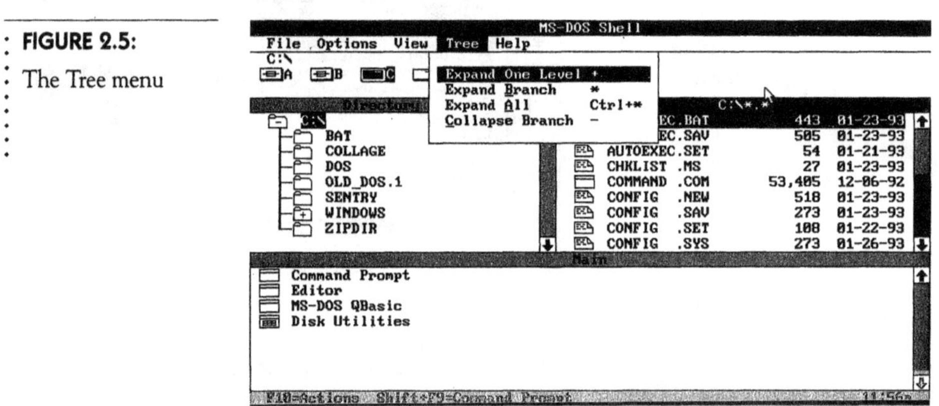

FIGURE 2.5:
The Tree menu

THE HELP MENU

The last menu on the menu bar is the Help menu, which I'll discuss in detail later in this lesson. The Help menu is shown in Figure 2.6.

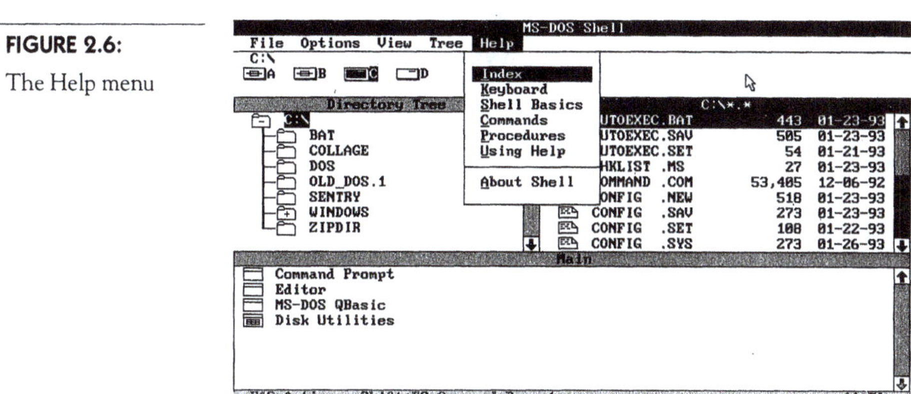

FIGURE 2.6: The Help menu

CANCELING A MENU

If you access a pull-down menu inadvertently (or change your mind), you can cancel that action quite easily. Suppose you've just selected the File menu, then decided not to use it after all. To cancel the menu, just click any blank area outside the menu near the top of the screen, such as the title bar, or the blank space beyond the last menu option. Alternatively, you can press the Esc key to cancel the menu.

Once a pull-down menu is displayed, you can switch to other menus on the menu bar. For instance, if you select the File menu, but then decide to use the Options menu instead, you can just click on the Option menu in the menu bar. If you prefer to use the keyboard, you can press → or ← to move from menu to menu.

USING THE DIRECTORY TREE WINDOW

The directory tree is a hierarchical structure (like a family tree or company organization chart) that DOS uses to organize your program and data files. Each directory in the directory tree holds files, other directories, or a combination of the two. The top of the directory tree is called the *root*.

The DOS Shell's Directory Tree window shows your directories hierarchically. For example, the Directory Tree window in Figure 2.7 illustrates three directories, named 123, DBASE, and WP. The DBASE directory has three subdirectories beneath it: LEDGER, PAYABLES, and RECEIVBL. These subdirectories contain files that are relevant only to the program in the DBASE directory.

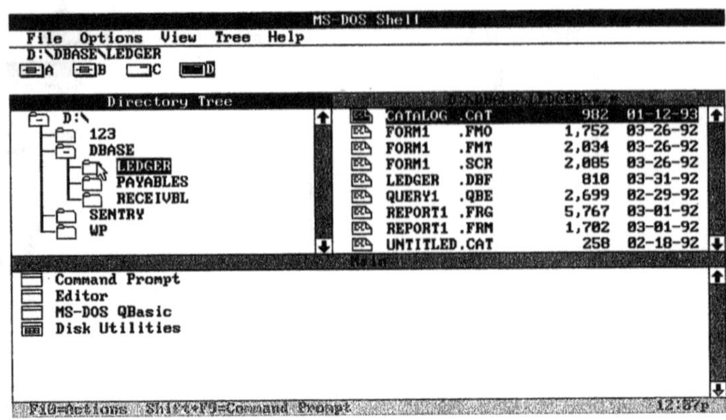

FIGURE 2.7:

A sample Directory Tree window

In the directory tree, each directory is called a *branch*. For example, 123, DBASE, and WP are individual branches beneath the root directory D:\. In the Directory Tree window, you can expand branches whose icons have a + sign in them, or collapse branches whose icons have a – sign in them, to view more or fewer levels of subdirectories. To do so, simply click on the + or – sign or press the + or – key.

To select a window in the DOS Shell, click the window's title or press Tab or Shift+Tab until the title is highlighted. You must select a window before you can work with it.

USING THE FILE LIST WINDOW

Next to the Directory Tree window, the File List window displays the names of the files on the currently selected drive and directory (or subdirectory). The File List window (see Figure 2.8) also shows the size of each file and the date the file was created or last changed.

You can refresh the list of files displayed in the windows by pressing F5 or selecting View ➤ Refresh whenever the File List window is selected. Sometimes this is necessary after switching disk drives or deleting files.

FIGURE 2.8:
A sample File List window

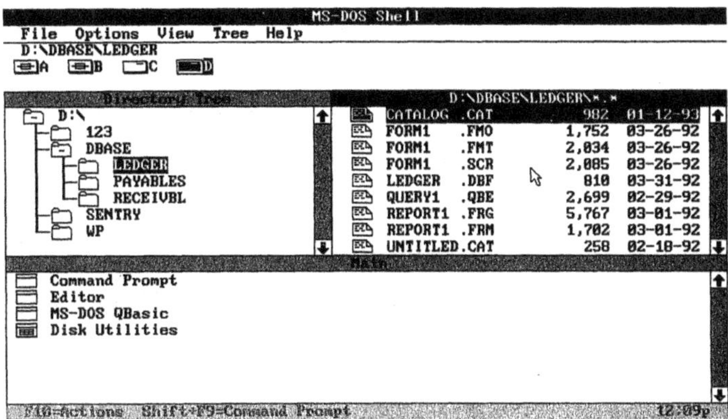

You'll learn how to manage files and directories in Lesson 4.

WHAT'S IN A NAME?

Files contain information that the computer uses. This information may be a program that you run or that is run automatically, data that you create, or some other information used by the system. Every file has a name and, optionally, an extension. Together, the name and extension are referred to as the *file name*. File names must adhere to the rules listed below:

- The name portion can have no more than eight characters; the extension can have no more than three characters.
- Only the letters A through Z, the numbers 0 through 9, and the following characters are allowed in file names and extensions:

  _ - ^ $ ~ ! # % & { } ( ) @ 'à

- Upper- and lowercase letters are treated the same.
- No spaces, commas, or backslashes are allowed in the file name. A period is required before the extension, if the file has an extension.

- The following file names are not allowed because they are reserved by DOS: CLOCK$, CLOCKS, CON, AUX, COM1, COM2, COM3, COM4, LPT1, LPT2, LPT3, NUL, and PRN.
- The rules for directory names are the same as for file names, although most people omit the extension from directory names.
- You cannot have two files of the same name in the same directory.

The following are examples of valid file names without extensions:

```
test
1derful
pc_arts
11-11-93
```

The file names listed below have extensions:

```
1.bat
command.com
octopus.txt
2_bseen.147
wp.exe
```

You can use the Options menu (shown in Figure 2.3) to customize the way that files are listed in the File List window. For instance, you can isolate groups of files, sort them (by name, extension, date, size, and order placed on the disk), and display hidden files or system files.

Sometimes you will be prompted to tell DOS exactly how to reach a certain file or directory by specifying its *path*. To specify this information, you type the drive letter followed by a colon (for example, **c:**) and then type each level in the hierarchy, preceded by a backslash character. For example, the path to the file named CATALOG.CAT, shown in Figure 2.8, could be specified like this:

```
d:\dbase\ledger\catalog.cat
```

This means that the file CATALOG.CAT is stored on drive D in the directory named LEDGER, which is just below the directory named DBASE. Notice that no spaces appear anywhere in the path. The full path name starts with the drive letter, then names the topmost directory, then the next directory down, and finally the name of the file.

OPENING PROGRAMS AND DATA FILES

A *program* or *application* is a series of instructions or commands that the computer can execute to accomplish a specific task. Word processors, database programs, spreadsheet programs, games, and DOS batch programs all fall into the category of "programs." In contrast, a *data file* is information that you create or change when you use a program. For instance, the data file for a word processing program is typically a document such as a letter, memo, report, or chapter. Programs and data are stored in files on the computer.

From the Shell screen, you can start a program or open a data file within the File List window, from the File menu, or within a group in the Program List window. The method you choose is pretty much up to you. If you use a mouse, you can also drag a file icon to its program file. And, as always, you can start a program from the command prompt, outside the Shell (see Lesson 3). I'll explore some of these techniques in the following sections.

STARTING A PROGRAM FROM THE FILE LIST WINDOW

The most straightforward way to start a program is to select its file name from the File List window of the Shell. To do so, you need to know the exact location and name of the program file. Once you know that, just follow these steps:

1. In the disk drives area, select the drive on which the program is stored (for example, drive C). You can click on the drive letter or press Tab or Shift+Tab until a drive letter is highlighted, and then press ← or → to highlight the drive you want.
2. In the Directory Tree window, select the directory that holds the program file, for example, \WP51. That is the program's *home directory*. You can select the directory by clicking on it with your mouse, or by selecting the Directory Tree window and pressing the ↑ or ↓ key until the appropriate directory name is highlighted.
3. In the File List window, double-click the program's file name, or highlight the file name and press ↵. The file name must have the extension .EXE, .COM, or .BAT to be *executable*, or runnable.

To double-click, move the mouse pointer to the item you're interested in, and then click the left mouse button twice in rapid succession.

When you exit the program, you'll be returned to the Shell.

STARTING A PROGRAM FROM THE FILE MENU

An alternative method for starting a program is to select File ➤ Run from the pull-down menus. Here are the steps to follow:

1. Select File ➤ Run.
2. In the dialog box that appears, type the command line and any parameters that the program needs (check the program's documentation, if necessary).
3. Click OK or press ↵.

Remember to include the drive and the directory path, if the file name is not visible in the File List window. For example, if you wanted to run a program named FUNGAME.EXE that was stored in the directory \GAMES\WIZARDS on drive C, you'd type the name as **c:\games\wizards\fungame** in Step 2 (you can include or omit the .EXE extension, as you wish).

Try using this method to start the same program you used in the previous example, such as WP.EXE.

STARTING PROGRAMS FROM THE PROGRAM LIST WINDOW

Yet another way to run a program is from the Program List window near the bottom of the screen. In DOS's off-the-shelf configuration, the Program List contains only a handful of program item options in the Main program group, and a few options in a group called *Disk Utilities*. For now, just be aware that you can run a program item simply by double-clicking it or by highlighting it and pressing ↵.

You can also customize the Program List by adding new program groups and program items that you use frequently. I'll explain how in the next section.

A program item contains startup instructions for a program. It's not the actual program file.

Adding a Group to the Program List

A *program group* is a collection of program items in the Program List window. You can add new program groups for your favorite programs quite easily, by following the steps below.

1. Select the Program List window.
2. If the title bar of the Program List window doesn't display the name of the group that should contain your new group, double-click the group name you want. The selected group's name will appear in the Program List title bar. (Most people simply add new groups to the Main group).
3. Select File ➤ New.
4. Select Program Group from the dialog box that appears, then select OK or press ↵.
5. Type a name for the new group, up to 23 characters long including spaces. The group name provides a way to describe the collection of program items within the group and can be any word or short phrase you want, such as **Mars Project** or **Word Processors**.
6. If you wish, you can type a help message (up to 255 characters, including spaces) and a password (up to 20 characters, including spaces) for the group.
7. Choose OK or press ↵. The name of the new group will appear in the Program List.

The Help text will appear when you highlight the group and press F1. The password will be required whenever you try to open the group.

Adding a Program Item to a Group

Here's how to add a program item to a group in the Program List window:

1. Double-click the program group to which you are adding the program (such as *Mars Project*, in the example above). (If you're using the keyboard, highlight the program group you want and press ↵.) The group name will appear in the Program List title bar.
2. Select File ➤ New.
3. Select Program Item, and then OK.
4. Type a title (up to 23 characters long including spaces) that describes the program item, such as **3-D Illustrator**. After you finish adding the program, this title will appear in the Program List window. The title you select can be any word or phrase that describes the program item.
5. Press Tab or click the Commands box. Then, type the exact command required to start the program, including any parameters. For example, type **3D** if 3D is an executable program in your path. The command you type here is exactly the same command you would enter at the DOS command prompt or when filling in the dialog box after choosing File ➤ Run from the DOS Shell menus.
6. Select OK or press ↵.

The path, which tells DOS where to search for commands and programs, is defined by the PATH command (Lessons 1 and 8). If the program is not in your path, be sure to type the complete path to it in Step 5. If, for example, the 3D program is located in C:\MAGIC\GAMES, type **c:\magic\games\3D** *in Step 5.*

When you complete the steps above, it's a good idea to test the program item you've just added by double-clicking the item or by highlighting it and pressing ↵.

Deleting a Program from a Group

You can delete a program from a group without disturbing the actual program stored on the disk. Just follow these simple steps:

1. Open the program group that contains the program item you want to delete, either by double-clicking it or by highlighting the group and pressing ↵.
2. Highlight the program item that you want to delete, such as 3D Illustrator. Select File ➤ Delete or press Del.
3. If the program item has a password, you'll need to enter it to proceed.
4. Select OK from the confirmation box.

To move a program from one group to another, first copy it to the new location, and then delete it from its original location. To copy a program item, highlight it, select File ➤ Copy, and then follow the instructions in the status line.

Deleting a Program Group

If you no longer need a program group, you can zap it from the Program List. First, however, the group must be completely empty of any program items or subgroups. Therefore, before deleting a group, you must follow the steps given in the previous section to delete program items in the group and in any subgroups of the group that you want to delete. Once you've done that, follow the steps below to delete any subgroups and to delete the group itself.

1. Highlight the program group you want to delete.
2. Select File ➤ Delete or press the Del key.
3. Select OK or press ↵ to confirm the deletion.

STARTING A PROGRAM BY DRAGGING

There's yet another way to start a program from the DOS Shell. Here's how to do it if both the program and the data file are on the same drive and directory and both are visible in the File List window. Highlight a data file for a program in the File List window, then drag that file to the appropriate program file in the File List. Release the mouse button and select *Yes* when asked if you want to start the program.

For example, if you want to start a word processing document file called NAMELIST.NEW, highlight its name and drag it to the program file named WP.EXE in the File List, as shown in Figure 2.9, then release the mouse button and answer Yes.

You can use this dragging technique when the program and data files are on different drives and directories if you customize the File List window so that both the program and file are visible at once. To see two file lists on the screen simultaneously, select View ➤ Dual File Lists. Your screen will look something like the arrangement in Figure 2.10.

Now, select the program and data file you want to work with by clicking their drive icons and directories in the dual file lists. When the program and data files are both visible in the File List windows, you can drag the data file icon from its File List window onto the appropriate program file icon in the other File List window. To display the File List and Program Group windows again, choose View ➤ Program/File Lists.

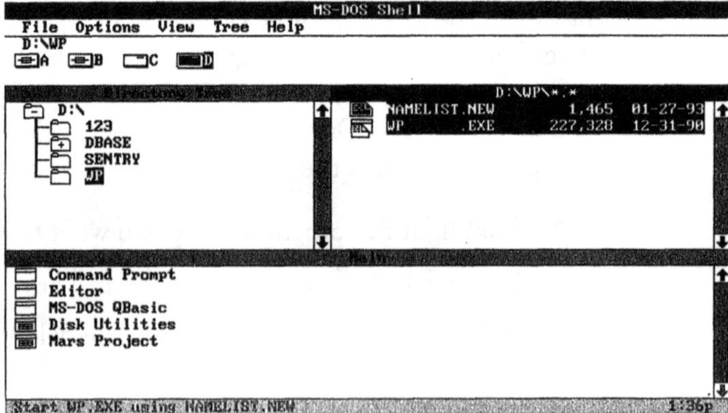

FIGURE 2.9: In the File List window, a highlighted file is dragged to a program file.

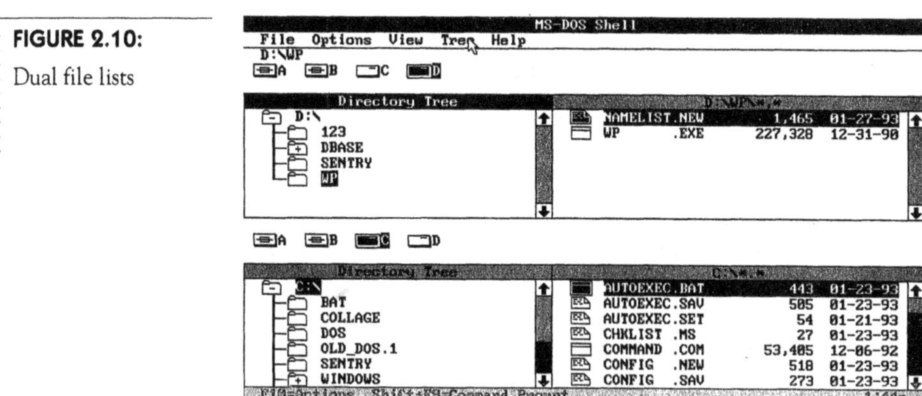

FIGURE 2.10: Dual file lists

ASSOCIATING PROGRAMS AND DATA FILES

If you frequently use data files created with a particular application, you can set up an *association* between the extension of the data files and the application. Once you've done that, you can run the program simply by opening one of the associated data files. Quite convenient!

Suppose that you use the file name extension .DOC to identify files created with the word processing program WP.EXE (WordPerfect). You can associate the .DOC extension with that word processing program so that later, when you open any .DOC file with a mouse or from the keyboard, the word processor will automatically open too.

Here's how to set up an association between a file name extension and a program:

1. Go to any directory that holds at least one of the files you want to associate with the program. For example, if you want to associate .DOC files with the WP.EXE program, you must move to a directory that has one or more .DOC files in it.
2. In the File List window, select a file name with the appropriate extension, such as NOVEL_1.DOC, either by clicking it once or by highlighting it with the arrow keys.
3. Select File ➤ Associate.
4. If the program's home directory is not in the current path, type the complete path for the program you want to execute, such as **c:\wp51\wp**.

(If the program's home directory is in the path, you can just type the program's command or file name, such as **wp.exe**.)

5. Click OK or press ↵ to leave the dialog box.

The path is defined by the PATH command, which is normally included in your AUTOEXEC.BAT file and executed automatically (see Lessons 1 and 8).

Once you've set up an association, try it out to make sure that it works. Double-click any file that has the associated file name extension, such as NOVEL_3.DOC, or highlight the file name and press ↵.

SOS: GETTING HELP FROM THE SHELL

DOS 6 provides useful, accessible Help right on your screen. Learning to use the built-in Help system can be a great time saver in finding new (or forgotten) information without referring to printed documentation.

GETTING IMMEDIATE HELP FROM THE SHELL

While in the DOS Shell, you can get help with whatever you're doing by following these steps:

1. Select the option with which you need help by highlighting it.
2. Press F1.

Figure 2.11 shows the Help screen that appears after clicking on the Options menu, pressing ↓ until Display is highlighted, and then pressing F1.

You can also use the Help button which is provided in many dialog boxes to get help that is specific to what you're doing in the dialog box.

GETTING GENERAL HELP FROM THE SHELL

The Help menu in the DOS Shell provides help on general topics (see Figure 2.6). For help in using Help, select Help ➤ Using Help or press Alt+H then U and scroll through the window that appears.

Shell Basics is a mini-tutorial on using the DOS 6 Shell, geared towards users who are already familiar with earlier versions of DOS. Select Help ➤ Shell Basics or press Alt+H then S to display this information.

USING THE HELP SCREEN

Once a Help screen appears, you can click the scroll bar or press the ↑, ↓, PgUp, and PgDn keys to scroll through the text. You can also click on the buttons shown at the bottom of the Help screen to review a previous screen (Back), show keystrokes that are relevant to the Help topic (Keys), display an index of Help topics (Index), explain how to use Help (Help), or close the Help screen (Close). To close the Help screen with a simple keystroke, press Esc.

If the current Help screen includes related procedures (as in Figure 2.11), you can double-click on a cross-referenced topic to go to the Help screen for that procedure. (If you're using the keyboard, press Tab to select the topic of interest, then press ↵.)

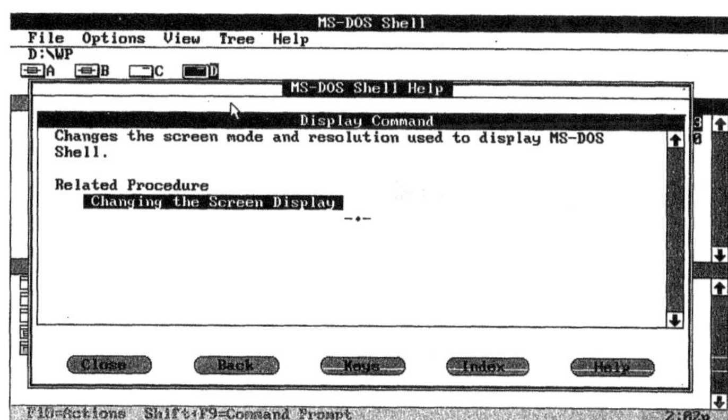

FIGURE 2.11: A sample DOS Shell Help screen

PRINTING DOS SHELL HELP

The Help system in the DOS Shell does not provide any explicit method for printing copies of online Help screens. However, you can obtain "rough" copies by following the steps below.

1. Select Options ➤ Display. Jot down the current setting, which will be highlighted in the Screen Display Mode dialog box that appears.
2. Now type **T** to highlight the *Text 25 lines Low Resolution* option, and click OK or press ↵. This places the screen in Text mode, which is usually necessary to print the screen legibly. In Text mode, your screen displays text characters only—no fancy icons or graphics.
3. Go to the Help screen that you want to print.
4. Press Shift+Print Screen. This copies the screen to your printer. (If you have a laser printer, you may need to press the Form Feed button to eject the page.)
5. Press Esc or click Close to exit the Help screen.
6. Select Options ➤ Display, highlight the original setting for your screen display, and click OK or press ↵.

If you need to capture the screen display on a frequent basis, you may wish to purchase a screen capture utility, such as Collage Plus.

EXITING THE DOS SHELL

When you're finished using the DOS Shell, choose File ➤ Exit or press Alt+F4. You'll be returned to the command prompt. Be sure to exit the Shell before turning off your computer.

SUMMARY

In this lesson you've learned how to use the Shell's menu bar, pull-down menus, program and file lists, and online Help. You've also learned how to open programs and files, and create your own program groups and items for programs that you use frequently.

REFERENCE ENTRIES

To learn more about the topics covered in this Lesson, see the following entries in the reference section:

- DIR
- DOSSHELL
- PATH
- SHELL
- TREE

Using the DOS Command Prompt and Online Help

INTRODUCING

The DOS command prompt
Getting help
The online Help and Reference entries syntax
Running programs from the command prompt
Looking at files
Redirecting input and output

In Lesson 2, you learned how to use DOS the easy way—through the Shell. In this lesson, I'll show you general techniques for using DOS from the command prompt. Although this method is less "friendly," it does let you access features that aren't available through the Shell.

If you've just completed Lesson 2, exit the Shell and return to the command prompt by selecting File ➤ Exit from the Shell menus or by pressing Alt+F4.

USING THE DOS COMMAND PROMPT

The *command prompt* is the message that DOS displays to tell you it's ready for the next command. On most computers, the command prompt appears as C> or C:\>. The C indicates that drive C is the default drive, that is, the drive where DOS will search for commands and data when you don't specifically instruct DOS to look elsewhere.

ENTERING DOS COMMANDS

Entering a DOS command is very easy: Simply type the name of the command, any required options or *switches* (separated from the command name and one another by a space), and press ↵. Thus, typing **ver** and pressing ↵ tells DOS to run the VER command, which displays the DOS version number. Likewise, if you enter the command **type c:\autoexec.bat**, you'll see the contents of AUTOEXEC.BAT displayed (typed) on your computer screen. In this example, **c:\autoexec.bat** tells the TYPE command which file you want to display.

DOS will do absolutely nothing until you press ↵ to send the command. So if DOS seems to be stalling, take a look at the screen and make sure you pressed ↵ after your command.

In many cases, the command you type will elicit some response from DOS. For instance, when you type **dir** and press ↵, DOS will display a list of file names and other information about files in the current directory.

DIR is known as the directory command, because it provides a directory of files available on your computer. Lesson 2 discussed the directory and file structure used in DOS.

In other situations, DOS may carry out your command without providing any feedback whatsoever (DOS is the strong silent type). When you issue the command to delete a file, for example, DOS deletes the file and returns to the command prompt without displaying any messages at all.

You cannot scroll the screen backwards when using the command prompt. Once the messages disappear from the screen, they're gone forever.

If you see the message "Bad command or file name" after typing a command, you've probably made a spelling mistake, or you typed a semicolon (;) instead of a colon (:), a forward slash (/) instead of a backslash (\ ), or made some similar error. A close look at the screen will usually reveal your mistake. Other error messages will appear if you try to delete a file that doesn't exist, specify an unknown option on a command line, or commit some other breach of computer etiquette. After you figure out the mistake, try typing the command again correctly.

Lesson 10 provides a guide to many common error situations and what to do about them.

EDITING THE COMMAND LINE

If you detect a mistake in the command line you're typing *before* you press ↵, you can make corrections by pressing the Backspace key to erase characters to the left of the cursor. After erasing as many characters as necessary, simply retype the rest of the line correctly and press ↵. If you prefer to erase the entire command line typed so far, press Esc. Remember that Backspace and Esc are effective only if you haven't pressed ↵ yet.

The cursor is the small blinking line or block that indicates where the next character will appear when you type it on the command line.

You can press F3 to recall the previous command typed, or press F1 to display the previous command one character at a time.

Zipping through Command Editing with DOSKEY

For more flexibility in editing the command line, you can use DOSKEY, a memory-resident program that allows you to edit command lines, recall DOS commands, and create macros. To install DOSKEY into memory, simply type **doskey** and press ↵. DOSKEY will stay in memory until you restart your computer.

DOSKEY is so handy that you'll probably want to place the command in your AUTOEXEC.BAT file so that it executes automatically whenever you start your computer. *See Lesson 8 for details.*

After placing DOSKEY in memory, you can use its editing features to recall and modify command lines. For instance, you can press ↑ to restore the previous command to the command line, so that you need only press ↵ to execute the command again. Each time you press ↑, the next oldest command will appear on the line. Pressing ↓ recalls the command you used after the one that's currently displayed.

You can use the ←, →, Ctrl+←, Ctrl+→, Home, and End keys to move the cursor through the command line. Once the cursor is positioned where you want it, you can press Backspace to delete the previous character, Del to delete the character above the cursor, or type any character to replace the character above the cursor. To insert a character in the command line, press the Ins key and type the new text; press Ins again to return to replace, or type-over, mode.

See DOSKEY in the Alphabetical Reference for additional information.

USING SPECIAL KEYS

Three additional keys and keystroke combinations can come in handy when you're working at the DOS command prompt, whether or not you've installed DOSKEY into memory. These three keyboard commands allow you to interrupt a command, pause the screen, and print a copy of the screen.

INTERRUPTING A COMMAND

Suppose you typed **dir**, pressed ↵, and then immediately regretted your decision to display a long list of file names. You can stop the command in its tracks and return immediately to the command prompt by pressing Ctrl+C or Ctrl+Break. This technique will interrupt just about any DOS command and will terminate batch programs. If you interrupt a batch program, the message "Terminate batch job (Y/N)?" will appear. Type **Y** to end the batch program or **N** to continue.

The characters ^C will appear on the screen when you press Ctrl+C or Ctrl+Break.

PAUSING THE SCREEN

If a DOS command is displaying information on your screen without giving you time to read it, you can pause the display temporarily by pressing the Pause key (or Ctrl+S). Press another key, such as the spacebar or ↵, to resume the display. This is particularly handy with the DIR and TYPE commands. (Later you'll learn about the MORE command, which provides a more refined way to pause the screen output.)

You can add the switch /p to the DIR command (as in **dir /p**) *to pause output automatically after each screenful.*

Printing the Screen

Whenever you're at the command prompt, you can print a copy of the screen by pressing either Print Screen or Shift+Print Screen (whichever works with your keyboard and computer). Try this technique as an alternative to copying down complex error messages with strange terminology or numbers that are meaningful only to programmers and other computer geeks. You can also use Print Screen to print copies of text screens and online Help displayed by DOS-based programs such as WordPerfect for DOS or Lotus 1-2-3 for DOS (sorry, this trick does *not* work in Windows and other "graphical" applications programs, and may even lock up your computer).

If you have a laser printer, you may need to press the Form Feed button to eject the page.

SOS: Getting Help from the Command Prompt

DOS 6 provides several levels of Help for commands that you type at the command prompt or place in the CONFIG.SYS file. At first, you may look at the Help screen and say, "This is Help? It looks more like computer gobbledygook!" It's true. Help does employ a confusing *syntax notation* to explain the rules for specifying commands. However, once you get used to the notation, you'll find the Help screens to be logical and relatively unambiguous, if not quite user friendly. If you've had a chance to flip to the reference section of this book, you will have encountered, and perhaps wondered about, this notation already. So let's take a look at the DOS Help and try to unravel its syntax notation.

DISPLAYING HELP SUMMARIES

You can display help about any DOS command by entering that command followed by */?* or by typing **doshelp** followed by the command. For example, to get help with the DIR command, which lists the contents of a directory, type **dir /?** or **doshelp dir** at the command prompt.

DOS responds with a short summary screen of help, and then displays the command prompt again. Usually the summary is short enough for you to see it while you're typing the next command line.

DISPLAYING DETAILED HELP

If you'd like more detailed help on a topic, type **help** followed by a space and the name of a command. For example, typing the command **help dir** displays detailed help for the DIR command (see Figure 3.1).

If you prefer to browse through a list of Help topics to see what's available, start at the command prompt and type **help**. The screen will display the Help table of contents (see Figure 3.2). Most Help topics include command <Syntax>, additional <Notes>, and <Examples>. You can click on any topic enclosed between < > symbols or highlight the topic and press ↵ to get information on that topic. (To click, move the mouse pointer to the appropriate spot on the screen, then press the left mouse button.)

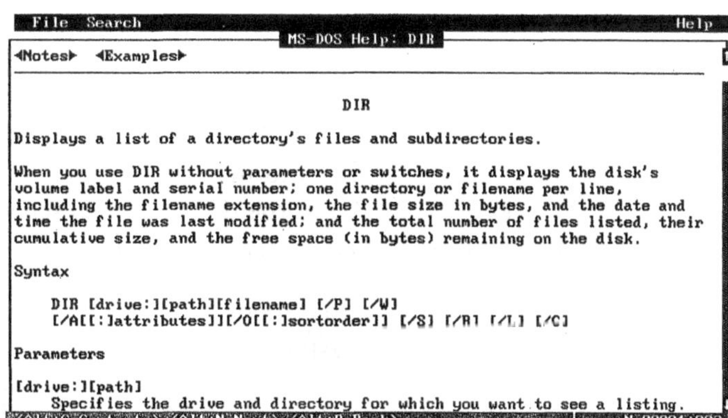

File Search
Help
MS-DOS Help: DIR
◄Notes► ◄Examples►
DIR
Displays a list of a directory's files and subdirectories.
When you use DIR without parameters or switches, it displays the disk's volume label and serial number; one directory or filename per line, including the filename extension, the file size in bytes, and the date and time the file was last modified; and the total number of files listed, their cumulative size, and the free space (in bytes) remaining on the disk.
Syntax
DIR [drive:][path][filename] [/P] [/W]
[/A[[:]attributes]][/O[[:]sortorder]] [/S] [/B] [/L] [/C]
Parameters
[drive:][path]
Specifies the drive and directory for which you want to see a listing.
<Alt+C=Contents> <Alt+N=Next> <Alt+B=Back>
N 00001:002

FIGURE 3.1:

The Help screen for the DIR command

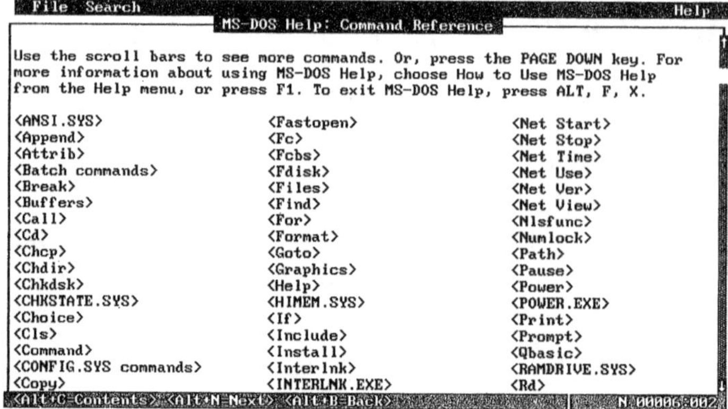

FIGURE 3.2: The Help table of contents

You can use any of the keys listed below to peruse the Help screens:

PgUp or PgDn	Scrolls up or down by a screenful
↑ or ↓	Scrolls up or down a line at a time
Tab or Shift+Tab	Moves to the next or previous topic enclosed between < > symbols; press ↵ to view Help for the topic
Alt+C	Returns to the Help table of contents
Alt+N	Continues to the next Help screen
Alt+B	Returns to the previous Help screen

As an alternative to using the keys listed above, you can click the scroll bar and scroll arrows at the right border of the screen and the Alt+C, Alt+N, and Alt+B "buttons" at the bottom of the screen.

Whenever you're in the detailed Help screens, you can select the following commands from the Help menus:

- To exit the Help screens and return to the command prompt, select File ➤ Exit or press Alt+F then X.
- To print the current Help topic, select File ➤ Print, then press ↵ or click OK.

- To search for a command name or a phrase in the Help topics, select Search ➤ Find, type the text you want to search for, and press ↵ or click OK. (You'll learn more about searching for text when I discuss the Editor in Lesson 8.)
- To find the next occurrence of the search text, press F3 or select Search ➤ Repeat Last Find.

You use the Help menus the same way you use menus in the DOS Shell (Lesson 2).

UNDERSTANDING THE HELP SYNTAX

Now that you know how to get help for a command, let's unravel the spaghetti of syntax rules you need to follow when you type the command. Consider the following syntax descriptions for a hypothetical command named SAMPLE. The first example below shows how this command might appear in DOS Help (either the summary Help or the detailed Help):

```
SAMPLE [+R | -R] [drive:][path]filename[...] [options]
```

The next example illustrates how the syntax might look in the reference section of this book.

sample [+r | -r] [*drive*:][*path*]*filename*[...] [*options*]

The reference section in this book often presents slightly simpler syntax descriptions, omits rarely used options, and reorders some options to make commands easier to understand.

The two sample representations above are equivalent, and can be explained as follows:

ELEMENT	**MEANING**
SAMPLE or sample	Specifies the name of the command.
[ ]	Indicates that the item is optional. To include the optional information, type the information within the brackets, but do not type the brackets themselves.
|	Separates two mutually exclusive choices. For example, the syntax *break [on | off]* allows either *break on* or *break off*.
drive: or *drive*:	The name of a hard disk or floppy disk drive, followed by a colon. Drives A and B are floppy drives, while drives C, D, and higher are hard disks and network drives. For example, in place of *drive*:, above, you could specify C: to reference hard drive C.
path or *path*	The path of directories, starting at the root directory, that DOS must take to locate a directory or file in another directory. If the file you want is located in the directory MYDATA below WP51, you would specify \WP51\MYDATA as the path.
filename or *filename*	The name and extension of a file. A file name can have up to eight characters and can be followed by a period and an extension of up to three characters (such as WOWEE.TXT). You can express file names in uppercase or lowercase letters, or in any combination of the two.

ELEMENT	MEANING
...	Indicates that the previous parameter or switch can be repeated. Type only the repeated information, not the ellipses.
options or *options*	Optional command parameters or switches that you can specify. Switches usually begin with a slash, as in **/p**.

In the online Help, text to be typed *exactly* as shown appears in uppercase letters (though you can type it in lowercase if you wish). In the Alphabetical Reference, such text is shown in lowercase letters that are not italicized. For instance, the command name SAMPLE and the +R and –R options above are to be typed exactly as shown (again, uppercase and lowercase letters are usually equivalent).

In the online Help, text to be substituted with a value that *you* choose appears in lowercase letters (you can usually type it in uppercase or lowercase letters). In contrast, the Alphabetical Reference shows replaceable text in italics. In the sample syntax shown earlier, *drive*, *path*, *filename*, and *options* are to be replaced by appropriate values.

One more thing: Blank spaces are important in DOS. Thus, in the example above, a space follows the command name SAMPLE, the optional +R or –R, and the drive, path, and file name. However, no spaces are allowed *between* the drive, path, and file name. Failing to put spaces in the correct place, or putting spaces in where they don't belong, is a common source of error for new and experienced DOS users alike.

Now, let's look at an example using the new batch program command CHOICE. This command displays a prompt and waits for the user to choose one of a set of choices (see Lesson 8). The CHOICE syntax that appears in the DOS online Help looks like this:

```
CHOICE [/C[:]keys] [/N] [/S] [/T[:]c,nn] [text]
```

In the Alphabetical Reference, the CHOICE syntax looks like this:

choice [*text*] [/c:*keys*] [/n] [/s] [/t*c*,*nn*]

Translating the syntax rules for CHOICE from computerese into English, your options are as follows: You can type **choice** and press ↵, or you can follow the command name with a space and several other switches and options. The *text* option can be replaced with any text, such as **So what's it gonna be**. The switch /c is followed optionally by a colon and then a list of keys the user can press, as in **/c123** or **/c:ynq**. The /n and /s switches can be typed as shown. Finally, the /t switch is followed optionally by a colon, and then a character (*c*), a comma, and a one- or two-digit number (*nn*), as in **/t:y,5** or **/tq,10**. (See CHOICE in the Alphabetical Reference for a complete explanation of each option and switch.)

Generally, an option is typed without a preceding slash (/), whereas a switch is preceded by a slash.

Here are some of the ways you can specify the CHOICE command, according to the syntax rules given above:

```
choice /c123
choice What is your choice /c:ynq
choice
choice So what's it gonna be /c:ynq /s /ty,5
```

You can try out these CHOICE commands at the command prompt if you wish. When the CHOICE command's text message appears, type one of the letters or numbers shown in square brackets to clear the message. (The computer will beep if you make a mistake, so just try again. If you get really stuck, press Ctrl+C or Ctrl+Break to interrupt the command.)

RUNNING PROGRAMS FROM THE COMMAND PROMPT

Program files, which usually have the extension .EXE or .COM, contain the instructions that your computer runs, or *executes*. Lotus 1-2-3 (123.EXE), Microsoft Excel (EXCEL.EXE), dBASE IV (DBASE.EXE), and WordPerfect for DOS (WP.EXE) are all examples of program files. Batch programs, which have the extension .BAT, also are considered program files since they, too, contain instructions for your computer to run. (In batch programs, the instructions are DOS commands and special batch program commands.)

To run a program from the DOS prompt, you simply type the program's file name, without the .EXE, .COM, or .BAT extension, and press ↵. As you can see, running a program is no different from entering any DOS command. So, for example, you can run the WordPerfect word processor simply by typing **wp** and pressing ↵ at the command prompt (assuming, of course, that WordPerfect is installed on your computer and DOS knows where to find it).

Most people omit the .EXE, .COM, and .BAT extensions when running programs; however, including them does no harm.

Like DOS commands, some programs require (or allow) you to provide additional information on the command line. To do this, you type the program name, a space, the information the program is expecting, and then press ↵ as usual. Using a WordPerfect example again, you could type **wp letter.wp** to start WordPerfect and open an existing file named LETTER.WP.

The one catch to all this is that DOS must be able to find the program you want to run somewhere on the disk. If the program can't be found in memory (that is, the program isn't a built-in, or *internal*, DOS command), DOS looks for it on the disk. When trying to locate a program on disk, DOS first looks in the current directory; if the program isn't there, it searches the *path*, which is established by the PATH command. If the program still can't be found, you'll get the message "Bad command or file name." (This message will also appear if you've typed the program name incorrectly.)

You should place a PATH command in your AUTOEXEC.BAT file so that you won't need to specify the path for programs that you use frequently. Lesson 8 explains how to do this.

You can usually run a program that isn't in your path if you tell DOS exactly where to find it when you type the program name. For example, the Show program that comes with Collage Plus normally is stored in the directory named \COLLAGE on drive C. So, to run Show when C:\COLLAGE is not in the current path, you would type **c:\collage\show** and press ↵.

Note that very large programs, such as WordPerfect for DOS (WP.EXE), typically require other files in order to run. If those files are not in the current directory or path, the program will not run, even if you specify the entire path when typing the program name. The solution to this problem is either to use the PATH command (Lesson 8) to establish a path to the directory that contains the program and the files it needs, or to use the command CD (or CHDIR) to make that program's directory the current directory (Lesson 4).

LOOKING AT FILES FROM THE COMMAND PROMPT

As you learned in Lesson 2, a *file* is simply a collection of information stored on the computer. There are many ways to "look" at a file in DOS. The DIR command, for example, shows you the *names* of files, along with certain vital statistics such as size and the date the file was last modified. The DIR command is useful whenever you want to determine which files are available, how large they are, and when they were last changed.

But from time to time you'll also want to look at or change the *contents* of a file. The procedures for doing this depend on the type of file you're interested in.

LOOKING AT TEXT FILES AND BATCH PROGRAMS

Text files and batch programs (which are special kinds of text files) contain letters, numbers, and other printable characters. You can look at the contents of any text file by using the TYPE command. For instance, the following command displays the AUTOEXEC.BAT file on your screen:

```
type c:\autoexec.bat
```

If the text file is very long, it may scroll off the screen before you have a chance to read it. In this case you can press the Pause key to pause the output temporarily, or you can use the MORE command, which pauses output after each screenful. I'll discuss MORE later in this lesson.

Most computer programs, including DOS, represent text using the American Standard Code for Information Interchange, or ASCII (pronounced "askey"). Text files often have a .TXT or .BAT extension.

To view and change the contents of a text file, you need a text editor or a word processor that can edit ASCII files. For example, the EDIT command, which calls up DOS's very own text editor, is commonly used to update the CONFIG.SYS and AUTOEXEC.BAT startup files (see Lessons 1 and 8).

LOOKING AT PROGRAMS

Program files that have .COM or .EXE extensions cannot be viewed or changed directly because they are stored in executable form, which is not readable by humans. Executable files contain special machine instructions that only DOS and your computer can interpret.

NEVER, NEVER, NEVER change the contents of an executable program file. Doing so will make the program as useless as an air conditioner on a cold winter day—and your computer may freeze if you try to run the altered program later.

If you accidentally use the TYPE command to view the contents of a program file, your screen will display lots of weird graphic characters, like happy faces and musical notes, and may even beep uncontrollably. No harm done; simply press Ctrl+C or Ctrl+Break to stop the racket, or wait until the command prompt reappears.

LOOKING AT OTHER KINDS OF FILES

Other files on your computer fall into the category of *data files*. Typically, these are files that you create in an application program—such as spreadsheets, databases, word processing documents, graphics files, and so forth. To look at and change these files, you must use the application program that created them. Consult the application's documentation to find out exactly how to open, retrieve, or change one of its data files.

Data files also may be used to provide information to programs, and these may or may not be readable by humans, depending on the data file and the application that uses it. The file CONFIG.SYS, for example, is a human-readable data file that DOS uses to establish your computer's initial configuration. Files with the extension .INI typically are used to initialize application programs (hence the extension .INI).

The terms program *and* application *often are used interchangeably. Generally, the term* program *refers to DOS-based programs, and the term* application *refers to Windows-based programs, but there are no hard-and-fast rules here.*

REDIRECTING INPUT AND OUTPUT

Many commands, such as DIR, DOSHELP, MORE, SORT, and TYPE, take information from the keyboard and send it to your screen. But you can change this if you wish, through a clever technique known as *redirection*. Redirection can be used to divert the display of most DOS commands to a file or to the printer, and to take input from a file or even from another DOS command.

REDIRECTION SYMBOLS

The following characters are used to redirect the output of a command:

>	sends output of a command to a file or a device such as the printer
>>	adds output of a command to the end of a file without deleting information already in the file

These characters redirect the input for a command:

<	takes command input from a file instead of the keyboard
|	sends (filters) the output of the previous command on the command line to the next command (the | symbol is called a *pipe*)

SENDING OUTPUT TO THE PRINTER

To send output of a DOS command to the printer, add the redirection symbol **>** followed by **prn** to the end of the command. For example, the command **dir > prn** sends the output of the DIR command to the printer.

You can use either of the commands below to send the summary Help for the DIR command to the printer:

```
dir /? > prn
doshelp dir > prn
```

If you're using a laser printer, you'll probably need to eject the page.

SENDING OUTPUT TO A FILE

To send command output to a text file, type **>** followed by the name of the file that should receive the output.

Be careful with this! Any information already in the file will be replaced by the output of the DOS command. For this reason, it's a good idea to pick a "junk" name, like TMPFILE, X, or JUNK when redirecting output. The command below stores the output of a DIR command in the file named X:

```
dir > x
```

TIP

After creating the file that contains command output, you can edit the file in the DOS Editor or a word processor if you wish.

SENDING OUTPUT TO THE END OF A FILE

You can add redirected output to the end of a text file, without overwriting any existing information in the file, by using two greater-than signs, like this:

```
dir >> x
```

In the example above, the output of the DIR command will be added to the end of the file named X. If X doesn't exist, it will be created.

WARNING

Never add DOS command output to the end of a data file created by an application program such as Lotus, WordPerfect, Excel, or dBASE, or to an executable program file.

GETTING INPUT FROM A FILE

The < symbol redirects the input to commands so that the commands read data from a file instead of from the keyboard. This is especially handy when used with the MORE command, which pauses after each screenful of output and waits for you to press a key (such as the spacebar or ↵) before displaying the next screenful.

For example, the command below takes the input from a file named GOODSTUF.TXT and displays GOODSTUF.TXT on the screen, one screen at a time:

```
more < goodstuf.txt
```

As you can see, MORE offers a useful alternative to looking at long text files with the TYPE command.

The next example uses the SORT command to sort a text file named MIXEDUP so that its lines appear in alphabetical order on the screen:

```
sort < mixedup
```

You can even combine the input and output redirection symbols, as in this example

```
sort < mixedup > sorted
```

which sorts the mixed-up input from the file named MIXEDUP and creates a new, sorted file named SORTED.

FEEDING THE OUTPUT OF ONE COMMAND INTO ANOTHER COMMAND

DOS offers three *filter* commands—MORE, FIND, and SORT—which divide, rearrange, or extract portions of the information that passes through them. MORE, as you know, displays the contents of a file or output of a command one screenful at a time. FIND searches through files and command output for text that you specify. And SORT alphabetizes files and command output.

Here are some examples of each of these commands being used as a filter for the previous command on the command line. Recall that the | symbol sends output from one command to the next.

type autoexec.bat | more Takes output from the TYPE command and displays it a screenful at a time. (This is the same as **more < autoexec.bat.**)

dir | find "01-18-93" Takes output from the DIR command and displays only those file names that were created or changed on January 18, 1993.

type mixedup | sort Takes output from the TYPE command and sorts it alphabetically (same as **sort < mixedup**).

SUMMARY

In this lesson you have learned how to enter DOS commands, display (and understand) the online Help provided for DOS commands, run programs, look at files, and redirect command input and output.

REFERENCE ENTRIES

To learn more about the topics covered in this lesson, see these entries in the Alphabetical Reference:

- CHOICE
- DIR
- DOSHELP
- DOSKEY
- EDIT
- FIND
- HELP
- MORE
- PATH
- SORT
- TYPE
- VER

Managing Your Files and Directories

INTRODUCING

The DOS directory tree
File name wildcards
Using directories
Copying and moving files and directories
Renaming and deleting files and directories

A messy hard disk is a lot like a messy desk: It bogs you down with needless searches for important information and causes you to waste precious time. In this lesson, you'll learn how to manage your files and directories efficiently so that you'll never be caught with messy disks again (sorry, I can't do much about those messy *desks*).

Many application programs, such as WordPerfect and Windows, provide their own tools for managing files and directories.

CLIMBING THE DOS DIRECTORY TREE

In Lesson 2, you learned that the DOS directory structure is organized hierarchically, like a company organization chart or a tree. The root directory (\) is at the top. Below the root are files and additional branches called *directories* and *subdirectories*.

VIEWING THE DIRECTORY TREE

You can view the directory tree quite easily. Figure 4.1 shows the result of typing the command **tree c:** at the command prompt to display the directory structure of drive C. Figure 4.2 shows this same directory structure displayed in the Directory Tree window of the DOS Shell after selecting View ➤ Single File List, then Tree ➤ Expand All from the menus.

See Lessons 2 and 3 for a review of the DOS Shell and the command prompt, respectively.

VIEWING FILE NAMES AND FILE INFORMATION

To display information about files on the current drive and directory from the command prompt, you use the DIR command. Simply type **dir** and press ↵. To see a sorted list of files in the current directory and pause after each screenful, type the command **dir /on /p**.

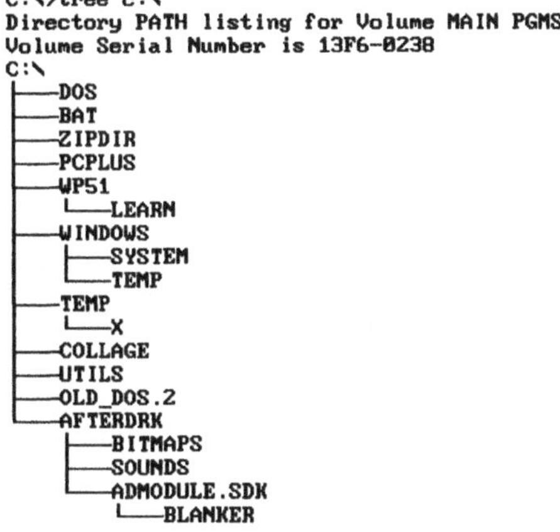

```
C:\>tree c:\
Directory PATH listing for Volume MAIN PGMS
Volume Serial Number is 13F6-0238
C:\
├──DOS
├──BAT
├──ZIPDIR
├──PCPLUS
├──WP51
│   └──LEARN
├──WINDOWS
│   ├──SYSTEM
│   └──TEMP
├──TEMP
│   └──X
├──COLLAGE
├──UTILS
├──OLD_DOS.2
└──AFTERDRK
    ├──BITMAPS
    ├──SOUNDS
    └──ADMODULE.SDK
        └──BLANKER

C:\>
```

FIGURE 4.1: The command TREE C:\ shows a graphical representation of the directory structure of drive C. (Of course, the files and directories on your own computer will be different.)

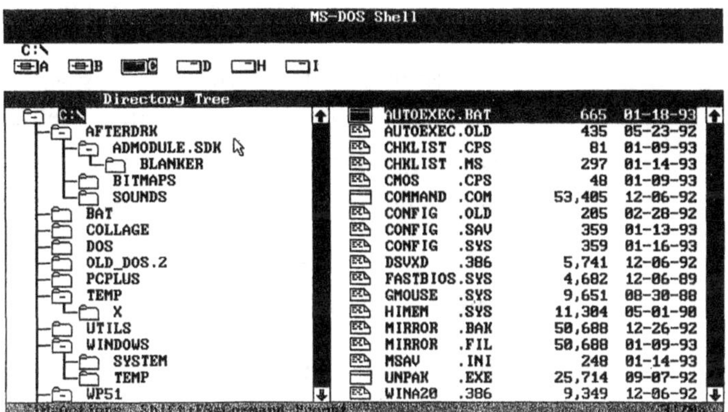

FIGURE 4.2: The same information as in Figure 4.1, displayed by the DOS Shell

A sample directory listing, sorted by file name, appears in Figure 4.3. Notice that the listing consists of general information about the disk and the five columns described below.

File name or directory name Appears in the first column.

File extension Appears in the second column (if the file or directory name has an extension). For esthetic reasons, the directory listing shows a space instead of a period between the file name and extension. However,

```
Volume in drive C is MAIN PGMS
Volume Serial Number is 13F6-0238
Directory of C:\

AFTERDRK     <DIR>       01-17-93  10:08a
AUTOEXEC BAT         665 01-18-93  10:47a
AUTOEXEC OLD         435 05-23-92   5:11a
BAT          <DIR>       01-19-91   4:12p
CHKLIST  CPS          81 01-09-93   4:15p
CHKLIST  MS          297 01-14-93  11:11a
CMOS     CPS          48 01-09-93   4:08p
COLLAGE      <DIR>       01-05-93  12:14p
COMMAND  COM       53405 12-06-92   6:00a
CONFIG   SAV         359 01-13-93  11:32a
CONFIG   OLD         205 02-28-92   8:31a
CONFIG   SYS         359 01-16-93   3:44p
DOS          <DIR>       01-19-91   4:10p
DSVXD    386        5741 12-06-92   6:00a
FASTBIOS SYS        4682 12-06-89   6:06p
GMOUSE   SYS        9651 08-30-88  12:00a
HIMEM    SYS       11304 05-01-90   3:00a
MIRROR   FIL       50688 01-09-93   4:08p
MIRROR   BAK       50688 12-26-92  10:07a
Press any key to continue . . .
```

FIGURE 4.3:

A sample directory listing, sorted by file name

you must include the period—*not* a space—when typing a file name and extension in a DOS command or in a Shell dialog box.

File size or <DIR> Shows the size of the files in bytes (characters) or the symbol <DIR> to indicate that an entry is for a directory instead of a file.

Date Shows the date that the file or directory was created or last changed.

Time Shows the time that the file or directory was created or last changed.

After displaying the file names, DOS will report the number of files listed, the number of bytes they occupy, and the number of bytes still available on the disk.

In the DOS Shell, the DIR command is unnecessary. You simply click on the drive and directory you're interested in, and the file names, extensions, and other information will appear in the File List window.

If necessary, you can refresh the list of names shown in the DOS Shell's File List window so that you're seeing the latest information. To refresh the list, click on the File List window and press F5 or select View ➤ Refresh from the menus.

The File List window will not be visible if you select View ➤ Program List from the menus. Try experimenting with options on the View menu to discover which view is best for you.

THE JOKER'S WILD: USING WILDCARDS IN FILE NAMES

Many DOS commands and DOS Shell options allow you to include wildcards, which let you work with groups of files. A wildcard acts as a placeholder for a name or extension and can be used just about anywhere that you can specify a simple file name. The two wildcards are as follows:

* represents a whole word or group of characters

? represents a single character

Suppose, for example, that you want to list files that begin with the letter C and have the extension .BAT. To list these files with the DIR command, you would type **dir c*.bat** and press ↵. The command **dir c*.*** lists all files that start with C and have *any* extension (notice that I've used the * wildcard in the extension as well).

*The wildcard *.* (pronounced* star dot star*) stands for all file names and all extensions.*

In the DOS Shell, you can use wildcards to restrict the files displayed in the File List window by selecting Options ➤ File Display Options and typing a file name wildcard (such as **c*.***) in the dialog box that appears. Select OK or press ↵ to complete your selections. To redisplay all files in the File List window, select Options ➤ File Display Options again, type ***.*** in the dialog box, and press ↵.

Here are two more examples of wildcards:

my*.txt	matches file names such as MYSTUFF.TXT, MY.TXT, and MYOHMY.TXT
???.*	matches three-character file names with any extension, including ABC.COM, ABC, and 135.TXT

CHANGING THE CURRENT DRIVE

The current (or default) drive tells DOS where to look for files and directories. If the files or directories you want to work with are located on the current drive, you don't have to specify the drive when typing commands or supplying information to the DOS Shell. If the files or directories aren't on the current drive, you must specify the drive you want. Assuming for a moment that the current drive is C, the command **dir a:** lists a directory of files on drive A.

On most systems, the current or default drive is drive C initially.

As an alternative to specifying the drive you want to work with, you can change the current drive. You can do this either from the DOS Shell or from the command prompt:

- To change the current drive from the DOS Shell, simply click on the desired drive letter in the disk drives area.
- To change the current drive from the command prompt, type the drive letter, a colon, and press ↵. Thus, to change the default drive to the floppy disk in drive A, you would place a disk in drive A (important for avoiding error messages), then type **A:** or **a:** and press ↵. (The DOS Prompt usually will change to reflect the new current drive.)

CREATING A DIRECTORY

You can create directories on a hard disk or floppy disk to organize your files further. For example, suppose you use WordPerfect to edit files for three different projects: ACCTG, BUDGET, and FUN. The directory structure below might provide a useful organization.

```
H:\>tree
Directory PATH listing for Volume HOST_FOR_C
Volume Serial Number is 1A29-8446
H:.
├───WP51
└───WP-PROJ
    ├───ACCTG
    ├───BUDGET
    └───FUN

H:\>
```

Figure 4.4 shows how this structure might look when represented as an organization chart.

In this example, the \WP51 directory on drive H contains the WordPerfect program files. The directory \WP-PROJ organizes all the WordPerfect projects, and the directories ACCTG, BUDGET, and FUN, below \WP-PROJ, represent the three projects for which you're using WordPerfect.

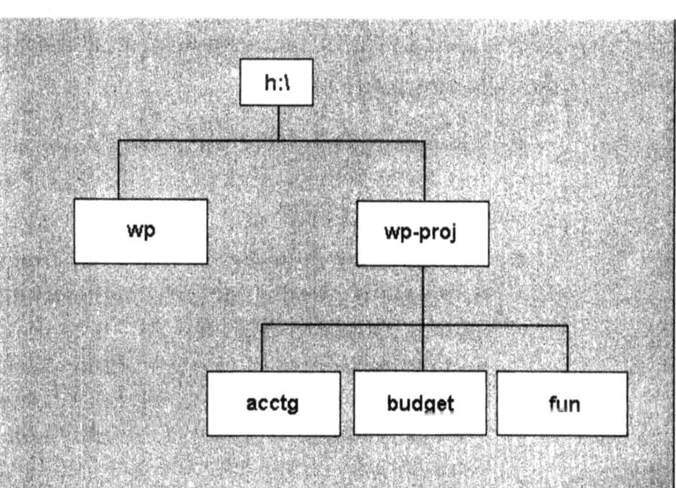

FIGURE 4.4: The sample directories shown in organization chart format

If your computer doesn't have a drive H, you should substitute an appropriate hard drive letter (such as C or D) or floppy drive letter (such as A or B) when trying the examples shown in this lesson.

The directory named WP-PROJ is said to be the *parent directory* of ACCTG, BUDGET, and FUN. Looking at the structure from a slightly different point of view, ACCTG, BUDGET, and FUN are *child directories* of WP-PROJ. The *root* (\) is the parent directory of WP51 and WP-PROJ in this example. The directories WP51 and WP-PROJ are children of the root, and both WP51 and WP-PROJ are at the same level of the directory tree (immediately below the root).

Like file names, directory names can have up to eight characters. You can also specify an extension of up to three characters, though few people do. (An unwritten law compels seasoned DOS users to omit extensions from directory names.)

The setup programs for many applications create directories automatically when you install the application.

Note that there is no single "right" way to organize directories on your hard disk. You should decide on a structure that appeals to you. However, please observe the following guidelines:

- You must create directories from the top down. Thus, you would need to create the WP-PROJ directory before creating the subdirectories ACCTG, BUDGET, or FUN.
- Avoid storing data files in the same directory with program files. This will make it easier to upgrade applications later, without deleting data files accidentally. Also, keeping data files separate from programs can prevent accidental deletion of important program files when you're cleaning up unwanted data. In the WP examples above, the directory \WP51 contains WordPerfect *programs* and related files, and is created automatically by the WordPerfect installation procedure. The \WP-PROJ directory and the directories below it store WordPerfect *data files*.

CREATING A NEW DIRECTORY FROM THE SHELL

To create a new directory from the DOS Shell, follow the steps below.

1. In the drives area and Directory Tree window, select the drive and (optionally) the directory where you want to add the new directory. If you select a directory, the new directory will be created *below* the selected directory; that is, it will become a *subdirectory* (or child directory) of the selected directory.
2. Select File ➤ Create Directory.
3. Type the name of the new directory, then press ↵ or click OK.

CREATING A NEW DIRECTORY FROM THE COMMAND PROMPT

To create a directory from the command prompt, you use the command MKDIR (or its abbreviated form, MD). The general form of this command is **md** *dirname* where *dirname* is the name of the directory you want to create.

The commands shown below will create the \WP-PROJ directory and subdirectories on the current drive:

```
md \wp-proj
md \wp-proj\acctg
md \wp-proj\budget
md \wp-proj\fun
```

Notice that I created the top-level directory first, then the directories below it. When specifying the complete *path* to the directory, I started at the root (\ ), typed the name of each directory in order from top to bottom, and separated each directory from the directory just above it with a backslash (\ ).

To create a directory on a drive other than the current one, simply precede the directory name with the drive letter, as in **md h:\wp-proj**.

SWITCHING DIRECTORIES

Just as the active drive is called the current drive, the directory you're working in at a given time is called the *current directory* for the drive. You can change to another directory at any time, making it the current directory. The current directory on any drive is the root, unless you change it.

TIP

To display the current drive and directory location in the DOS prompt message, type the command **prompt pg** *or place this command in your* AUTOEXEC.BAT *file.*

One advantage to switching to a different directory is that you can restrict your operations to that directory only. For example, the simple command **dir** shows just the files located in the current directory. Thus, after you switched to the directory \WP-PROJ\ACCTG (**cd wp-proj\acctg**), typing **dir** would show only those files in the ACCTG subdirectory of \WP-PROJ.

If you've switched directories, you can work with files in another directory simply by including a complete path name in the command. For example, the command **dir \wp-proj\fun*.dat** would list all files with a .DAT extension that are stored in the directory \WP-PROJ\FUN. Similarly, if an application program, such as WordPerfect, asked you to supply a file name, you could specify the complete path to the file—as in **h:\wp-proj\fun\mystuf.wp** or **a:\autoloan.let**—regardless of the current directory or drive.

DOS will remember the current directory for a drive, even after you switch to a different drive. To illustrate, suppose the current drive is C and the current directory is \WP-PROGS\ACCTG. If you make drive D the current drive, by typing **d:** and pressing ↵, DOS will still know that C:\WP-PROGS\ACCTG is the current directory on drive C. If you then entered the command **dir c:** and pressed ↵, you'd see a list of files in the \WP-PROGS\ACCTG directory of drive C. Switching the current drive back to C would return you to the directory \WP-PROGS\ACCTG (not to the root directory of drive C).

SWITCHING DIRECTORIES FROM THE SHELL

To switch to another directory in the Shell, simply click on the desired directory in the Directory Tree window. The title bar and contents of the File List window will reflect the change.

If you need to expand a directory so that you can see directories below it, click the plus sign (+) to the left of the directory name or activate the Directory Tree window and type **+**.

SWITCHING DIRECTORIES FROM THE COMMAND PROMPT

To switch to another directory from the command prompt, type **chdir** or its short form **cd**, a space, and the name of the directory you want to switch to. For instance, typing **cd \wp-proj\acctg** makes the \WP-PROJ\ACCTG directory current. If you were already in the directory \WP-PROJ, you could type **cd acctg** to switch to the ACCTG directory, which is one level down in the directory tree.

When you omit the leading backslash (\) in a directory name (for example, **cd acctg***), DOS assumes you're referring to a directory that's just below the current directory. When you type the leading backslash (for example,* **cd \wp-proj\acctg***), DOS assumes that the specified directory path starts at the root, regardless of the current directory.*

Here are some other useful forms of the CD command:

- Type **cd** by itself to show the name of the current directory.
- Type **cd ** to switch quickly from any directory back to the root directory.
- Type **cd ..** to switch quickly to the parent directory of the current directory.

UNDERSTANDING . AND ..

Whenever you create a new directory, DOS automatically creates two entries that represent the directory itself and the parent directory one level above the new directory. You'll see those entries whenever you use the DIR command to list files in any directory except the root. These two entries, . and .., appear in the example below:

```
H:\WP-PROJ>dir

 Volume in drive H is HOST_FOR_C
 Volume Serial Number is 1A29-8446
 Directory of H:\WP-PROJ

.            <DIR>      01-18-93   4:16p
..           <DIR>      01-18-93   4:16p
ACCTG        <DIR>      01-18-93   4:17p
BUDGET       <DIR>      01-18-93   4:17p
FUN          <DIR>      01-18-93   4:17p
        5 file(s)              0 bytes
                         2506752 bytes free

H:\WP-PROJ>
```

The . character refers to the current directory, while .. refers to the parent directory. You can use .. as a shortcut when specifying path names. For instance, you could type **dir ..** to list the files in the parent directory of whatever directory you're in, or **cd ..** to switch to the directory that's one level higher. Similarly, if the current directory were \WP-PROJ\FUN, you could switch to the subdirectory \WP-PROJ\ACCTG by typing the shortcut command **cd ..\acctg**.

COPYING FILES

The COPY command offers an important tool for organizing files and making copies of files. You can copy files from one directory to another or one drive to another (to make backup copies, for example). You can also copy a group of files using wildcards, and rename a file as you copy it.

COPYING FILES FROM THE SHELL

With the DOS Shell, you can easily copy files by using the keyboard, or by dragging selected files with your mouse. The steps for the keyboard method are as follows:

1. In the File List window, select the file or files you want to copy. To select one file, click on it. To select additional files, hold down the Ctrl key while clicking the files you want.
2. Select File ➤ Copy or press F8.
3. In the To box, type the drive and directory where you want to copy the file or files.
4. Select OK or press ↵.

To copy files by dragging them with your mouse, follow these steps:

1. Select View ➤ Dual File Lists if you want to copy the file or files to a drive or directory that isn't visible at the moment. Then make sure the source files and their destination directory are visible in the Directory Tree window and File List window. If they are not visible, select the desired drive and directories by clicking in the disk drives area and the Directory Tree window as necessary.
2. In the File List window, select the file or files you want to copy.
3. Press and hold down the Ctrl key (very important) while dragging the file or files to the appropriate directory in the Directory Tree window. (To drag, hold down the left mouse button while sliding the mouse to another location.)
4. Release the mouse button when you've dragged the files to the correct location.
5. When asked to confirm the mouse operation, click Yes to complete the operation or No to cancel it.

WARNING

To prevent COPY from overwriting an existing file without warning, select Options ➤ Confirmation and make sure an X appears in the Confirm On Replace and Confirm Mouse Operation check boxes. (If no X appears, click the check box). For utmost safety when working in the Shell, place X's in all the confirmation check boxes.

COPYING FILES FROM THE COMMAND PROMPT

When typed at the command prompt, the COPY command offers many options. But basically COPY follows the format

copy *from to*

where *from* is the name (or wildcard name) of the file you're copying from and *to* is the name (or wildcard name) of the file you're copying to. You can copy files from any drive or directory to any drive or directory (though, of course, you can't copy a file to itself).

WARNING

The COPY command will overwrite an existing file of the same name. Therefore, before making copies, use the DIR command to see whether the file or files being copied already exist in the destination directory.

Taking a simple example, the command **copy a:whatsup.doc b:** copies the file named WHATSUP.DOC from drive A to WHATSUP.DOC on drive B. To copy WHATSUP.DOC to a file named NOTMUCH.DOC on drive B, you could use this command:

```
copy a:whatsup.doc b:notmuch.doc
```

The command **copy a:*.* c:\mystuff** copies all the files from the current directory of drive A to the directory MYSTUFF on drive C. The command **copy *.txt a:** will copy all files with an extension of .TXT from the current directory to a floppy disk in drive A.

Keep in mind that floppy disks cannot hold as much data as a hard disk can. If COPY runs out of room when copying files to a floppy disk, you'll see the message "Insufficient disk space" and the COPY command will stop. To copy the remaining files, you'll either need to delete some files from the floppy disk or insert a fresh (formatted) floppy disk and use COPY again, this time copying only the files that didn't fit on the first floppy disk. (In Lesson 5, you'll learn how to use MSBACKUP to create backup copies of hard disk files and how to format disks.)

If you run out of space when copying files through the DOS Shell, you'll see a message and the copying will stop.

Here's one more example. Suppose you want to copy all the files from the directory \WP-PROJ\ACCTG to the \WP-PROJ\FUN directory. The following command will do the trick:

```
copy \wp-proj\acctg\*.* \wp-proj\fun
```

There are, in fact, other ways to accomplish this task, but the method above is relatively foolproof.

You can also use the XCOPY command to copy files in the current directory and its subdirectories. Turn to the Alphabetical Reference for details.

RENAMING FILES AND DIRECTORIES

You can change the name of an existing file or directory quite easily, so you're never stuck with one name forever. The next few sections will show you how.

RENAMING FILES AND DIRECTORIES FROM THE SHELL

To rename files or directories from the Shell, follow the steps below:

1. To rename files, select the file or files you want to rename in the File List window. (Remember to hold down the Ctrl key when selecting more than one file.) To rename a directory, select the directory in the Directory Tree window.
2. Select File ➤ Rename.

3. Type the new name into the Rename dialog box, then select OK or press ↵.

If you select more than one file to rename at one time, a separate Rename dialog box will appear for each file you've selected.

RENAMING FILES FROM THE COMMAND PROMPT

You use the RENAME command (or its abbreviated form, REN) to rename a file or group of files from the command prompt. The basic form is

```
rename from to
```

where *from* is the old name of the file and *to* is the new name. You can use wildcards in the *from* and *to* file names, but all files must be in the same drive and directory. You cannot specify a drive or directory in the *to* file name.

Suppose you want to change the name of a file from LITTER.DAT to LETTER.DAT. Simply type **ren litter.dat letter.dat** and press ↵.

The command **ren l*.txt l*.wp** renames all files beginning with *l* and having a .TXT extension. The new files will have the same file names but new .WP extensions. To verify that the rename command worked properly, type **dir l*.*** or just **dir**.

The following command renames LSN1.WP on drive B to LSN-01.WP (also on drive B):

```
ren b:lsn1.wp lsn-01.wp
```

To rename a *directory* from the command prompt, you must use the MOVE command, which is described below.

MOVING FILES

As you learned in the previous section, renaming is a useful way to change the name of an existing file. However, it doesn't provide any way to move files to different drives or directories. So how can you move files? One way is to copy files to a new location and then delete them from the old location. Fortunately, however, DOS 6 provides easier alternatives.

MOVING FILES IN THE SHELL

Moving files in the Shell is similar to copying. The keyboard method is as follows:

1. In the File List window, select the file or files you want to move.
2. Select File ➤ Move or press F7.
3. In the To box, type the drive and directory where you want to move the file or files.
4. Select OK or press ↵.

To move files by dragging them with your mouse, follow these steps:

1. Select View ➤ Dual File Lists if you want to move the file or files to a drive or directory that isn't visible at the moment. Bring the source and destination drive and directories into view by clicking in the appropriate windows.
2. In the File List window, select the file or files you want to move. Remember to press and hold the Ctrl key if you need to select several files.
3. Press and hold down the Alt key (very important) while dragging the selected files to the desired directory in the Directory Tree window.
4. Release the mouse button when you've dragged the files to the correct location.
5. When asked to confirm, click Yes to complete the operation or No to cancel it.

MOVING FILES AND DIRECTORIES FROM THE COMMAND PROMPT

You can use the MOVE command to move files and directories from the command prompt. The format of MOVE is similar to COPY and RENAME, as shown below:

move *from to*

In the command above, *from* indicates the original location and *to* indicates the new location. MOVE also can be used to change the name of a directory. Some examples will illustrate the techniques you can use.

To move a file named BATMAN.BAT from the root directory of drive A to the file named CATBOY.BAT in the current directory of drive C, type the command **move a:\batman.bat c:catboy.bat**.

The command **move *.txt h:\wp-proj\fun** moves all files with the extension .TXT from the current directory to the \WP-PROJ\FUN directory on drive H.

The command **move c:\av8tor \flier** renames the directory \AV8TOR on drive C to \FLIER. Note that you cannot move a directory to another drive or to a different level in the directory tree.

Moving a file to an existing file overwrites that file. For safety, use the DIR command to see if there's any danger of overwriting the destination file.

DELETING FILES AND DIRECTORIES

You can remove files from your hard disk or floppy disk to recover some space and clean house when necessary.

After removing unwanted files, you might want to consider using the DoubleSpace and MS-DOS Defragmenter programs, which can "buy" you lots of extra hard disk space without costing you a single penny. See Lesson 6 for details.

Before deleting files, you should use the DIR command or the Shell to review the names of the files you'll be deleting, just to make sure that there aren't some you want to keep. Although it's often possible to retrieve deleted files with the UNDELETE command (discussed in Lesson 5), you shouldn't delete files unless you really mean it. If necessary, use the copy or move techniques discussed earlier or the MSBACKUP command covered in Lesson 5 to make backup copies of files on floppy disks or backup drives.

The following sections list some kinds of files you might want to delete if you're sure you no longer need them.

NEVER delete COMMAND.COM or any hidden files in the root directory. If you delete them, you won't be able to start your system. Also, if you're not absolutely certain about the purpose of a file in the \DOS directory (or any other directory for that matter), do not delete it.

PROGRAM AND DATA FILES

Many people can easily part with old spreadsheets, text files, databases, and other data that they rarely use. You can retain programs that are rarely used on floppy disks rather than using the hard disk for dead storage.

TEMPORARY FILES

When a program ends suddenly (for instance, if the power fails), your application may create temporary files (these often have the extension .TMP). Once your system is running and you've restarted the program and retrieved the data, you can delete the temporary file from the hard disk (if it's still there).

Environment variables control the behavior of some batch programs, DOS itself, and certain application programs. These variables often point to the temporary file directories. To list the current environment variables, type **set** at the command prompt and press ↵. The variables TEMP and DBTEMP are commonly used to specify directory names that store temporary files. You can then use DIR to look in those directories for stray temporary files, and delete the files if you're sure they're unnecessary.

DELETING FILES AND DIRECTORIES FROM THE SHELL

Here are the steps for deleting files and directories from the Shell:

1. Select the file or files you want to delete in the File List window, or select the directory you want to delete in the Directory Tree window.
2. Select File ➤ Del or press the Del key.
3. If you're deleting several files, choose OK or press ↵ to continue.

4. When the confirmation box appears, choose Yes to delete the file or No to leave the file alone.

When deleting directories and files, keep these guidelines in mind:

- You can delete a directory only if it doesn't contain any files or subdirectories. If necessary, delete all files and subdirectories of that directory first, then delete the directory.
- Confirmation messages appear only if the Confirm On Delete box contains an X. To verify or change the setting, select Options ➤ Confirmation.

DELETING FILES FROM THE COMMAND PROMPT

You can use the DEL or ERASE command to delete files. The general form is **del** *filename* or **erase** *filename*, where *filename* specifies the file or files to be deleted. For added safety, you can add the switch /P to the end of the command. You'll then be prompted to confirm the deletion of each file. Now let's look at some examples.

Suppose you no longer need the file named JUNKFILE.DAT in the directory \WP-PROJ\FUN on drive H. Here are two equivalent ways to delete the file. In the first method, I use the CD command to switch to the directory I want, then I delete the file, like this:

```
cd \wp-proj\fun
del junkfile.dat
```

Although the following command takes longer to type, it will delete the file successfully regardless of the current drive or directory:

```
del h:\wp-proj\fun\junkfile.dat
```

Now, suppose that you want to delete all the files with the extension .JNK in the current drive and directory. The command **del *.jnk** will do the trick. Be especially careful when using wildcards with DEL or ERASE, since many files could go to file heaven with this method. For added safety when using wildcards, add the /P option, as in this example:

```
del *.jnk /p
```

With this form of the command, DOS will display a message like the one below for each file that will be deleted:

```
H:\WP-PROJ\FUN\THISIS.JNK,    Delete (Y/N)?
```

Type **Y** if you're sure you want to delete the file, or **N** to leave the file alone.

If you're very brave, you can use the command **del *.*** or **erase *.*** to delete all files in the current directory. When you use the wildcard *.* with DEL or ERASE, DOS will prompt you for confirmation, as follows:

```
All files in directory will be deleted!
Are you sure (Y/N)?
```

Respond by typing **Y** (to delete the files) or **N** (to leave the files alone) and pressing ↵. If you answer Y, all files will be deleted without further comment. For added safety, you can use the form **del *.* /p** or **erase *.* /p** to have DOS prompt you before deleting each file.

Beware of Del . and Del ..

You learned earlier that . represents the current directory and .. stands for the parent directory. When you use those symbols with the DEL and ERASE commands, you risk losing many files because...

- The commands **erase .** and **del .** are the same as **erase .*.*** and **del .*.***. That is, they erase all files in the current directory.
- The commands **erase ..** and **del ..** are the same as **erase ..*.*** and **del ..*.***. These commands erase all files in the parent directory.

Of course, DOS will prompt you before deleting all files in the current directory or parent directory. But don't get trigger happy and press the Y key until you're sure you really want to delete all the files.

DELETING DIRECTORIES FROM THE COMMAND PROMPT

You can use the RMDIR or RD command to delete a directory from the command prompt. The general form is **rd *dirname***, where *dirname* is the name of the directory to be deleted. As when deleting a directory from the Shell, the directory to be deleted cannot contain any files or subdirectories. If it does, you first must delete the files and subdirectories contained within the directory. What's more, the directory you're deleting cannot be the current directory.

Returning to our \WP-PROJ example again, let's assume we no longer need any of the files in \WP-PROJ or any of its subdirectories. Assuming you've made copies of files that you want to keep, you could use the following commands to remove the \WP-PROJ branch of the directory tree.

```
cd \wp-proj
del acctg\*.*
del budget\*.*
del fun\*.*
rd acctg
rd budget
rd fun
cd ..
rd \wp-proj
```

Remember to type **Y** *(or* **N***) when asked if you're sure that you want to delete all files (*.*) in a directory.*

CHOPPING THE TREE WITH DELTREE

DOS 6 includes a new command named DELTREE which provides a quick, but potentially dangerous, way to chop off an entire branch of the directory tree in a single step. The basic form of this command is **deltree *treename***, where *treename* is the drive and directory name of the branch you want to remove.

DELTREE will delete all files and subdirectories of treename.

The following commands would delete \WP-PROJ and all of its files and subdirectories in just two steps:

```
cd \
deltree \wp-proj
```

Before taking such drastic action, DOS would display this warning message:

```
Delete directory "\wp-proj" and all its subdirectories? [yn]
```

If you're absolutely sure you want to delete all these files and directories, type **Y** and press ↵. To cancel the command, type **N** and press ↵.

SUMMARY

In this lesson you've learned how to use the basic file and directory management techniques available in the DOS Shell and at the command prompt. These include creating and switching directories, copying, moving, renaming, and deleting files and directories, and displaying information about the files and directories on any disk.

REFERENCE ENTRIES

To learn more about the topics covered in this lesson, see these entries in the Alphabetical Reference:

- CHDIR or CD
- COPY
- DEL or ERASE
- DELTREE
- DIR
- DOSSHELL
- FORMAT
- MKDIR or MD

- MOVE
- RENAME or REN
- RMDIR or RD
- SET
- TREE
- UNDELETE
- XCOPY

*K*EEPING THE WOLVES AT BAY: AVOIDING DISASTER

INTRODUCING

Checking your disks for errors
Backing up and restoring files
Recovering files deleted accidentally
Formatting and unformatting disks
Protecting your computer from viruses

Murphy's Law clearly states "Disaster strikes every computer system eventually." You may delete files or format disks accidentally, your hard disk may go bad, or your computer may contract a nasty and potentially devastating virus that puts all of your data at risk. In this lesson you'll learn how to prepare for and cope with disaster, and how to protect your system against future catastrophes.

THE DOCTOR IS IN: USING CHKDSK TO CHECK THE HEALTH OF A DISK

DOS uses a *file allocation table* or FAT to track the locations of all files on the disk. Errors can occur in the FAT when a program is interrupted unexpectedly—for example, if you reboot or have a power failure when the computer is in the middle of writing files to disk. You should not let such errors remain on the disk because they can interfere with the normal operation of some programs and can waste space on your hard disk.

An allocation unit is the smallest amount of disk space that can be allocated to a file. These units can be lost when a program creates a temporary file due to unexpected conditions.

You can use the CHKDSK command to display a status report for the disk drive and to recover lost allocation units, if any exist. To display a status report for drive C, type **chkdsk c:** and press ↵. Figure 5.1 shows a sample report from CHKDSK (the numbers reported for your disks will probably be different).

FIGURE 5.1:

CHKDSK report screen

```
C:\>chkdsk c:

Volume MAIN PGMS   created 01-11-1993 12:45p
Volume Serial Number is 13F6-0238

   56344576 bytes total disk space
      90112 bytes in 3 hidden files
     163840 bytes in 20 directories
   33120256 bytes in 1038 user files
   22970368 bytes available on disk

       8192 bytes in each allocation unit
       7397 total allocation units on disk
       3323 available allocation units on disk

     655360 total bytes memory
     507456 bytes free

C:\>
```

RECOVERING LOST FILE ALLOCATION UNITS

To correct file allocation errors and update the file allocation table, add the /F switch to CHKDSK, as in **chkdsk c: /f**. Some data may be lost when you use CHKDSK to correct disk errors, so be sure to back up your files first.

Before using CHKDSK with the /F switch, you should exit all programs, including memory-resident (TSR) programs. If any TSRs are listed in your CONFIG.SYS or AUTOEXEC.BAT file, you must disable them in those files by opening the files through the DOS Editor, changing relevant lines into comments (see Lesson 8), and restarting your computer.

If file allocation errors exist, you'll see a message like this one:

```
10 lost allocation units found in 3 chains.
Convert lost chains to files?
```

If you type Y (for Yes) in response to the message, DOS will save lost file allocation units as a series of numbered files in the root directory, using the file name format FILE*nnnn*.CHK. If you respond with N (for No), DOS will fix the disk errors but won't save the lost units.

It's a good idea to add CHKDSK commands (without the /F switch) to AUTOEXEC.BAT to check the health of each hard disk whenever you start your computer. If CHKDSK reports errors, you can then back up your files and use CHKDSK /F to correct the errors.

When CHKDSK is through, you can change to the root directory (type **cd **) and view the saved files (assuming you chose to save them). To view the first file, use the TYPE command as shown below:

```
type file0000.chk
```

Use the DEL command to erase any of these files, or open the data file's application and resave the file under a different name. You can also use the MOVE command to give the file another name and move it to another directory.

FIXING CROSS-LINKED FILES

CHKDSK can detect *cross-linked files*—two files or directories that are recorded as using the same disk space. However, it cannot fix these errors, even if you use the /F switch. To fix a cross-linked file, copy the files or directories listed in the cross link message elsewhere and then delete the originals. Note that some information in these files may be lost.

CHKDSK can't fix physical errors such as bad disk sectors, either. Bad sectors are rendered harmless when you format the disk, so they pose no danger.

BUY SOME CHEAP INSURANCE: BACK UP YOUR HARD DISKS

A computer hard disk that isn't backed up is an accident waiting to happen. Therefore, hard disk backups are a must for any computer.

Making the job easier is MSBACKUP, a fully interactive DOS 6 utility program that allows you to back up and restore files from one disk to another. You can run the program from the DOS command line or from Windows (assuming you have installed both versions provided with DOS 6).

The BACKUP command was used in prior versions of DOS to back up files, and it's provided in DOS 6 for compatibility with earlier versions. You must use the RESTORE command, not MSBACKUP, to restore files created by BACKUP.

MSBACKUP provides three backup methods. This gives you lots of flexibility for controlling which files are backed up when. But regardless of which method you choose, it's essential to stick with a regular backup regimen. Even though DOS provides commands like CHKDSK, UNDELETE, and UNFORMAT, there's no substitute for complete backups. Here's why:

- Hard disks fail occasionally, making it nearly impossible to recover data using DOS commands.

- If you purchase a new hard disk, you may need a quick way to restore files to your new disk.
- You may need to transfer many files from one DOS 6 computer to another. MSBACKUP provides one of the most efficient ways to do this.
- UNDELETE and UNFORMAT may not be able to recover data if you've made changes to files on the hard disk or have added or deleted files.

Although most people back up onto and restore from floppy disks, you can speed up the job by using other drives, such as network drives, for your backups.

UNDERSTANDING THE BACKUP METHODS AVAILABLE

MSBACKUP allows you to choose from the following backup methods:

Full Backup Backs up every file you select (default setting). Use Full Backup for initial backups and whenever you want to back up all selected files, whether they've changed or not.

Incremental Backup Backs up files that have changed since your last full or incremental backup. This method switches the archive flag to prevent the same files from being backed up in the next incremental backup unless they change again. Use this method if you want to keep interim copies of all files that you've changed. Be sure to save all incremental backup sets made between full backups.

Differential Backup Backs up files that have changed since your last full backup. This method leaves the archive status unchanged so that the same files can be backed up again during the next differential backup. Use Differential Backup if you want a single backup set that contains all files changed since the last full backup.

UNDERSTANDING SETUP FILES

Before beginning your backups, you must make selections that control how the backups will be performed. These selections are stored in setup files with an extension of .SET (the default setup file name is DEFAULT.SET). You can define various setup files to handle each type of backup you wish to perform. For example, you might define FULLBACK.SET for full backups, DAILY.SET for differential daily backups, and WEEKLY.SET for incremental weekly backups.

UNDERSTANDING BACKUP SETS AND BACKUP CATALOGS

During the backup process, MSBACKUP creates *backup sets* and *backup catalogs*. Backup sets contain the actual data that has been backed up, and they're stored on the backup disk or disks.

The backup catalog, which lists relevant information about the files that have been backed up, is stored on the last floppy disk of each backup set and in the \DOS directory of drive C (or wherever the MSBACKUP program files are located). If you need to restore files, you must load the appropriate backup catalog first.

Backup catalog file names uniquely identify each backup set. For example, the name CD31109A.INC provides the following information:

- C is the first drive backed up in the set (drive C).
- *D* is the last drive backed up in the set (drive D).
- *3* is the last digit of the year, as determined by the system date (*3* for 1993).
- *11* is the month the backup set was created (*11* for November).
- 09 is the day the backup set was created.
- A is the sequence letter (from A to Z) of the backup. This letter is incremented each time you take another backup of the same disks on the same day. In this example, A refers to the first backup set made on November 9, 1993.
- The file name extension reflects the type of backup you made: .INC (incremental), .FUL (full), or .DIF (differential).

BACKING UP FILES WITH MSBACKUP FOR DOS

The simplest way to use MSBACKUP for DOS is to type **msbackup** and press ↵ at the command prompt. If you haven't performed a disk compatibility test, an Alert message will remind you that reliable system backups cannot be guaranteed until you've completed the test successfully. Press ↵ to begin the test, then follow the on-screen prompts. (Normally, you'll just have to press ↵ to continue with each step of the compatibility test). You'll need two floppy disks of the same type to complete the test, and all data on those disks will be overwritten.

The main Backup screen includes a File menu, a Help menu, and these five buttons:

Configure Allows you to adjust video and mouse settings, define the drives used for backup and restore procedures, and run a compatibility test to make sure that your system will work properly with MSBACKUP.

Backup Allows you to select the type of backup you want (full, incremental, or differential), define backup options, select files to back up, save your setup file (choose File ➤ Save), and perform the backup.

Compare Allows you to compare the backed up files to the original files to verify that the backup process went smoothly.

Restore Allows you to select restore options, load the backup catalog, select files to be restored, and perform the restore.

Quit Exits MSBACKUP. Alternatively, you can select File ➤ Exit.

The keyboard procedures for selecting options with MSBACKUP are summarized below. If you prefer, you can use your mouse instead.

- To select a button or open a menu, press Alt plus the highlighted or colored letter in the name. For example, press Alt+B to select the Backup button. After opening a menu, select an option by typing its highlighted letter.
- To move from button to button or to various areas on the screen, use the Tab or Shift+Tab keys.
- To move the selection highlight up or down within a list of options, press the ↑ or ↓ keys.
- To check or uncheck a selected item in a list, press the spacebar. The spacebar toggles your selection on or off.
- To select a radio button option, type the option's highlighted character.

To get help, highlight the option you're interested in and look at the status line at the bottom of the screen. For more detailed help, press F1 or select options from the Help menu.

To exit MSBACKUP, select File ➤ Exit from the menus, or select the Quit button from the main Microsoft Backup screen.

The steps for backing up a file are as follows:

1. Start MSBACKUP and select the Backup button. You'll see the Backup screen shown in Figure 5.2. If you've already defined and saved your default Setup file, you can skip directly to Step 8.

Unlike COPY, which quits when it fills up a floppy disk, MSBACKUP will prompt you when it needs another backup disk, and it will format disks automatically as needed.

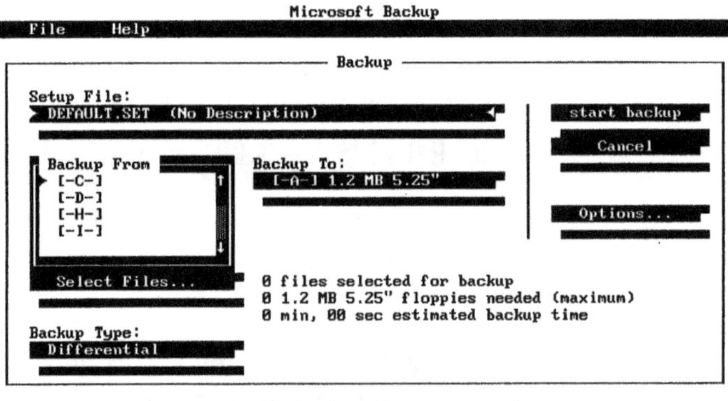

FIGURE 5.2:
The Backup screen

2. If you want to load a different setup file, select Setup File, highlight the file you want, and press ↵.
3. If you want to back up from a different drive, or an additional drive, select Backup From, highlight the drive you want, and press the spacebar. (If you select the drive and press the spacebar again, that drive will be cleared from the list to be backed up.)
4. If you want to back up to a different drive, select Backup To, type the highlighted letter or number of the drive you want, and press ↵.

5. To select the files to be backed up, choose Select Files. The Select Backup Files screen shown in Figure 5.3 will appear. Use the Tab (or Shift+Tab) key to move to the drive, directory, or file you're interested in, then press the spacebar to select (check) or deselect (uncheck) it in the backup list. You can also use the buttons for finer control over selection criteria. Choose OK when you've finished making your selections.

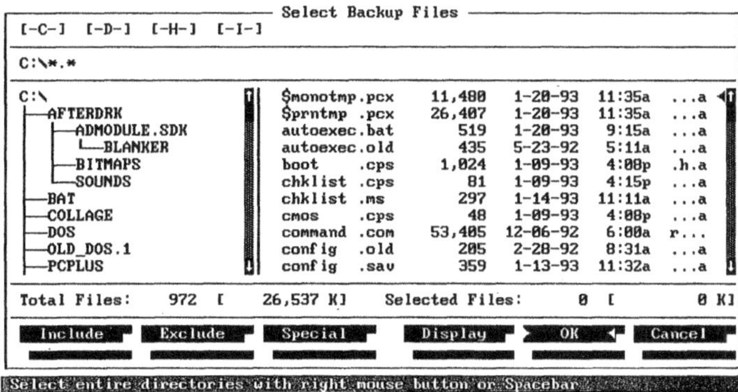

FIGURE 5.3:

The Select Backup Files screen

6. If you want to select a different backup type, select Backup Type, highlight the type of backup you want (Full, Incremental, or Differential), and press ↵. Full, the default option, backs up *all* selected files.

7. If you want to change any backup options, select Options, then select or deselect the options you want (the defaults should be adequate for most people). Press ↵ when you've finished.

8. To start the backup, select Start Backup and follow the instructions that appear on the screen.

As you remove each backup disk, be sure to label it with the name of the backup catalog file and disk number within the backup set, so that you'll know which disks to use if you need to restore files later. (Use the DIR command, if necessary, to find out the catalog file name.)

Backing Up Altered Files Only

After the initial backup, you can save a lot of time by backing up only files that are new or were modified since the last backup. To perform a partial backup, follow the first five steps above. In Step 6, select either Incremental or Differential, then complete the remaining steps.

BACKING UP FILES WITH MSBACKUP FOR WINDOWS

Using MSBACKUP for Windows is almost the same as using MSBACKUP for DOS. To begin the backup process, double-click the Backup icon (shown below) in the Microsoft Tools group of Program Manager.

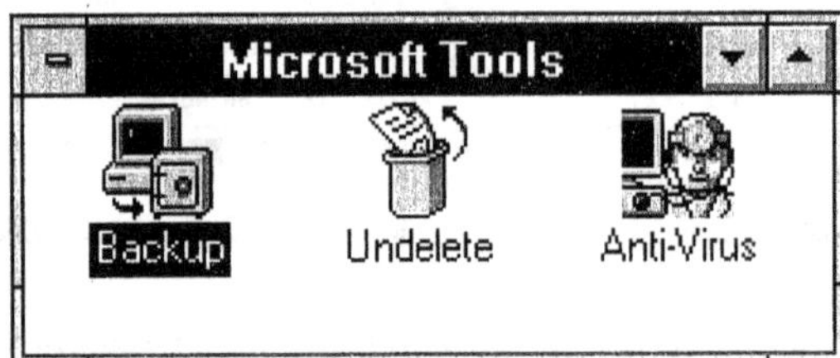

Figure 5.4 shows the Microsoft Backup window. Notice that this window features Backup, Compare, Restore, Configure, Quit, Start Backup, Options, and Select Files buttons. These work the same way as their MSBACKUP for DOS counterparts. Simply use your left mouse button to choose the button you want.

Figure 5.5 shows the Select Backup Files window that appears after you click the Select Files button. You can select files and directories to back up using the methods described earlier for MSBACKUP for DOS.

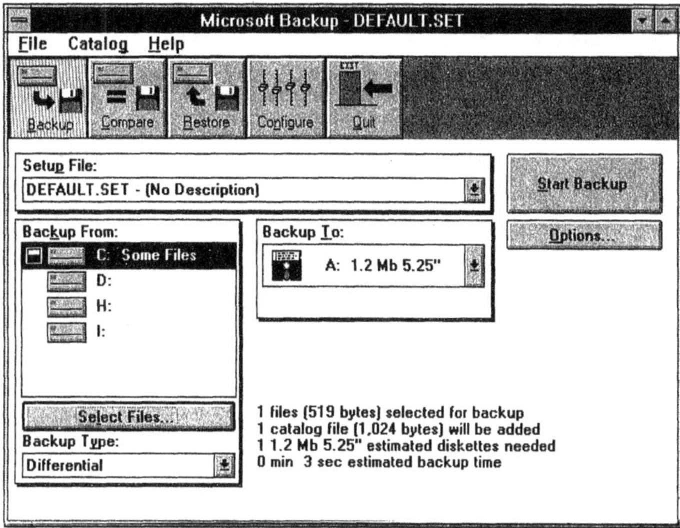

FIGURE 5.4:

The Microsoft Backup window

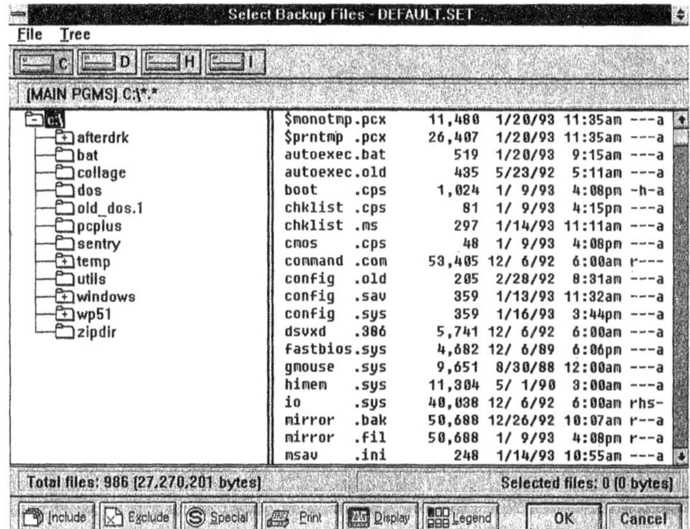

FIGURE 5.5:

The Select Backup Files window

CASHING IN ON THE POLICY: RESTORING DATA FROM BACKUPS

If your hard disk crashes and needs to be replaced or formatted, or you need to transfer files to another computer or hard disk, you can restore files from backups either from the DOS command prompt or from Windows. Before restoring files, you'll need to find the appropriate backup set and know which backup catalog includes the files to be restored. (If you've lost or deleted the hard disk copy of the backup catalog, you can select the Catalog option from the Restore screen and rebuild the catalog.)

It doesn't matter whether files were backed up with the DOS or Windows version of MSBACKUP—both versions of MSBACKUP back up and restore files, and they're completely interchangeable.

Remember that RESTORE is provided for compatibility with versions of DOS prior to 6.0. Use RESTORE, not MSBACKUP, if you need to restore files that were backed up with the BACKUP command.

RESTORING FILES WITH MSBACKUP FOR DOS

To restore a file with MSBACKUP for DOS, start the program by typing **msbackup** and pressing ↵ at the command line. Then select the Restore button. Figure 5.6 illustrates the Restore screen that appears. Notice how similar it is to the Backup screen shown in Figure 5.2.

The basic steps for restoring files are as follows. (If you want to accept all the default selections, skip directly to Step 6.)

1. If you want to select a different backup catalog, select Backup Set Catalog, highlight the catalog you want, press the spacebar, and press ↵.
2. If you want to restore from a different drive, select Restore From, highlight the drive you want, and press ↵.
3. If you want to restore the files to a location other than their original location, select Restore To, select the option you want, and press ↵.

FIGURE 5.6:

The Restore screen for MSBACKUP for DOS

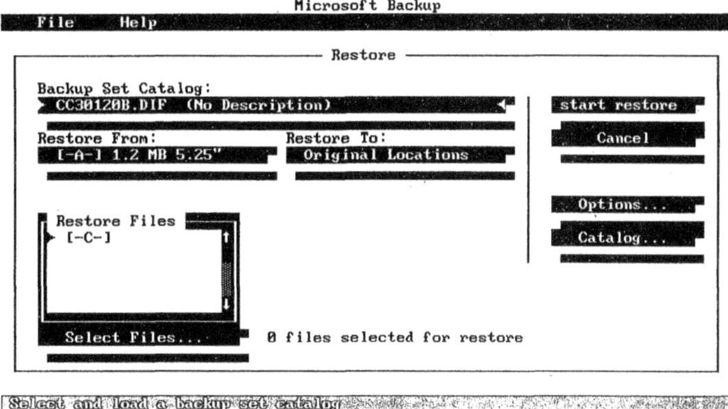

4. If you want additional control over how the restore will be done, choose Options, check the options you want, and press ↵.
5. If you need to find, load, retrieve, rebuild, or delete catalogs, or find catalogs that contain specific files, you can select the Catalog option.
6. To select the files to be restored, choose Select Files and check the files you want, using the same techniques used to select files for backup. Press ↵ when you've finished.
7. When you're ready to restore the selected files, select Start Restore and follow the screen prompts.

RESTORING FILES WITH MSBACKUP FOR WINDOWS

The procedures for restoring files with MSBACKUP for Windows are almost identical to the corresponding DOS restore procedures. Begin the restore operation by double-clicking the Backup icon in the Microsoft Tools group of Program Manager. Then click the Restore button. Figure 5.7 shows the Restore screen that appears. Notice its similarity to the Restore screen shown in Figure 5.6 for the DOS version. The restore screen features the usual Backup Set Catalog, Restore From, Restore To, Select Files, and Options selections. However, the Catalog options are located on the Catalog *menu*.

FIGURE 5.7:

The Restore screen for MSBACKUP for Windows

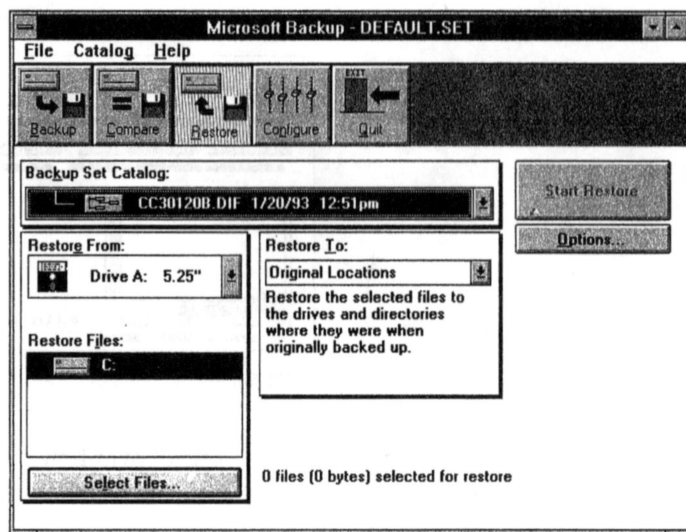

SAVING THE BACON: HOW TO RECOVER DELETED FILES

Two different commands—UNDELETE and UNFORMAT—allow you to recover deleted files and directories. But even though these commands are provided, you shouldn't rely on them exclusively. Instead, you should make complete backups, and you should be very careful when deleting files and formatting disks. Furthermore, you should be aware that UNDELETE and UNFORMAT aren't foolproof. If other files have been created or changed on a disk, you may not be able to recover lost files or directories. Therefore, if you delete or format a disk accidentally, use UNDELETE or UNFORMAT without delay.

SELECTING UNDELETE FILE PROTECTION IN UNDELETE FOR DOS

You can use Undelete to restore files that you removed with the DEL or ERASE command. This is possible because DOS 6 provides three levels of file protection when you delete a file.

Delete Sentry: Highest Protection Level

When you select Sentry protection, DOS creates a hidden directory named SENTRY, to which deleted files are moved without changing their locations in the file allocation table. When you use Undelete, the deleted file is restored to its original position on disk. Sentry operates through the TSR (memory-resident) portion of Undelete.

By default, Sentry is allocated only about 20% of the total disk space. Once this space is used up, the oldest files are purged to make room for the new ones.

Delete Tracker: Intermediate Protection

For this intermediate protection method, DOS creates a small hidden file named PCTRACKR.DEL, where it records the location of a deleted file. When you delete a file, DOS changes the file allocation table so that the deleted file's former location is available for a new file. You can recover the deleted file only if another file has not been placed in its former location. Like Delete Sentry, Delete Tracker operates through the TSR portion of Undelete.

MS-DOS: Lowest Protection Level

MS-DOS deletion protection is available automatically when you turn on your computer. As long as the original disk location of a deleted file hasn't been taken by a new file, you may be able to recover all or part of it. No additional memory, disk space, or command is needed to activate MS-DOS protection.

Activating Undelete Protection

The simplest way to activate the memory-resident portion of Undelete is to type **undelete /load** and press ↵ at the command prompt. The /LOAD switch loads Undelete into memory and directs the program to use options specified in the file UNDELETE.INI (UNDELETE.INI will be described in just a moment). If you prefer to load deletion tracking automatically, you can place the UNDELETE /LOAD command in your AUTOEXEC.BAT file, preferably following other commands that load memory-resident programs.

The MS-DOS level of deletion protection is activated automatically when you ***do not*** *use the UNDELETE command.*

As an alternative to using the /LOAD switch, you can use the /S or /T switch. The /S switch loads Undelete into memory and activates Delete Sentry for the current drive or a specified drive. For example, you can type **undelete /sd** to enable Sentry tracking for drive C (the default) and drive D. Similarly, the /T switch loads Undelete into memory and activates Delete Tracker protection for the current drive or a specified drive. Thus, the command UNDELETE /TD implements Delete Tracker protection for drive C (the default) and drive D. Only one deletion tracking method can be loaded at any time.

All drives specified in the \DOS\UNDELETE.INI file are protected, regardless of the drives you specify when you start Undelete.

To unload Undelete from memory, type **undelete /u** and press ↵. (If Undelete wasn't the last memory-resident program loaded, you won't be able to unload it.)

Controlling Undelete Protection

When you load Undelete into memory, the program uses settings in the file \DOS\UNDELETE.INI. This file is divided into these five sections:

- The **[sentry.drives]** section specifies which drives are protected by the Delete Sentry method.
- The **[sentry.files]** section specifies which files are protected by the Delete Sentry or Delete Tracker method. A hyphen (-) preceding a file name prevents that file from being protected. Wildcards (* and ?) are allowed in the file names.
- The **[mirror.drives]** section specifies the drives protected by the Delete Tracker method.

- The **[configuration]** section defines whether files are protected when the archive bit is set, the number of days files remain on disk before they are purged, and the amount of total disk space reserved for deleted files.
- The **[defaults]** section specifies the default method of file tracking (either Sentry or Tracker).

The default UNDELETE.INI file settings are as follows:

- Use the Delete Sentry method of file tracking on the current drive.
- Save all files except *.TMP, *.VM?, *.WOA, *.SWP, *.SPL, *.RMG, *.IMG, *.THM, and *.DOV.
- Do not save files that have the archive bit set.
- Purge files after seven days.
- Restrict the amount of disk space available for deleted files to 20% of the total disk space.

You can change settings by carefully editing the UNDELETE.INI file in the \DOS directory with the DOS Editor or another text editor. For example, to add Delete Sentry tracking for drive D, place the following line in the [sentry.drives] section of the UNDELETE.INI file:

```
D=
```

Type **help undelete** *for more information on editing the UNDELETE.INI file.*

RECOVERING DELETED FILES WITH UNDELETE FOR DOS

If you need to recover a file, use the CD command to switch to the directory where it was located. Then type **undelete** and press ↵ if you want Undelete to recover all deleted files in the current directory one at a time. You'll be prompted for confirmation of each file, and Undelete will use the highest level of deletion tracking available.

Alternatively, you can specify the name of a file to recover as well as one of these switches: /DS (for Delete Sentry), /DT (for Delete Tracking), /DOS (for MS-DOS protection), or /ALL (for all three protection methods). For example, the command **undelete c:\wp-files*.txt /all** recovers all deleted files with a .TXT extension in the \WP-FILES directory of drive C, without prompting for confirmation of each file.

USING UNDELETE FOR WINDOWS

If you want to use the Windows version of Undelete, double-click the icon in the Windows Tools group in Program Manager.

Selecting Undelete File Protection in Undelete for Windows

As with the DOS version of Undelete, the Windows version allows you to select the level of protection for files that you delete. After double-clicking the Undelete icon, choose Options ➤ Configure Delete Protection. In the dialog box that appears, select Delete Sentry, Delete Tracker, or Standard and click OK. If you chose Delete Sentry or Delete Tracker, other dialog boxes will ask you to select the drive and files you want to protect, and will ask for permission to update your AUTOEXEC.BAT file. The protection will be in effect after you quit Windows and restart your computer. To exit UNDELETE, select File ➤ Exit or press Alt+F4.

Recovering Deleted Files with Undelete for Windows

When you start Undelete for Windows, the program will list files that have been deleted from the current directory in reverse chronological order (most recent first). If necessary, use the Drive/Dir button to switch to the directory where the file was located. The example in Figure 5.8 shows the window after I selected drive H on my computer.

The Undelete window also displays the condition of each file—Perfect, Excellent, Good, Poor, or Destroyed.

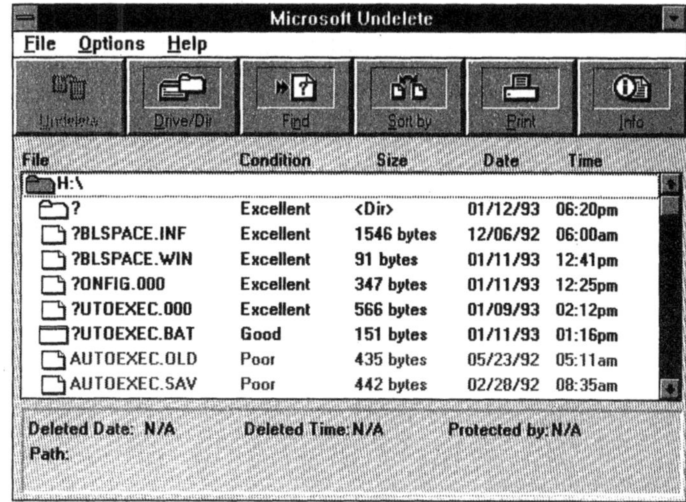

FIGURE 5.8: Undelete for Windows shows deleted files that you may be able to recover.

The Find, Sort By, Print, and Info buttons provide some handy tools for limiting the files that are listed, sorting files, printing the list of files available to recover, and getting information about individual files.

Undeleting Poor or Destroyed Files Files designated Poor or Destroyed cannot be undeleted with Undelete for Windows. However, you can try deleting them with the DOS version of Undelete.

Undeleting Good, Excellent, or Perfect Files To undelete files, select one or more files and choose the Undelete button. If the name of the file to be undeleted begins with a ? character, you'll need to replace that character in the name and choose OK. If another file with the same name as the file being undeleted currently exists on disk, choose OK to clear the warning message, supply a new name for the recovered file in the Rename File dialog box, and choose OK.

Undelete will not let you overwrite an existing file.

Undeleting Directories To undelete a directory, switch to its parent directory (with the Drive/Dir button), select the deleted directory, and then select the Undelete button. You may need to repeat the Undelete procedure for lower-level directories and files in the undeleted directory.

FORMATTING AND RECOVERING DISKS

Before you can use a brand new floppy disk that wasn't formatted by the manufacturer, or a hard disk that has never been formatted before, you must use the FORMAT command to format the disk. The FORMAT command creates a new root directory and file allocation table for the disk. To format a floppy disk in drive A, you could type **format a:** and press ↵. To format the disk in drive B, you could type **format b:** and press ↵. You can also format disks by using the Quick Format and Format options in the Disk Utilities program group of the DOS Shell.

If you reformat a disk accidentally, you may lose all the files on that disk. Depending on the type of formatting you used, it may be possible to recover the files with the command UNFORMAT.

WARNING

Reformatting and unformatting a hard disk is rarely necessary, and it can be tricky unless you know precisely what you're doing. To be safe, reformat and unformat floppy disks only!

FORMATTING DISKS

To understand how UNFORMAT works, you should be aware of the three FORMAT options available:

Quick Formatting If you use the /Q option of FORMAT or the Quick Format option from the Shell's Disk Utilities program group on a previously formatted disk, DOS will recreate the file allocation table and root directory, but won't delete any other data. This method allows you to unformat the disk later. Since quick formatting doesn't check for bad sectors, you should use it only on disks that are in good physical condition.

Safe Formatting If you do not specify any switches when formatting a disk, DOS will perform a "safe format," which creates a root directory and FAT, leaves the data, and also checks for bad sectors. This option also allows you to unformat the disk later.

Unconditional Formatting Using the /U switch with FORMAT deletes all data on the disk, leaving nothing to be recovered with UNFORMAT.

If you used quick or safe formatting, you might be able to recover data as long as it hasn't been overwritten by new files.

UNFORMATTING DISKS

If you think your disk has recoverable files, type **unformat** at the command prompt, followed by the letter of the drive containing the disk; for example, **unformat a:** will unformat the disk in floppy drive A.

Any files you've written to the disk since it was reformatted will be destroyed in the unformatting process.

Whenever you unformat a disk, DOS uses information from the file allocation table and root directory to reconstruct files that weren't fragmented.

If DOS finds a fragmented file—one that's stored in several places—it will ask you whether you want the truncated portion (the first part) recovered or whether it should be deleted (DOS will proceed only after you respond). If you aren't questioned about a particular file, it probably has been recovered (though there are no guarantees!). As unformatting proceeds, the subdirectories that are recovered will be displayed.

Keep in mind that unformatting should be done immediately and only as a last resort.

VIRUS VIGILANCE: PROTECTING YOUR SYSTEM FROM VIRUS ATTACKS

Viruses are computer programs silently installed on your computer for the sole purpose of disrupting its operations. Like a biological virus, a computer virus attaches itself to a larger entity and either multiplies or spreads to other entities (in this case, programs). Some viruses are merely mischievous, while others can destroy your programs, your data, or both. Three general types of viruses can attack your computer:

- *Boot sector viruses* replace the portion of the disk that controls the operating system startup, then spread from disk to disk
- *File infectors* add on to executable files, so that they are activated when the file is run, then spread to program files
- *Trojan horses* seem to be ordinary programs, but damage or destroy files and disks

Virus-damaged files may be recoverable, though often data is lost, particularly if the attacker was a Trojan horse virus. DOS 6 provides two types of antiviral protection: one that scans the system for programs that act like viruses and protects against them, and another that you can use to examine disks for specific viruses and disinfect them.

MONITORING YOUR COMPUTER FOR VIRUSES

VSafe is a memory-resident program that guards your system against viruses and displays a warning if it identifies one. VSafe is available for both MS-DOS and Windows, depending on choices you make when installing DOS 6.

Loading VSafe for DOS

You can load VSafe into memory simply by typing **vsafe** and pressing ↵ at the command prompt. When loaded into memory, VSafe will warn you automatically about formatting that could erase the hard disk (option 1), check executable files as they are opened (option 4), check for boot sector viruses (option 5), and warn you when an attempt is made to change the boot sector or the hard disk's partition table (option 6).

Configuring VSafe for DOS

If you want to change any VSafe options after the program is loaded, just press the hotkey Alt+V to open the VSafe pop-up menu, and then type the number of the option you want to change. Each time you select an option, the option will either be turned on (an X will appear next to it) or off (the X will be cleared).

In addition to the options listed above, you can have VSafe warn you if a program is trying to remain in memory (select option 2), prevent programs from writing to the disk (option 3), warn of attempts to write to a floppy disk's boot sector (option 7), and warn of attempts to modify executable files (option 8). Press Esc to clear the pop-up menu.

You can also specify options on the VSafe command line if you'd like more control over how VSafe operates or if you want to change the hotkey. *See VSAFE in the Alphabetical Reference for more information.*

Removing VSafe for DOS from Memory

You can remove VSafe from memory in either of two ways:

- Type the command **vsafe /u** and press ↵.
- Press Alt+V, then press Alt+U.

Using VSafe with Windows

To activate VSafe for use with Windows, first add the command **load=mwavtsr.exe** to your \WINDOWS\WIN.INI file. Then run VSafe in one of these ways:

- Type **vsafe** at the command prompt before starting Windows.
- Place the command VSAFE in your AUTOEXEC.BAT file, before any command that starts Windows. Use this method if you want VSafe to run automatically whenever you boot your computer.

WARNING

If you've already loaded VSafe into memory and you plan to install Windows (or other programs), you should disable VSafe first so that it won't interfere with the installation.

SCANNING DISKS FOR VIRUSES

Microsoft Anti-Virus, or MSAV, is a program that you should run periodically to search for over 1000 specific viruses. If a virus is found, you can direct the program to clean or disinfect the disk. You can also use the program to learn more about the viruses it can detect. As with VSafe, versions of Microsoft Anti-Virus are provided for DOS and for Windows.

Microsoft Anti-Virus is licensed from Central Point Software, and you can order updates of the list of viruses that Anti-Virus detects from that company. See your DOS manual for further information on ordering updates.

Using Anti-Virus from the DOS Command Line

You can run Anti-Virus interactively, or add it to your AUTOEXEC.BAT file so that it runs automatically whenever you start up your system.

To run Anti-Virus interactively, type **msav** and press ↵ at the command prompt. When the Main Menu appears (see Figure 5.9), you can select any of the options listed below.

Detect Scans the entire current work drive, reports any viruses found, and gives you the option of removing them. Usually, the work drive is C, unless you specify a drive letter on the command line (for example, by typing **msav d:**).

Detect & Clean Same as Detect, but this option removes viruses automatically.

Select New Drive Allows you to select a different drive. Use the arrow keys to highlight the drive and press ↵, or click your mouse on the drive letter you want.

Options Allows you to exercise more control over Anti-Virus's behavior.

Exit Allows you to save configuration options and exit to DOS.

To select an option, highlight it with the arrow keys and press ↵, or press (or click) one of the function keys listed on the status line at the bottom of the screen. The function keys are F1=Help, F2=Select New Drive, F3=Exit, F4=Detect, F5=Detect & Clean, F7=Delete Checklist Files from the Current Drive, F8=Options, and F9=List (described later in this lesson).

FIGURE 5.9:

The Microsoft Anti-Virus Main Menu

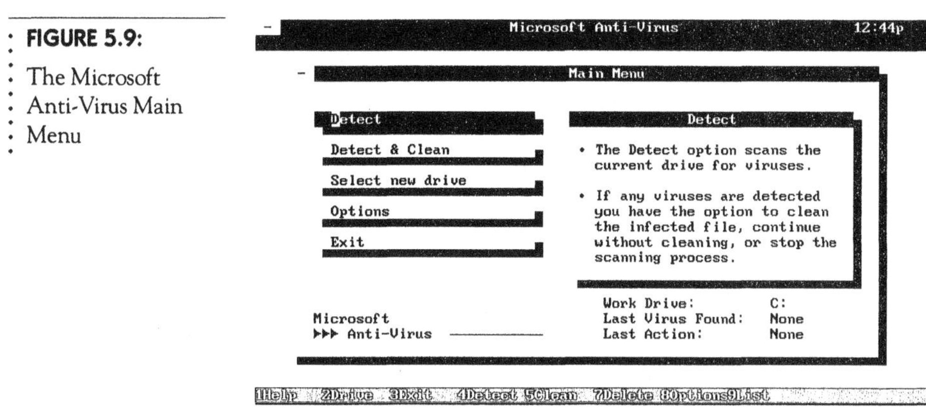

Running Anti-Virus from AUTOEXEC.BAT

To run Anti-Virus automatically every time you turn on the computer, place the MSAV command in your AUTOEXEC.BAT file and specify the drives and command line switches you want to use (see MSAV in the reference section for a complete list of switches).

The following command line runs Anti-Virus on drives C and D, removes any viruses detected (/C switch), and turns off the information display during scanning (/N switch):

```
msav c: d: /c /n
```

If your computer is connected to a network, follow the MSAV command with the switch /L to confine the scan to local drives.

Using Anti-Virus with Windows

The Anti-Virus program for Windows is similar to the DOS version, but prettier. To start the program from Windows, double-click the Anti-Virus icon in the Microsoft Tools group of Program Manager. Figure 5.10 illustrates the opening screen.

If you want to change the configuration options (which are the same as the options in the DOS version), choose Options ➤ Set Options from the menus, then click the desired option with your mouse. Or, use the Tab or arrow keys to move to an option and press the spacebar to toggle the option on or off. Choose OK when you're done.

After selecting configuration options, you can scan a single drive or multiple drives. To select a drive or drives, click on the drive or drives you want to scan in the Drives area, or use the arrow keys and make your selection with the spacebar. If you choose the Detect And Clean button, Anti-Virus will detect viruses and clean them automatically. If you want to be prompted after a virus is detected, select the Detect button instead.

When you're finished with the program, select Scan ➤ Exit Anti-Virus from the menus.

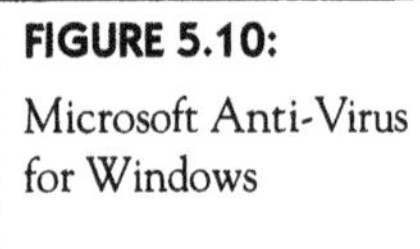

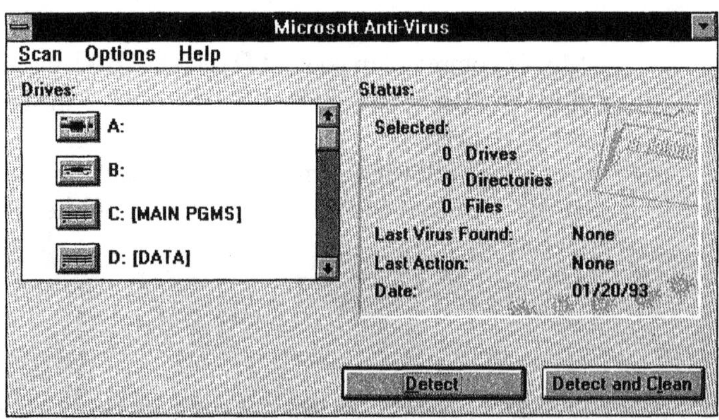

FIGURE 5.10:
Microsoft Anti-Virus for Windows

Running Anti-Virus Automatically from Windows

You can scan a specified drive automatically when you start Anti-Virus for Windows. First click on the Anti-Virus icon in the Microsoft Tools group, then select File ➤ Properties from the Program Manager menus. When the Program Item Properties dialog box appears, enter the name **mwav.exe**, followed by the drive or drives (such as **mwav.exe c: d:**) into the Command Line box. Then choose OK.

If you're running Windows 3.1, you can copy or move the Anti-Virus icon to the StartUp group to have Anti-Virus scan disks automatically when you start Windows.

Getting Virus Information from the DOS Version

Both versions of Anti-Virus can provide you with information about the viruses it protects against. To learn more about one of the viruses from the DOS version, go to the Anti-Virus Main screen and press F9 to see the list of viruses. Use the ↑ and ↓ keys to highlight the one you want and then press ↵. Alternatively, you can click the name with your mouse, or type the virus name (or partial name) and press ↵. After viewing the virus information, press ↵ to clear the message. Press Esc to return to the Main Menu screen.

Getting Virus Information from the Windows Version

To display virus information from the Windows version of Anti-Virus, choose Scan ➤ Virus List. Then use the arrow keys to highlight the name of the virus you're interested in, click on the virus name, or type the name in the Search For box. When you choose OK or press ↵, the information will be displayed. Choose OK or press ↵ to clear the message, then press Esc when you're finished viewing the list.

SUMMARY

In this lesson you've learned how to use CHKDSK to check for and repair logical errors in the file allocation table, MSBACKUP to back up and restore files on your hard disk, Undelete to protect deleted files and restore them, FORMAT to format disks, UNFORMAT to restore data on reformatted disks, VSafe to protect disks from virus attacks, and Microsoft Anti-Virus to detect and eradicate existing viruses.

REFERENCE ENTRIES

To learn more about these topics, see the following entries in the Alphabetical Reference:

- CHKDSK
- FORMAT
- LABEL
- MSAV
- MSBACKUP
- UNDELETE
- UNFORMAT
- VSAFE

Squeezing the Most from Your Hard Disk

INTRODUCING

Doubling the space available on your hard disks

Speeding up and defragmenting a sluggish hard disk

In this lesson you'll learn how to squeeze more space and speed from your disks without having to spend a cent on bigger or faster drives.

COMPRESSING FILES ON YOUR HARD DISK

By compressing files, you can store the same data in half or even one-third the original space. Thus, file compression is an economical way to increase disk storage without going to the expense of purchasing a higher-capacity hard disk. There are various file compression programs on the market, some of which require a special compression procedure once the file has been saved. However, the DOS 6 program DoubleSpace compresses files as they are written and uncompresses files as they are read, so that your normal computing process is just that—completely normal. After you've compressed a drive, you refer to it by its drive letter, just as you do for uncompressed drives.

Once you compress a drive, you cannot uncompress it without reformatting the disk completely. Please refer to your DOS manual for detailed troubleshooting procedures.

CLEANING HOUSE BEFORE COMPRESSING YOUR FILES

Before compressing files with DoubleSpace, you should...

- Exit any programs you are running
- Back up and then delete unneeded files; for added safety, you can back up the entire hard disk that you'll be compressing
- Run CHKDSK to repair any logical disk errors

You must exit all programs, including the DOS Shell, Windows, and memory-resident programs (TSRs) before running DoubleSpace or CHKDSK. Do not exit SMARTDrive.

When you're ready to run DoubleSpace for the first time, type **dblspace** and press ↵ at the command prompt and, after the introductory screen, press ↵ to display the next screen. If you want to compress files on drive C, choose the Express Setup option by pressing ↵. If you want to compress files on a different drive, select Custom Setup by pressing ↓ and then pressing ↵.

The first time you run DoubleSpace, the DoubleSpace Setup program is run. The next time you run DoubleSpace, the DoubleSpace Manager program starts. Compressed drives are managed by DBLSPACE.BIN, a portion of DOS that is loaded into memory automatically when you start your computer.

USING DOUBLESPACE EXPRESS SETUP

Once you select the Express Setup, a screen will show approximately how long the procedure will take. When you're ready to continue, type **C**. DoubleSpace will perform the following operations:

- Run CHKDSK
- Update CONFIG.SYS with the device driver DBLSPACE.SYS and restart your computer
- Create a new drive for files that must remain uncompressed, including the Windows permanent swap file 386SPART.PAR
- Display information about the amount of space available on drive C before and after compressing

When you're ready, press ↵ to restart the computer. Now go ahead and use your computer just as you did before compressing the disk. Most of your files will remain on drive C. The uncompressed files will be moved to the uncompressed remainder of the hard disk (the *host*), designated with the next unused drive letter, such as drive H. If you use Windows, DoubleSpace will add the swap file's new drive designation to the SYSTEM.INI file automatically.

DOUBLESPACE CUSTOM SETUP

You can choose Custom Setup if you want to compress an existing drive other than drive C or create a new (empty) compressed drive. DoubleSpace will follow a procedure similar to Express Setup.

USING THE DOUBLESPACE MANAGER

After you have compressed the files, you can use the DoubleSpace Manager to check on the status of a compressed drive, change the size and compression ratio of compressed drives, create new compressed volumes (even on floppy disks), run CHKDSK, and defragment your disk. To start the Manager, type **dblspace** and press ↵ at the DOS command prompt. DoubleSpace will search for existing compressed drives and display the DoubleSpace Manager screen and menus, as shown in Figure 6.1.

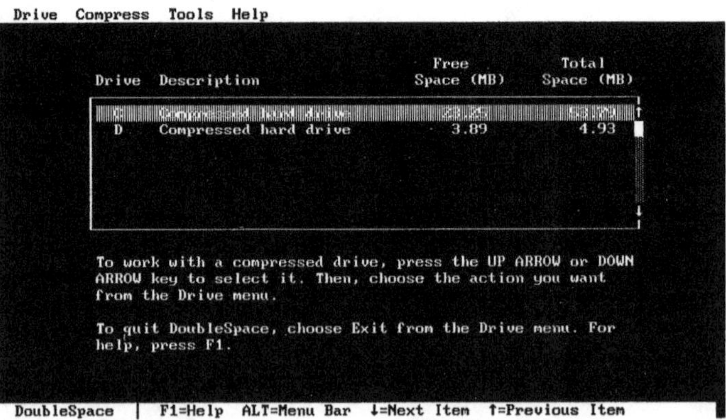

FIGURE 6.1: The DoubleSpace Manager

You can use the DoubleSpace Manager screen as follows:

- To select the drive you want to work with, click on it in the drives area, or use the ↑ or ↓ keys to highlight it.
- To get help, select options from the Help menu or press F1.
- To exit the DoubleSpace Manager, select Drive ➤ Exit.

Displaying Information about Compressed Drives

You can display detailed information about any compressed drive. To do this, select the drive in the drives area of the DoubleSpace Manager, then choose Drive ➤ Info. Figure 6.2 shows a sample Compressed Drive Information screen for drive C. From here, you can select OK to return to the DoubleSpace Manager screen, or you can select the Size or Ratio button to adjust the size of the compressed drive or the estimated compression ratio.

You can also display the Compressed Drive Information screen for a drive by double-clicking the compressed drive or highlighting it and pressing ↵.

FIGURE 6.2: The Compressed Drive Information screen

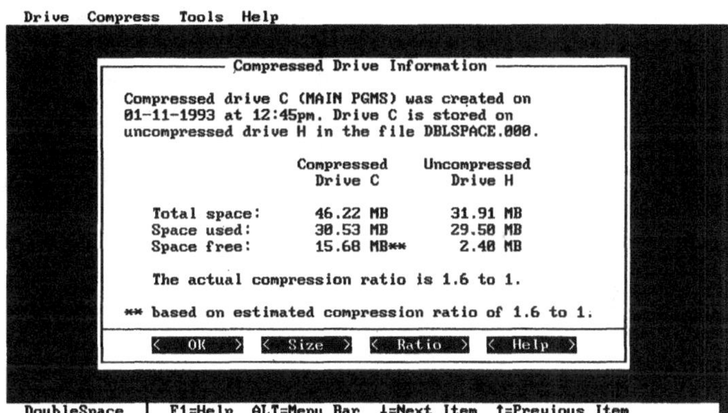

Changing the Size of Compressed Drives

You can change the size of a compressed drive by adjusting the amount of free space on the uncompressed (host) drive. Select the compressed drive you want to change, then select Drive ➤ Change Size from the menus. Alternatively, you can select the Size button from the Compressed Drive Information screen shown in Figure 6.2.

When the Change Size screen appears (Figure 6.3), you can type in a new amount of free space for the uncompressed drive. Increasing the free space on the host drive decreases the size of the compressed drive (assuming free space is available on the compressed drive). Conversely, decreasing the free space on the host drive increases the size of the compressed drive.

When you enlarge a compressed drive, you'll gain more free space on the compressed drive than you lose on the host drive. This is because the space on the compressed drive is also compressed.

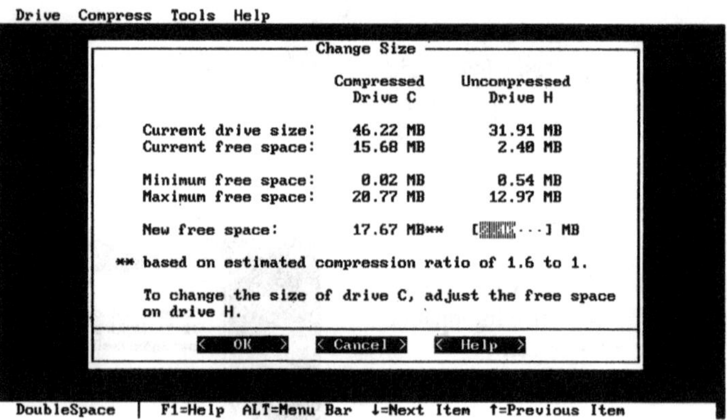

FIGURE 6.3:
The Change Size screen allows you to change the amount of free space on the uncompressed host drive.

Compressing Additional Drives

You can compress files on a floppy disk or hard disk that hasn't been compressed yet by following the steps below.

1. If you're compressing a floppy disk, insert the disk into the floppy drive.
2. Select Compress ➤ Existing Drive from the main menu. DoubleSpace will scan your computer for compressible drives, which must be formatted and have at least 0.65 MB of free space (or 1.2 MB for a startup hard disk).
3. Select the drive you want to compress and press ↵.
4. Press C to begin the process.

A compressed floppy disk must be "mounted" before you can use its files. To mount a floppy disk manually, insert the disk into the drive and select Drive ➤ Mount. To unmount the disk, select Drive ➤ Unmount, then remove the disk.

The mounting procedure simply informs DOS that the floppy disk is compressed. If you don't mount the floppy disk, DOS will assume that the floppy disk isn't compressed.

If you've just compressed the floppy drive, DoubleSpace will mount it automatically. Thereafter, you'll need to use manual procedures to work with the compressed floppy disk. For instance, you'll need to unmount the disk before using an uncompressed floppy disk, and you'll need to remount the compressed disk if you want to use it again after unmounting it or restarting the computer.

Creating New Compressed Drives

You can follow the steps below to create a new compressed drive from free space on an uncompressed hard disk drive. The newly created drive will be compressed, but empty.

1. Select Compress ➤ Create New Drive from the DoubleSpace Manager menus.
2. Highlight the host drive you want to use and press ↵. DoubleSpace will convert that drive's free space to a new compressed drive.
3. DoubleSpace will display the settings it will use for the new drive. Press ↵ to accept the settings and create the new compressed drive.

Running CHKDSK from the DoubleSpace Manager

To learn the status of the compressed drive's logical integrity and repair errors, you can run CHKDSK by selecting Tools ➤ Chkdsk. Then select the Check button to check the drive without fixing errors, or the Fix button to check the drive and fix any errors that are detected.

RUNNING DEFRAG FROM THE DOUBLESPACE MANAGER

To defragment your compressed drive, select Tools ➤ Defragment from the menu, then choose Yes. (Defragmenting is explained in detail in the following sections.)

SPEEDING UP A SLUGGISH HARD DISK WITH MS-DOS DEFRAGMENTER

You can speed up disk access by rearranging the files on the disk so they're stored more efficiently—a process called *defragmenting.*

HOW FILES BECOME FRAGMENTED

Fragmentation can occur when you frequently load, add to, delete from, and then save files. The problem is caused by the way files are stored on a disk. You can visualize how fragmentation occurs by imagining that the original file is a piece of string: If the string is 10 inches long, it is stored in 10 inches of space. If you substitute an 11-inch piece of string, the extra inch must be stored elsewhere.

The same is true of a DOS file. When you add to a stored file, DOS stores the new data elsewhere on the disk. The more you add to the file, the more scattered its contents become on disk. This lengthens the time required to load and save the file. Such fragmentation of a much-changed file can occur even if your disk has lots of free storage space.

The cure for fragmentation is defragmenting. This process reorganizes the disk so that, ideally, each file is stored in just one disk area. You can use the MS-DOS Defragmenter program to accomplish this.

Defragmenter can't be used on network drives or on drives created with the INTERLNK command.

PREPARING TO DEFRAGMENT A DISK

Before starting the defragmentation process, you should delete any unnecessary files (Lesson 4), run CHKDSK to make any needed logical repairs (Lesson 5), back up the disk you want to defragment (Lesson 5), and exit all programs.

Never run MS-DOS Defragmenter without first exiting all active programs, including memory-resident programs (TSRs), the DOS Shell, and Windows. Do not exit SMARTDrive

USING MS-DOS DEFRAGMENTER

When running Defragmenter, you can choose whether to leave empty spaces between files and how to sort the files in the directories.

To begin the defragment procedure, type **defrag** and press ↵ at the command prompt. Defragmenter will test system memory and then ask which disk you want to optimize. Highlight or click on the desired disk and press ↵ (or simply type the drive letter, such as **C**).

MS-DOS Defragmenter provides lots of online help. For assistance, highlight a menu option or go to the dialog box you need help with and press F1.

MS-DOS Defragmenter will analyze the selected disk. If the drive contains fragmented files, a recommendation screen will appear and you can either press ↵ to begin optimization immediately, or press **C** if you wish to modify the optimization method or type of sorting used.

After optimization is complete, and whenever you select Configure from a dialog box, the Optimize menu will appear, as illustrated in Figure 6.4.

If you have compressed the selected drive, Defragmenter will run the DoubleSpace defragment program automatically.

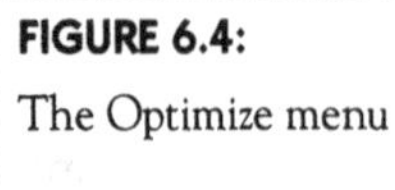

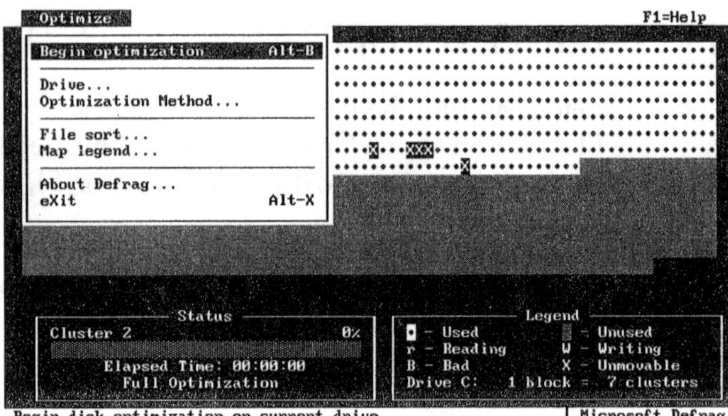

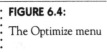

FIGURE 6.4: The Optimize menu

Configuring Defragmenter

The Optimize menu shown in Figure 6.4 provides various options for controlling the defragmentation process. The most important options are listed below.

Begin Optimization Defragments the selected disk with the configuration options you have selected.

Drive Allows you to select the drive you wish to optimize.

Optimization Method Allows you to select one of two optimization methods (described below).

File Sort Allows you to sort all files in all directories according to criteria that you choose (described below).

Exit Returns to the command prompt.

As an alternative to specifying the configuration options interactively, you can run Defragmenter from the command line and specify all the options you want. Type **help defrag** *from the command prompt for more information.*

Selecting an Optimization Method

The Optimization Method option on the Optimize menu lets you select one of two optimization methods.

Choose Full Optimization if you want the best performance gain and you're willing to wait a while for the process to complete. Full optimization moves directories to the front of the disk, defragments all files, and moves all gaps to the end of the disk.

Choose Unfragment Files Only if you're in a hurry and you're not worried about squeezing that last iota of performance out of the system. This option does not optimize directory placement and leaves unfilled gaps scattered around the disk, but it's very fast to run.

Selecting the File Sort Order

By default, MS-DOS Defragmenter stores files in the same order they were in when the process began. If you want to change the sorting order used for file names, select Optimize ➤ File Sort. The File Sort dialog box will appear.

File sorting does not affect the physical positioning of the data on the disk.

To select a sort criterion, type the first letter of the sort criterion you want. The available sort criteria are listed below.

Unsorted Uses the current order on the disk.

Name Sorts by file name.

Extension Sorts by the file extension.

Date & Time Sorts by the date and time the file was created or last modified.

Size Sorts by the size of the files.

After choosing your sort criterion, press ↓ and select a sort order—**A** for Ascending (A to Z) or **D** for Descending (Z to A). Finally, press ↵ to complete your selections.

You can also use your mouse to select a sort criterion and sort order.

SUMMARY

In this lesson you've learned how to make more disk space available by compressing disk files with DoubleSpace, and how to speed up and defragment your disk with MS-DOS Defragmenter.

REFERENCE ENTRIES

To learn more about the topics covered in this lesson, see these entries in the Alphabetical Reference:

- CHKDSK
- DBLSPACE
- DEFRAG

*T*HANK YOU FOR THE MEMORY

INTRODUCING

Why memory is important

How DOS divides the memory pie

Getting the most out of your computer's memory

Driving smarter and faster with SMARTDrive

In this lesson you'll learn about your computer's memory, how it is divided up, how to configure it most efficiently, and how to use SMARTDrive to speed up your system.

UNDERSTANDING COMPUTER MEMORY

Memory consists of the computer chips (RAM chips) where data is held temporarily while you are working with it. All programs must be loaded into memory to run, and data passes through memory on its way to and from the disk. Typically, memory is measured in *kilobytes* (thousands of bytes) or *megabytes* (millions of bytes). Information is deleted from memory when you turn off or restart your computer. Therefore, before rebooting, you should be sure to save any work to a disk for permanent storage.

Memory provides the fastest way to store information on a computer, but it is only temporary. Hard disks are much slower than memory, and floppy disks are slower yet. However, disk storage is permanent.

OPTIMIZING MEMORY FOR PEAK PERFORMANCE

By default, DOS uses specific memory areas for different purposes. However, these default areas may not be right for everyone's needs. For instance, you may have only a few applications that use many data files. Or perhaps you run many applications, memory-resident programs, and disk management programs that could compete for memory and slow down operations. Fortunately, DOS 6's memory management tools can help you configure memory automatically, so that your system uses memory efficiently and accesses data and programs as quickly as possible.

Memory-resident programs are also known as terminate-and-stay-resident programs, or TSRs.

DIVIDING UP THE MEMORY PIE

The computer memory pie is composed of five types of memory—conventional, upper, extended, high, and expanded—which should be freed up as much as possible to provide space that your applications can use to process data. DOS 6 offers several painless ways for you to take advantage of the larger amounts of memory available with modern computer systems. Even better, DOS does most of the work for you. Let's take a quick look at the types of memory available, as illustrated in Figure 7.1.

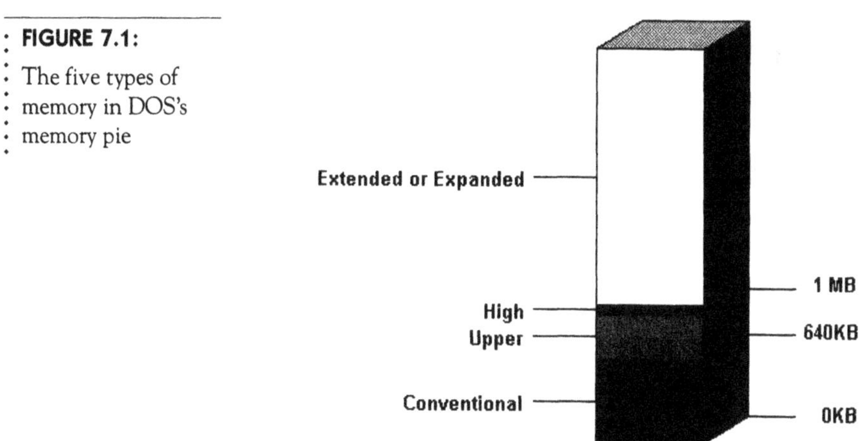

FIGURE 7.1: The five types of memory in DOS's memory pie

Memory Directly Available to DOS

The first megabyte of memory can be used directly by DOS. This area is divided into two parts: conventional memory and upper memory.

Conventional Memory The first 640 KB of memory, called *conventional memory*, typically is used by applications. If your computer has less than 1 MB, all of its memory is conventional.

Most modern personal computers are equipped with at least 2 MB of memory, with 8 MB, 16 MB, or even a whopping 32 MB becoming increasingly common.

Upper Memory DOS can use the *upper* or *reserved memory* between 640 KB and 1 MB directly. This 384 KB of storage typically is reserved for monitor adapters and other system hardware, but often sections of it are unused. Several DOS utilities let you load information into upper memory, including LOADHIGH for programs and DEVICEHIGH for device drivers. If you have an 80386- or 80486-based system, you can use MemMaker to direct device drivers and memory-resident programs to these upper memory blocks (UMBs) rather than to conventional memory.

Additional Memory That Can Be Linked to DOS

Systems based on 80286, 80386, or 80486 microprocessors generally have memory beyond 1 MB. If you have such a system, you can configure DOS to use this additional memory automatically.

You can increase the amount of memory available on your system by plugging a memory board into a slot inside your computer, or by adding more memory to the main system board.

Extended Memory (XMS) *Extended memory*, which is used by Windows and Windows applications, is made available by a memory manager such as HIMEM.SYS.

High Memory *High memory*, the first 64 KB of extended memory, is used by Windows and some applications. You can load DOS into high memory, thereby freeing up space in conventional memory.

Expanded Memory (EMS) *Expanded memory* offers another way to provide memory beyond 1 MB. This type of memory, which was introduced before extended memory was invented, is used by Lotus 1-2-3 and other applications that conform to the Lotus/Intel/Microsoft Expanded Memory Specification (LIM EMS). Expanded memory is installed on a memory board and managed with a device driver called an *expanded memory manager*.

If you have extended memory and an 80386 or 80486 system, you can run programs that normally require expanded memory without installing an expanded memory board and driver. For example, the EMM386 utility uses extended memory to emulate expanded memory.

Expanded memory can be slower and more cumbersome for programs to use than extended memory.

How Windows Uses Memory

If you use Windows, the amount of memory your system requires will differ from that required by DOS alone. This is illustrated in Figure 7.2. For example, Windows needs large amounts of extended memory to hold the many applications that can be open at once.

When extended memory does not contain enough space to hold all of the opened Windows applications, Windows must swap some of those applications to special areas of the hard disk called *swap files*. (This "fake memory" on disk is also called *virtual memory*.) When you activate a swapped application by clicking on it or opening its window, Windows must then return it from disk to memory. As you might expect, lots of swapping can lead to a very sluggish Windows system. Therefore, if you use Windows and Windows applications exclusively, you may need to avoid using extended memory for other purposes.

Even though several Windows applications can be opened at once, only one can be active at any moment.

Learning about Your System's Memory Use

You can use the command MEM to learn how your system's memory is being used. MEM can show total memory in use, how much memory is free (available), and how programs are using memory. If you're running Windows, you should exit Windows and return to the DOS prompt before running MEM.

To find out how much memory is free, type **mem /free**.

You can display memory information one screen at a time by adding the switch /PAGE or /P to any MEM command. For example, type the command **mem /p** to pause the listing after each page.

FIGURE 7.2:

DOS uses memory differently from Windows.

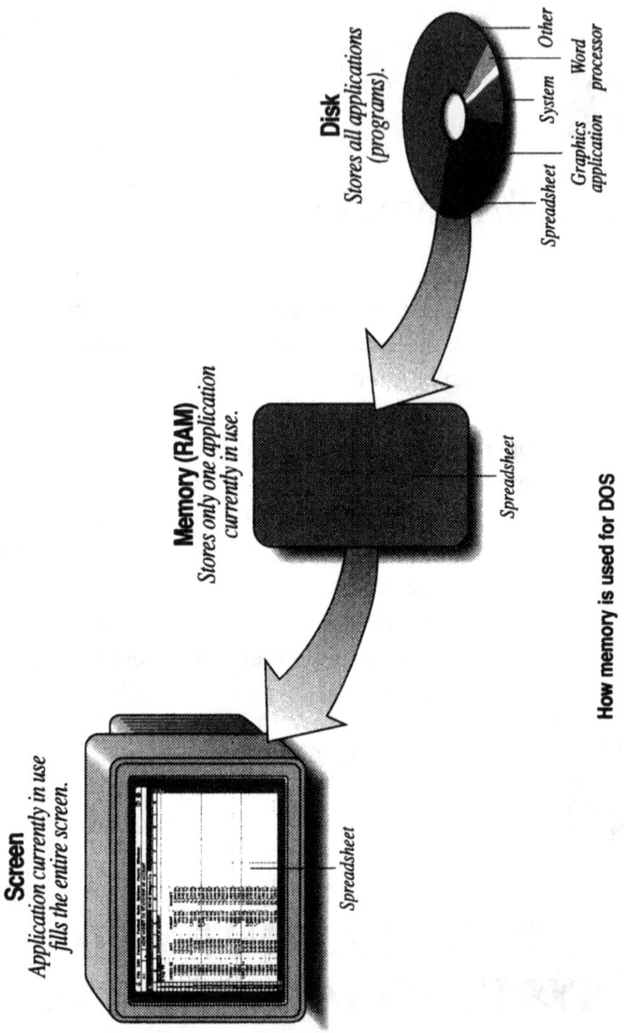

Screen
Application currently in use fills the entire screen.
Spreadsheet

Memory (RAM)
Stores only one application currently in use.
Spreadsheet

Disk
Stores all applications (programs).
Spreadsheet
Graphics application
System
Word processor
Other

How memory is used for DOS

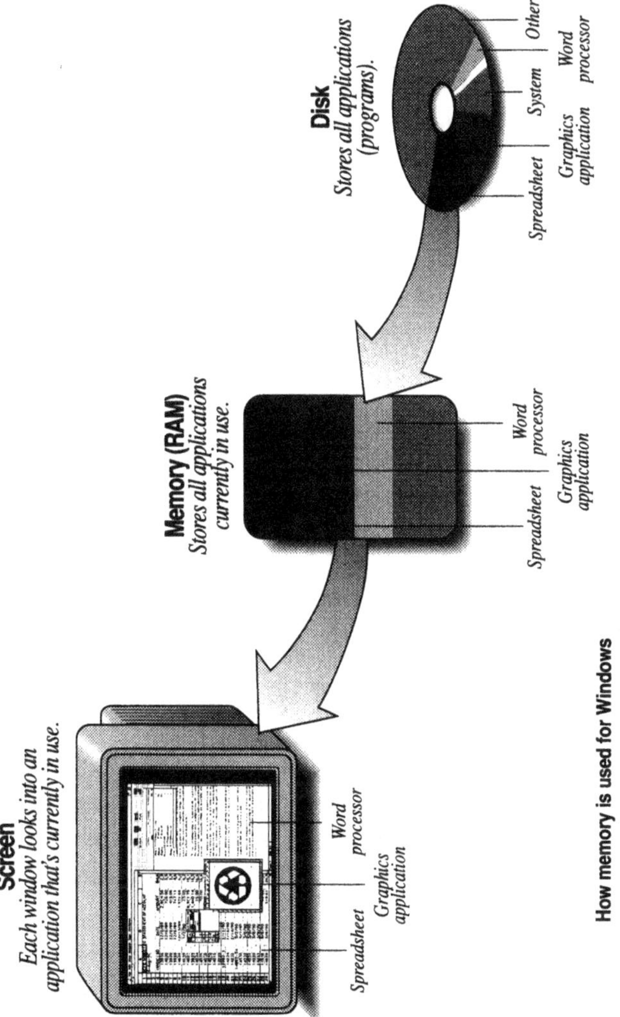
Screen
Each window looks into an application that's currently in use.
Spreadsheet
Graphics application
Word processor
Memory (RAM)
Stores all applications currently in use.
Spreadsheet
Graphics application
Word processor
Disk
Stores all applications (programs).
Spreadsheet
Graphics application
System
Word processor
Other

How memory is used for Windows

Typing **mem /classify** will give you a report similar to the one shown in Figure 7.3. Note that it lists the conventional, upper, and total memory below 1 MB for each module, as well as the amount of used and free conventional, upper, extended, and expanded memory. It also specifies where DOS is loaded, the largest executable program size, and the largest free upper memory block (UMB).

If you want information about a specific module's memory use, type **mem /module *pgmname***, where *pgmname* is the module name you're interested in. For example, type **mem /module msdos** to find out how much memory DOS is using. This form of the MEM command returns the segment addresses, segment sizes, and the total size occupied by the module.

MEM /DEBUG shows the status of all modules and internal drivers in memory. This option can be useful for configuring programs that require the base address of a memory-resident program.

OPTIMIZING MEMORY USAGE THE EASY WAY

Now that you know something about how your system uses memory, you can determine what changes, if any, you want to make. If you have an 80386- or 80486-based system and extended memory, you can optimize memory use with MemMaker, a DOS 6 program that takes nearly all the guesswork out of the job.

FIGURE 7.3: The MEM command's memory use summary

```
Modules using memory below 1 MB:

  Name         Total       =   Conventional   +   Upper Memory
  --------  ----------------   ----------------   ----------------
  MSDOS      14413     (14K)    14413    (14K)         0      (0K)
  SETVER       656      (1K)      656     (1K)         0      (0K)
  HIMEM       1104      (1K)     1104     (1K)         0      (0K)
  COMMAND     2912      (3K)     2912     (3K)         0      (0K)
  Free      636304    (621K)   636304   (621K)         0      (0K)

Memory Summary:

  Type of Memory       Total       =       Used         +       Free
  ----------------  -----------------   -----------------   -----------------
  Conventional        655360    (640K)     19056     (19K)    636304    (621K)
  Upper                    0      (0K)         0      (0K)         0      (0K)
  Adapter RAM/ROM          0      (0K)         0      (0K)         0      (0K)
  Extended (XMS)     3538944   (3456K)    196608    (192K)   3342336   (3264K)
  Expanded (EMS)           0      (0K)         0      (0K)         0      (0K)
  ----------------  -----------------   -----------------   -----------------
  Total memory       4194304   (4096K)    215664    (211K)   3978640   (3885K)

  Total under 1 MB    655360    (640K)     19056     (19K)    636304    (621K)

  Largest executable program size         636208    (621K)
  Largest free upper memory block              0      (0K)
  MS-DOS is resident in the high memory area.
```

MemMaker analyzes your system's memory, figures out how to move memory-resident programs and device drivers to unused upper memory blocks, and changes your CONFIG.SYS and AUTOEXEC.BAT files to implement the optimized configuration each time you restart your computer.

After using MemMaker, your computer's memory will remain optimized until you add or remove memory-resident programs or device drivers.

You should keep the following points in mind when working with MemMaker:

- After running MemMaker, DO NOT alter any switches or options included with DEVICEHIGH, LOADHIGH, and EMM386 commands in CONFIG.SYS or AUTOEXEC.BAT.
- After updating CONFIG.SYS with new or deleted drivers, you should re-optimize memory by running MemMaker again.
- Windows and Windows-based applications need as much extended memory as they can get. Therefore, if you run those applications exclusively, you should either avoid using MemMaker or choose the Custom Setup option described later in this lesson.

You can also use the DOS commands DEVICEHIGH, LOADHIGH, HIMEM, and possibly EMM386 to make memory adjustments manually. Refer to those entries in the Alphabetical Reference or DOS Help.

STARTING MEMMAKER

Before you use MemMaker, you should close Windows and the DOS Shell, returning to the command prompt. However, make sure that you *are* running all device drivers and TSRs that you want to optimize.

Device drivers, such as ANSI.SYS, HIMEM.SYS, and SMARTDRV.EXE, are loaded into memory when DOS executes commands in CONFIG.SYS. When you install a new device (for example, a network card), the device installation program usually updates CONFIG.SYS automatically so that the device driver will run whenever you start your computer. TSRs, such as DOSKEY, Undelete, and VSafe, typically are loaded by appropriate commands in the AUTOEXEC.BAT file or when you start them.

To start MemMaker, type the command **memmaker** and press ↵. After reading the welcome screen, press ↵ to continue.

The next screen, which appears in Figure 7.4, allows you to choose between Express Setup (the default) and Custom Setup. To toggle the selection between Express and Custom Setup, press the spacebar. (Generally, the Express Setup will be just what you want, so make sure it is selected and press *f*. If you wish to select Custom Setup, which is described later in this lesson, select Custom Setup and press *f*.)

USING EXPRESS SETUP

After selecting Express Setup, MemMaker asks whether you use programs that need expanded memory (EMS). If you do have programs that require expanded memory, press the spacebar to change the response to Yes. If you do not have programs that require expanded memory, or you're not sure, leave the response set to No (the default). Then press ↵ to continue.

After checking for the presence of Microsoft Windows, MemMaker prompts you to remove disks from your floppy disk drives and press ↵ to restart your computer.

If your computer doesn't restart properly, just turn it off and on again; MemMaker will continue automatically from where it left off. If a program other than MemMaker starts after your computer restarts, exit the program so that MemMaker can continue.

As it restarts your computer, MemMaker calculates a new configuration that optimizes memory use, then it updates your CONFIG.SYS and AUTOEXEC.BAT startup files accordingly. You're asked to press ↵ again so that MemMaker can restart your computer with the new configuration.

FIGURE 7.4:

The second screen in MemMaker lets you choose Express Setup or Custom Setup.

```
Microsoft MemMaker

 There are two ways to run MemMaker:

 Express Setup optimizes your computer's memory automatically.

 Custom Setup gives you more control over the changes that
 MemMaker makes to your system files. Choose Custom Setup
 if you are an experienced user.

            Use Express or Custom Setup? Express Setup


ENTER=Accept Selection  SPACEBAR=Change Selection  F1=Help  F3=Exit
```

After restarting your computer again, MemMaker asks you to confirm that the system works correctly by pressing ↵. (If there is a problem, consult your user's manual.) Finally, MemMaker displays a list of the new memory locations. To exit MemMaker and accept the changes, press ↵. (If you want to undo the changes and restore your original system files, press Esc instead, then press Y.)

USING CUSTOM SETUP

Express Setup works well for most systems and is the easiest method to use. However, Custom Setup may help free more conventional memory and provide better optimization in the following situations:

- A device driver or program has been causing problems or computer lock-ups during MemMaker operation.
- You use an EGA or VGA monitor.
- You don't use Windows to run non-Windows applications.

To run MemMaker's Custom Setup, start the program by typing **memmaker** and pressing ↵ as usual. Press ↵ to bypass the welcome screen, press the spacebar to select Custom Setup from the second screen (Figure 7.4), and press ↵ once more. As with Express Setup, you'll be asked whether you use programs that need expanded memory. Select No (the default) or press the spacebar to answer Yes, then press ↵.

Next, the Advanced Options screen, shown in Figure 7.5, presents a list of items for you to answer with either Yes or No. Each MemMaker option is discussed

FIGURE 7.5:
MemMaker's Advanced Options screen

```
Microsoft MemMaker

                          Advanced Options

Specify which drivers and TSRs to include in optimization?        No
Scan the upper memory area aggressively?                          Yes
Optimize upper memory for use with Windows?                       No
Use monochrome region (B000-B7FF) for running programs?           No
Keep current EMM386 memory exclusions and inclusions?             Yes
Move Extended BIOS Data Area from conventional to upper memory?  Yes

To select a different option, press the UP ARROW or DOWN ARROW key.
To accept all the settings and continue, press ENTER.

ENTER=Accept All  SPACEBAR=Change Selection  F1=Help  F3=Exit
```

briefly in the next section. To select different options, press the ↑ or ↓ key to highlight the option you want, then press the spacebar to toggle the response between Yes and No.

For additional details about the advanced options, press F1, the Help key.

When you're finished making your selections, press ↵ to proceed with the optimization. MemMaker will carry out the same process and display the same prompts it followed in the Express Setup.

UNDERSTANDING THE ADVANCED OPTIONS

There are several factors you should consider as you answer the questions posed by the advanced options shown in Figure 7.5. Here are the questions you'll be asked and some things to keep in mind:

1. *Specify which drivers and TSRs to include in optimization?*

   - Answer Yes if you had problems using the Express Setup. After MemMaker restarts the computer, you'll have a chance to specify which programs in your CONFIG.SYS and AUTOEXEC.BAT files should be excluded from optimization. (If you wish, you can exclude a program from the optimization process permanently by adding that program to the MEMMAKER.INF file in the \DOS directory.)

- Answer No (the default) if Express Setup has worked smoothly in the past.

2. *Scan the upper memory area aggressively?*

   - Answer Yes (the default) if you haven't had any problems running MemMaker and you want more upper memory available for running programs.
   - Answer No if you've had problems restarting the computer while using MemMaker.

3. *Optimize upper memory for use with Windows?*

   - Answer Yes (the default) if you use Windows to run non-Windows programs.
   - Answer No if you don't use Windows or you use it only to run Windows programs.

4. *Use monochrome region (B000-B7FF) for running programs?*

   - Answer Yes if you use an EGA or VGA (but not Super VGA) monitor and your video card does not use the region of upper memory between the addresses B000 and B7FF (most EGA and VGA monitors do not use this region).
   - Answer No (the default) if you use a monochrome or Super VGA (high resolution) monitor.

5. *Keep current EMM386 memory exclusions and inclusions?*

   - Answer Yes (the default), particularly if problems occurred previously when you answered No. This preserves your current EMM386 switches.
   - Answer No to have MemMaker remove I= and X= switches from the EMM386 command line and add new switches as necessary. This may be more efficient.

6. *Move Extended BIOS data area from conventional to upper memory?*
   - Answer Yes (the default) if you haven't had any problems using MemMaker and want to free more conventional memory for applications.
   - Answer No if you've had problems when you tried to move the extended BIOS data area (EBDA) to upper memory.

UNDOING MEMMAKER'S MEMORY RECONFIGURATION

If you need to restore your original memory configuration, quit all your programs, return to the command prompt, type **MemMaker /undo** and press ↵. When prompted, press ↵ to undo the changes. MemMaker will restore your original CONFIG.SYS and AUTOEXEC.BAT files and restart your computer.

WARNING

If you've made any changes to your CONFIG.SYS and AUTOEXEC.BAT files after MemMaker reconfigured them, those changes will be lost if you restore the original files.

DRIVING YOUR DISK SMARTER AND FASTER

If you want to reduce the time your computer spends reading from your hard disk, and your system has extended memory, you can put SMARTDrive in the driver's seat.

SMARTDrive reserves an area (or *cache*) in extended memory where it temporarily stores information read from your hard disk. When information is needed by an application, SMARTDrive supplies it directly from memory whenever possible, instead of going to the much slower hard disk. SMARTDrive also uses the reserved memory to temporarily store information to be written to your hard disk. Later, when system resources are in less demand, the information is stored permanently on disk. All this activity takes place safely and automatically behind the scenes. You simply need to make sure that SMARTDrive is installed when your system starts up.

SMARTDrive is added to AUTOEXEC.BAT automatically when you install DOS 6.

ACTIVATING SMARTDRIVE

You can activate SMARTDrive from your AUTOEXEC.BAT file or CONFIG.SYS file to ensure that the program starts when you start your computer. For example, when placed in your AUTOEXEC.BAT file, the following line will start SMARTDrive with default settings:

```
c:\dos\smartdrv
```

Do not use SMARTDrive after Windows has started, and do not use it with other disk-caching programs.

If you use a hard disk controller that cannot work with memory provided by EMM386.EXE or Windows when running in 386 enhanced mode, you may need to install SMARTDrive with the *double-buffering* feature. Double-buffering is most often necessary if you're using an SCSI hard disk or device, an ESDI device, or an MCA device. To install SMARTDrive with double-buffering, add the following line to your CONFIG.SYS file (*not* to AUTOEXEC.BAT):

```
device=c:\dos\smartdrv.exe /double_buffer
```

When adding SMARTDrive to the CONFIG.SYS file, be sure to list it after commands that install HIMEM.SYS and EMM386.EXE.

SUMMARY

In this lesson you've learned about the various types of memory available on your computer, how to find out information about memory usage, how to optimize your system's memory configuration, and how to speed up your system with SMARTDrive.

REFERENCE ENTRIES

To learn more about memory, see these entries in the Alphabetical Reference:

- DEVICE
- DEVICEHIGH
- EMM386
- LOADHIGH
- MEM
- MEMMAKER
- SMARTDRV

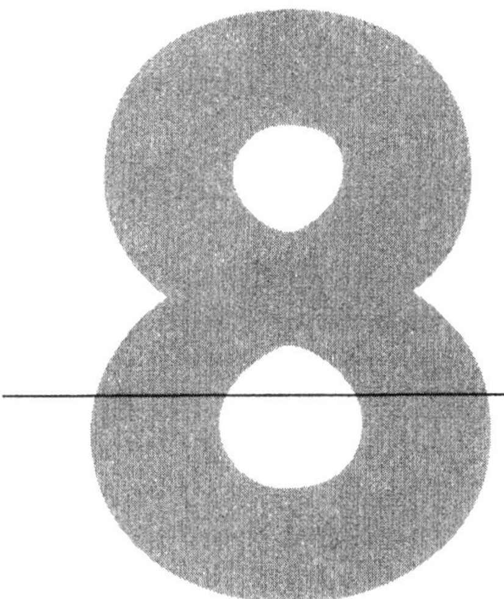

Smarter Startup Configurations & Batch Programs

INTRODUCING

The DOS Editor

Creating and running batch programs

More about CONFIG.SYS and AUTOEXEC.BAT

Bypassing startup commands

Multiple startup configurations in CONFIG.SYS and AUTOEXEC.BAT

Using the new CHOICE command

In this lesson you'll learn how to use the DOS Editor to create and change text files, including the CONFIG.SYS and AUTOEXEC.BAT startup files in the root directory. You'll also take a closer look at some useful CONFIG.SYS and AUTOEXEC.BAT files, learn how to set up multiple startup configurations, and discover how to bypass the startup files if necessary.

USING THE DOS EDITOR

If you've been using DOS 4 or an earlier version of DOS, you'll probably be glad to know that the ancient line editor EDLIN has gone to its just reward (though die hards can still use EDLIN should a wave of nostalgia strike). In its place is the DOS Editor.

The Editor is line-oriented and designed strictly for text files, so it doesn't have word wrap like a full-fledged word processor has. Therefore, when you get to the end of a line, you must press ↵ to begin the next line. You can use the Editor to change your CONFIG.SYS and AUTOEXEC.BAT files, write and change batch programs, and write lists and other small text files.

The CONFIG.SYS and AUTOEXEC.BAT files, which are executed automatically when you start your computer, provide configuration information to DOS and customize your computer. Be sure to back up these files before changing them, just in case something goes wrong.

The Editor is a self-contained program within DOS, independent of the Shell. You can start the Editor from the Shell's Main group in the Program List (see Lesson 2) or by typing **edit** and pressing ↵ at the command prompt. If you want to alter an existing file, follow the EDIT command with the file's path and file name. For example, type **edit \autoexec.bat** to edit the AUTOEXEC.BAT file in the root directory.

If you omit a file name, the Editor will display a dialog box that offers help in the form of a "Survival Guide." To display the Survival Guide, press ↵. Alternatively, you can exit directly to the Editor's screen by pressing Esc.

If you specify a text file name when you open the Editor, you can begin working with the file immediately. Otherwise, choose File ➤ Open from the blank Editor screen, type a file name in the dialog box, and press ↵.

The Editor's main screen is shown in Figure 8.1. Notice that the screen has a bar of menus at the top, from which you make selections, and a status bar at the bottom. When working with the Editor, you can use any of the cursor and scrolling keys that you use with the Shell, as well as a mouse. The keys used most often are listed in Table 8.1. You can also pull down menus and select options from open menus just as you can in the DOS Shell (Lesson 2).

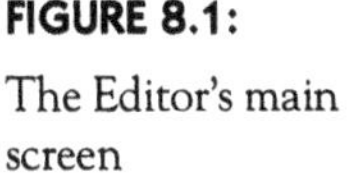

FIGURE 8.1: The Editor's main screen

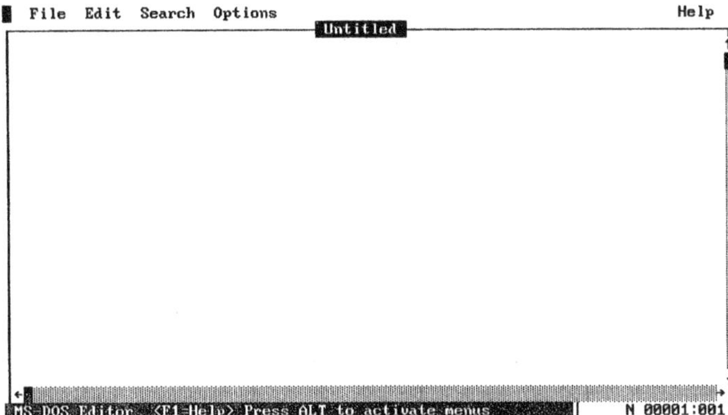

To change the foreground text color and background color of the Editor screen, choose Options ➤ Display from the menus.

You can use the Editor to add or edit text, search for a word or phrase, or search and replace a phrase either throughout the file or by verifying each change before it is made. You can also change existing text by highlighting or *selecting* it. Once text is selected, you can move, copy, or delete it.

TABLE 8.1: Keys Commonly Used with the Editor

FUNCTION	EDITOR KEY
To activate the menu bar	Alt
To access online Help	F1
To switch between Help and editing screens when the Help screen is displayed	F6
To back out of the current window, menu, or dialog box	Esc

ADDING TEXT

The *cursor* is the small blinking underline that indicates where the next character you type will appear or the next change you make will take effect. You can position the cursor by clicking your mouse in the text or by using cursor movement keys, including those listed in Table 8.2.

TABLE 8.2: Cursor Movement Keys Used in the DOS Editor

TO MOVE THE CURSOR...	PRESS THIS KEY...
Character left	←
Character right	→
Word left	Ctrl+←
Word right	Ctrl+→
Line up	↑
Line down	↓
Beginning of line	Home
End of line	End
Page up	PgUp
Page down	PgDn
Beginning of file	Ctrl+Home
End of file	Ctrl+End

The Editor also supports WordStar and Microsoft Word shortcut keys. For example, you can move the cursor one character to the left by pressing Ctrl+S (as in WordStar), or by pressing ←.

To add text to a file, simply move the cursor where you want the text to begin and start typing. When you want to start a new line, move the cursor to the beginning or end of an existing line and press ↵.

MOVING TEXT

Suppose you want to move chunks of text within a file. For instance, you may decide to reorganize CONFIG.SYS by moving the device drivers to the top of the file. The process known as *cut-and-paste* makes this job easy.

The first step is to select (block, or highlight) a portion of the text using the mouse or the keyboard, as illustrated in Figure 8.2. Here's how to select a block of text:

- To select text with the mouse, place the mouse pointer at the beginning of the block that you want to select, then hold down the left mouse button while dragging the mouse to the end of the block. When all the text you want to select is highlighted, release the left mouse button.
- If you prefer to use the keyboard to select text, move the cursor to the beginning of the block, then hold down the Shift key while pressing the arrow keys or other cursor movement keys listed in Table 8.2.

The next step is to choose Edit ➤ Cut or press Shift+Del (the highlighted text will disappear) and then position the cursor to the place where you want to move the text. Finally, choose Edit ➤ Paste or press Shift+Ins. The selected text will appear in its new location, as shown in Figure 8.3.

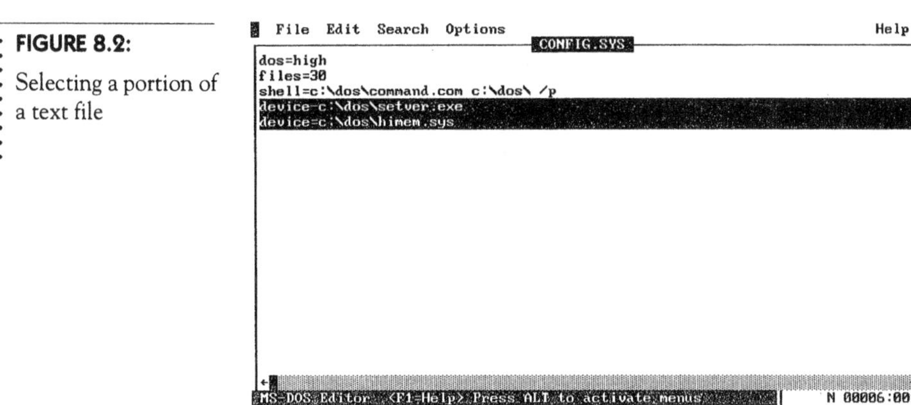

FIGURE 8.2: Selecting a portion of a text file

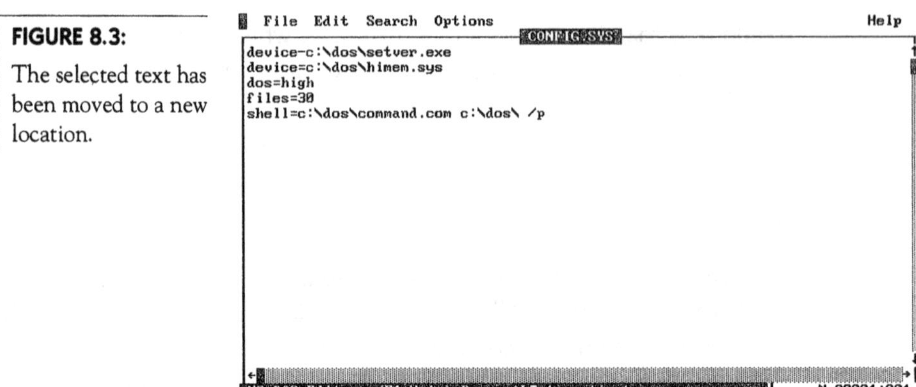

FIGURE 8.3:

The selected text has been moved to a new location.

COPYING TEXT

Copying text is similar to moving it, except that the highlighted text remains in its original location. Simply select the text, choose Edit ➤ Copy or press Ctrl+Ins, move the cursor to the new text location, and then choose Edit ➤ Paste or press Shift+Ins.

DELETING TEXT

To delete a block of text, select the text, then choose Edit ➤ Clear or press the Del key. To delete a single character above the cursor, press the Del key. To delete a single character to the left of the cursor, press the Backspace key.

FINDING AND REPLACING PHRASES

If your file is lengthy, you can let the Editor find or replace words so you don't have to make the changes manually. You can only search forward, so begin by placing the cursor in the text at the point where you want to begin searching.

For example, suppose you want to clean up your AUTOEXEC.BAT file by removing redundant ECHO commands. Choose Search ➤ Find, insert the word or phrase in the dialog box (in this case **echo**), select the Match Upper/Lowercase and Whole Word options if you wish, and select OK. The Editor will find the first occurrence of the phrase. To continue searching, select Search ➤ Repeat Last Find or press F3.

If you want the Editor to replace a word or phrase with another word or phrase, choose Search ➤ Change. Enter the original text in the Find What box and the replacement text in the Change To box, specify the Match Upper/Lowercase and Whole Word options (if you wish), then choose either Change All (to change all occurrences without confirmation) or Find And Verify (to change occurrences one by one). You also can use Search ➤ Change to delete a phrase by leaving the replacement text box empty.

SAVING A FILE

Once you've completed your changes, save them permanently. If you want to retain the same file name, simply select File ➤ Save. To save the file and rename it, select File ➤ Save As. If you wish, you can specify a new drive and directory for the saved file.

PRINTING A FILE

To print the entire file, choose File ➤ Print. Alternatively, you can print just part of the file by selecting the text you want to print, then choosing File ➤ Print.

EXITING THE EDITOR

To exit the Editor, simply select File ➤ Exit. If you forgot to save your file, you'll be prompted to save it before the Editor returns you to the Shell or command line.

WRITING AND USING BATCH PROGRAMS

Batch programs (sometimes called *batch files*) are files with the extension .BAT. These programs contain a series of commands that DOS executes automatically, from top to bottom. For instance, if you perform a series of commands routinely, such as copying or printing files, you can include them in a batch program. Then you can execute the commands automatically by entering the name of the batch program—without the .BAT extension—from the Shell or the command prompt, or you can execute the batch program from another batch program, such as AUTOEXEC.BAT.

Batch programs are text files, so you can write or edit them with DOS's text editor (described above) or with any other text editor or word processor.

If you edit a batch program with a word processor, be sure to save the file in a text (ASCII) format.

WRITING A BATCH PROGRAM

Suppose you wanted to display a different message each day during startup without disturbing AUTOEXEC.BAT. You could write a special "message" batch program and call it from AUTOEXEC.BAT. You could change the message in the message program each day. For example, the following commands in AUTOEXEC.BAT direct DOS to run the batch program named MESSAGE.BAT, and then return to execute the next command in AUTOEXEC.BAT. The first line is a remark about the purpose of MESSAGE.BAT.

```
rem message.bat is the daily greeting
call message
```

Because DOS ignores lines beginning with the REM command, you can use REM to include comments in a batch program or to disable commands temporarily. The CALL command transfers control to another batch program (MESSAGE.BAT in the example above). When the "called" program finishes, control returns to the original batch program (AUTOEXEC.BAT in this example).

To begin writing a batch program, start the Editor and open the File menu. If you're creating MESSAGE.BAT, select New. To change an existing MESSAGE.BAT file, select Open, type **message.bat** in the File Name box, and select OK. Now complete the batch program as in the example below, and select File ➤ Save to save it as MESSAGE.BAT in the same directory as AUTOEXEC.BAT.

```
@echo off
echo Welcome to the Star-Struck Improvise!
echo Today's goals are to finish yesterday's work.
echo -------------------------------------------
pause
```

To try this message program before adding it to AUTOEXEC.BAT, exit the Editor (File ➤ Exit), type **message** at the command prompt, and press ↵. When you're sure the program works properly, you can open your AUTOEXEC.BAT file and add the REM and CALL MESSAGE lines shown earlier to display the message automatically whenever you start your system.

If you need to stop a batch program before it completes, press Ctrl+C *or* Ctrl+Break*, then type* **Y** *in response to the confirmation message.*

Commands Used in Batch Programs

You can use any DOS command in a batch program. In addition, the programming commands listed in Table 8.3 are specific to batch programs, and usually are not used (or cannot be used) at the command prompt.

Using Batch Program Variables

When you run a batch program, you can specify additional text (or *parameters*) after the program name. Batch program *variables* named %1 through %9 are replaced with text from the command line in order from left to right. For instance, if you typed the command **dobat file1 file2** to run a batch program named DOBAT, the variable %1 in the batch program would get the value *file1*, and the variable %2 would get the value *file2*. The variable %0 always contains the name of the batch command that you type (*dobat* in this example).

TABLE 8.3: Programming Commands for Batch Programs

FUNCTION	BATCH PROGRAMMING COMMAND
To call one batch program from another	CALL
To allow the user to choose from a set of options after a specified prompt creates a pause in program execution	CHOICE
To display commands or text during program execution, or to turn off such display	ECHO ON *or* ECHO OFF
To run a command for a designated file or set of files	FOR
To execute a specified program line other than the next one	GOTO
To specify conditional command execution	IF
To stop program execution until user input is received	PAUSE
To add remarks or comments to a program without their being executed	REM
To change the position of replaceable parameters	SHIFT

The simple batch program shown below illustrates how batch program variables are used and how they're substituted with real values when you run the program.

```
@echo off
echo The batch program name (%%0) is %0
echo %%1 = %1
echo %%2 = %2
echo %%3 = %3
echo %%4 = %4
echo %%5 = %5
```

```
echo %%6 = %6
echo %%7 = %7
echo %%8 = %8
echo %%9 = %9
```

If you saved these lines in a batch program file named TEST.BAT, you could execute the program by typing the following command at the command prompt:

```
test first second third 4th 5th 6th
```

This would cause the following lines to appear on the screen:

```
The batch program name (%0) is test
%1 = first
%2 = second
%3 = third
%4 = 4th
%5 = 5th
%6 = 6th
%7 =
%8 =
%9 =
```

The first line of the batch program, @ECHO OFF, turns off the display of remaining command lines in the batch program. The @ character prevents DOS from displaying the ECHO OFF command.

The ECHO commands in the remaining lines of the batch program display on the screen whatever text follows the command. Each message includes some text and a percent variable that gets filled in with the text you typed on the command line. For example, the line

```
echo The batch program name (%%0) is %0
```

displays the message "The batch program name (%0) is test." Notice how DOS interprets the two percent signs in %%0 literally, so that only %0 is displayed. When it gets to the %0 in the message, it replaces that with the name of the batch command (*test* in this example).

Similarly, when DOS encounters the line

```
echo %%1 = %1
```

it displays the text %*1* = (remember, %%1 is interpreted simply as %*1*) and replaces the variable %1 with the text of the first parameter typed on the command line. In this example, the first parameter is the word "first."

Because you didn't supply values for the seventh, eighth, and ninth parameters on the command line, the values for %7, %8, and %9 are empty (or *null*).

Of course, more practical batch programs are often used to substitute file names for command line variables, as in the following example for a hypothetical batch program named C.BAT:

```
copy %1 %2
```

If you executed C.BAT by typing the command

```
c wombat baboon
```

DOS would copy the file named WOMBAT to the file named BABOON (assuming, of course, that WOMBAT exists).

ANATOMY OF AN AUTOEXEC.BAT BATCH PROGRAM

AUTOEXEC.BAT is a batch program that's executed automatically when you start your computer. Figure 8.4 shows an example of an AUTOEXEC.BAT file that might be useful on your own computer.

You can try out an AUTOEXEC.BAT program without restarting your computer. Simply type **c:\autoexec** *at the command prompt (assuming that AUTOEXEC.BAT is located on drive C).*

FIGURE 8.4:

A sample AUTOEXEC.BAT file

```
@echo off
c:\dos\smartdrv.exe
set dircmd=/on /p
prompt $p$g
path c:\dos;c:\windows;c:\;c:\wp51
c:\dos\chkdsk c:
c:\dos\chkdsk d:
set temp=c:\windows\temp
set winpmt=Type 'EXIT' to return to Windows $_$p$g
mode con rate=32 delay=1
c:\dos\doskey
undelete /load
```

Now let's dissect the AUTOEXEC.BAT file shown in Figure 8.4 line by line.

- The command @ECHO OFF prevents DOS from displaying each command as it is executed in the batch program. Most people place an @ECHO OFF command at the beginning of every batch program.
- The command C:\DOS\SMARTDRV.EXE executes the SMARTDrive disk-caching program, which was described in Lesson 7.
- The SET DIRCMD=/ON /P sets the DIRCMD environment variable to specify two automatic switches for the DIR command. The switch /ON sorts file names alphabetically and /P pauses after each screenful of file names. With DIRCMD set, typing **dir** alone is the same as typing **dir /on /p**.
- The command PROMPT PG defines the message displayed by the command prompt. This example shows the most widely used form of the PROMPT command, which displays the current drive and path name followed by the greater-than symbol (>). Thus, when you're in the Windows directory of drive C, the command prompt will display **C:\WINDOWS>** as it awaits your next instruction. You can use any text (*hello*, for example) as well as a variety of special character combinations in the message following the PROMPT command, as shown in Table 8.4.
- The PATH command tells DOS which drives and directories to search, and the order in which to search them if a command or program can't be found in memory or in the current directory. To enter several paths on the same line, separate them with semicolons (;). Do not include any spaces in the line. (If you haven't installed Windows, you can omit C:\WINDOWS; from your PATH command.)
- The two CHKDSK commands check drives C and D for logical errors (see Lesson 5).
- The command SET TEMP=C:\WINDOWS\TEMP associates the directory named C:\WINDOWS\TEMP with the TEMP environment variable. The TEMP variable is used by DOS and other programs to determine the location of temporary files. (If you haven't installed Windows, you should substitute a different, existing directory name for C:\WINDOWS\TEMP.)

TABLE 8.4: Character Combinations for the Prompt Command

<table>
<tr><th>TO DISPLAY THIS...</th><th>USE THIS CHARACTER...</th></tr>
<tr><td>$ (dollar sign)</td><td>$$</td></tr>
<tr><td>< (less-than sign)</td><td>$l</td></tr>
<tr><td>= (equal sign)</td><td>$q</td></tr>
<tr><td>> (greater-than sign)</td><td>$g</td></tr>
<tr><td>| (pipe)</td><td>$b</td></tr>
<tr><td>ASCII escape (code 27)</td><td>$e</td></tr>
<tr><td>Backspace (for deleting a character written to the command line)</td><td>$h</td></tr>
<tr><td>Current time</td><td>$t</td></tr>
<tr><td>Current date</td><td>$d</td></tr>
<tr><td>Current drive and path</td><td>$p</td></tr>
<tr><td>Enter-Linefeed (for starting text on the next line)</td><td>$_</td></tr>
<tr><td>Version of DOS</td><td>$v</td></tr>
</table>

- The SET WINPMT command defines the prompt that will appear when you exit temporarily from Windows to the DOS prompt. (Omit this line if you're not using Windows.) In this example, we would see the following prompt after exiting to DOS:

```
Type 'EXIT' to return to Windows
C:\WINDOWS>
```

- The MODE CON RATE=32 DELAY=1 command sets the keyboard's typematic (repeat) rate to the fastest speed available.
- The commands C:\DOS\DOSKEY and UNDELETE /LOAD load the DOS programs DOSKEY and UNDELETE into memory.

If you want to run Windows whenever you start your computer, add the command WIN to the end of the AUTOEXEC.BAT file. To run the DOS Shell, add the command DOSSHELL to the end of the file.

UNDERSTANDING CONFIG.SYS FILES

As you know, the CONFIG.SYS file is read whenever you start up your computer and contains special commands used to configure your computer's hardware components. A CONFIG.SYS file can include any of the commands listed in Table 8.5.

TABLE 8.5: CONFIG.SYS File Commands

FUNCTION	CONFIG.SYS COMMAND
To specify where DOS should look for keyboard interrupts	BREAK
To specify the number of buffers and caches	BUFFERS
To designate the time, date, decimal separators, and other conventions used in a particular country	COUNTRY
To tell DOS which drivers to load	DEVICE
To load drivers into upper memory	DEVICEHIGH
To specify where to load DOS	DOS
To define block device parameters	DRIVPARM

TABLE 8.5: CONFIG.SYS File Commands (continued)

FUNCTION	CONFIG.SYS COMMAND
To specify how many file control blocks (FCBs) can be open at the same time	FCBS
To specify how many files you can have open at the same time	FILES
To include the contents of a configuration block for a specific menu block	INCLUDE
To load memory-resident (terminate-and-stay resident, or TSR) programs	INSTALL
To specify the number of drives	LASTDRIVE
To set the startup menu colors	MENUCOLOR
To specify the default item in the startup menu	MENUDEFAULT
To define up to nine startup menu items	MENUITEM
To set the numlock key on or off	NUMLOCK
To include comments or remarks	REM
To display, set, or remove environment variables	SET
To specify the name and location of the command interpreter	SHELL
To use data stacks for hardware interrupts	STACKS
To define a set of menu items under a startup menu item	SUBMENU
To provide special device options	SWITCHES
To verify accuracy of a file written to a disk	VERIFY

Figure 8.5 illustrates a bare-bones CONFIG.SYS file that was created automatically when DOS was installed on an 80386 system with extended memory.

FIGURE 8.5:

A bare-bones CONFIG.SYS file

```
device-c:\dos\setver.exe
device=c:\dos\himem.sys
dos=high
files=30
shell=c:\dos\command.com c:\dos\ /p
```

In the next few sections, I'll discuss some of the commands most commonly used in CONFIG.SYS files. Other CONFIG.SYS commands are discussed in the Alphabetical Reference and in the Help topics available from DOS (see Lesson 3).

Keep in mind that you may never need to update CONFIG.SYS manually since the installation programs for MS-DOS, various hardware devices, and most applications update the file automatically. Moreover, if your computer has an 80386 or higher microprocessor and extended memory, you can use MemMaker (discussed in Lesson 7) to update the CONFIG.SYS file so that its commands make the most efficient use of memory.

DEVICES

DEVICE indicates the name and path of device drivers to be loaded into memory. For example, the command DEVICE=C:\DOS\SETVER.EXE loads the DOS version table into memory. The command DEVICE=C:\DOS\HIMEM.SYS loads the driver that manages extended memory.

Your devices should always appear in the order shown below (of course, you can omit any devices that don't apply to your system):

- HIMEM.SYS
- expanded memory manager (for example, EMSDRIV.SYS)
- EMM386.EXE (for simulating expanded memory while using extended memory and an 80386 or higher processor)
- drivers for other devices, such as a mouse or RAM drive

For devices that you want loaded into upper memory, use the command DEVICEHIGH. Or better yet, leave memory management to MemMaker, which will insert the necessary DEVICEHIGH commands for you.

BUFFERS

The BUFFERS command allocates memory for a specified number of disk buffers, which temporarily hold data while it's being read and written. The BUFFERS=20 command generally provides good performance with programs such as word processors. If you plan to create many subdirectories, BUFFERS=30 might be more efficient. You can specify up to 99 buffers, but don't go overboard. Specifying more than 50 can slow down your system. Note that MemMaker and the installation programs for most applications will update and optimize the BUFFERS setting for you.

If you are using SMARTDRV.EXE, either use a relatively small value for BUFFERS or omit the BUFFERS command altogether.

FILES

The FILES command lets you specify how many files DOS can access at once, in the range from 8 to 255. A setting of FILES=25 is typical. Again, MemMaker and various setup programs will optimize this setting, so you'll seldom need to fiddle with it.

BYPASSING CONFIG.SYS AND AUTOEXEC.BAT COMMANDS

On rare occasions you may need to start your computer without running the commands in CONFIG.SYS and AUTOEXEC.BAT. For instance, you may be experiencing problems caused by inappropriate settings in these files.

You can use any of the three methods listed below to bypass startup commands.

- To bypass both CONFIG.SYS and AUTOEXEC.BAT, press F5 or press and hold down the Shift key as soon as you see the "Starting MS-DOS..." message when restarting your computer.
- To be asked whether you want to execute individual CONFIG.SYS commands and whether to run AUTOEXEC.BAT, press F8 as soon as you see

the "Starting MS-DOS..." message when restarting your computer. You'll then be prompted to answer Y (Yes) or N (No) before each command is executed.

- To have DOS confirm a specific CONFIG.SYS command each time your computer starts, follow the DEVICE command name with a question mark (?), as in **device?=c:\windows\gmouse.sys 2**.

Before restarting your computer as described in Lesson 1, be sure to exit all programs, including Windows, and return to the command prompt.

PROVIDING MULTIPLE STARTUP CONFIGURATIONS FOR YOUR SYSTEM

Several people in your office may share a computer, and each user might have different memory management, networking, device, and software needs. If you're the local DOS guru, and understand the role played by CONFIG.SYS, you can define *configuration blocks* in the CONFIG.SYS file so that each user can select a custom configuration option from a menu at startup. DOS 6 provides six new commands—MENUITEM, INCLUDE, MENUDEFAULT, MENUCOLOR, SUBMENU, and NUMLOCK—that you can use in the CONFIG.SYS file to display a startup menu and provide alternative configurations.

Figure 8.6 shows a sample CONFIG.SYS file that presents the user with three choices for startup configurations. Figure 8.7 shows the menu that appears when the computer is started with this sample CONFIG.SYS file in place.

When the startup menu appears, you can select a menu option by typing the option number you want or highlighting the option with the ↑ and ↓ keys, then pressing ↵. Alternatively, you can bypass the startup files CONFIG.SYS and AUTOEXEC.BAT altogether (press F5), or confirm whether to run each line in CONFIG.SYS and whether to run AUTOEXEC.BAT (press F8).

FIGURE 8.6:

A sample CONFIG.SYS file with three startup configurations

```
[menu]
menuitem=Windows,Windows configuration
menuitem=DOS,DOS configuration
menuitem=network,Network configuration
menudefault=Windows,15

[common]
device=c:\dos\himem.sys
dos=high
files=40

[Windows]
set path=c:\dos\windows;c:\dos
set temp=c:\windows\temp
numlock=off

[DOS]
set path=c:\dos
device=c:\dos\emm386
numlock=on

[Network]
device=c:\net\net.sys
set path=c:\dos;c:\network
include=DOS

[common]
```

menu block - specifies selections on the configuration menu that appears at startup

common block - specifies commands that alternate configurations can use

Windows, DOS, and Network blocks - specify commands that are executed after user chooses an option from the configuration menu

Notice that the [Network] block uses the INCLUDE command to include the [common] commands specified earlier

empty common block - allows installation programs to add commands that alternate configurations may require

FIGURE 8.7:

The screen that appears with the sample CONFIG.SYS file in place

```
MS-DOS 6 Startup Menu
═════════════════════

   1. Windows configuration
   2. DOS configuration
   3. Network configuration

Enter a choice: 1        Time remaining: 15




F5=Bypass startup files     F8=Confirm each CONFIG.SYS line [N]
```

DEFINING THE STARTUP MENU ITEMS

As Figure 8.6 illustrates, the startup menu items are listed in the [menu] block. Following the [menu] block is an alternate configuration for each menu item. Every configuration must be introduced by a named *block header* enclosed in square brackets. The block headers in our example are [menu], [common], [Windows], [DOS], and [Network].

Defining the Blocks

The first block is always named **[menu]**, and it lists the menu block names that can be selected from the startup menu. For example, if you want the user to be able to choose one of three options—Windows, DOS, or Network—you would define the menu block names of those options with the command MENUITEM, as shown below.

```
[menu]
menuitem=Windows
menuitem=DOS
menuitem=Network
```

You can add menu text to each definition, for example,

```
menuitem=Windows, Windows configuration
```

In this case, the startup menu text for the first item will be **Windows configuration** (see Figure 8.7). If you omit the menu text, DOS will display the block name by itself, for example, **Windows**.

Creating the Blocks

To define the commands for each block, type the block header (e.g. **[Windows]**), press ↵, and then enter lines to be executed in sequence for that block. You can see the commands used for the [Windows], [DOS], and [Network] menu blocks in Figure 8.6.

USING COMMANDS IN COMMON

If you want to use specific commands in *all* configurations, you can include these under the special block heading named **[common]**, as shown in Figure 8.6. The [common] block is especially handy when you want certain memory management commands to be executed for every configuration. You can have as many [common] blocks as you want. DOS will run the [common] commands in the order in which they appear.

You should end your CONFIG.SYS file with a [common] block, even if it's empty, because some installation programs may need it for commands that should be carried out for all configurations.

INCLUDING ONE MENU BLOCK IN ANOTHER

The command INCLUDE lets you include the commands of one menu block within another, so that you don't need to type a bunch of redundant commands in each menu block. For example, to include the [DOS] block's commands in the [Network] block, I added the command INCLUDE=DOS to the [Network] block (see Figure 8.6).

SETTING THE NUM LOCK KEY ON OR OFF

You can use the NUMLOCK command to define the initial Num Lock key setting within a menu block. For instance, if users of one configuration perform data entry as their primary task, you can turn Num Lock on with NUMLOCK=ON, as I did for the [DOS] menu block shown in Figure 8.6. For text entry, Num Lock can be set off with NUMLOCK=OFF as in the [Windows] menu block example.

SPECIFYING A DEFAULT MENU ITEM

The command MENUDEFAULT lets you specify a default configuration to be loaded if a user doesn't select a menu item within a given time period. To select [DOS] automatically if the user doesn't respond within 15 seconds, I added the command MENUDEFAULT=DOS,15 to the [menu] block, as shown in Figure 8.6.

SELECTING THE MENU'S TEXT AND BACKGROUND COLORS

If your computer has a color monitor, you can use the command MENUCOLOR in a menu block to specify the menu's text and background colors. For example, to specify bright white text (number 15) on a blue background (number 1), add the line MENUCOLOR=15,1 to the [menu] block. If you want a black background, specify only the text color, as in MENUCOLOR=15. (For a complete list of colors, see MENUCOLOR in the Alphabetical Reference.)

CREATING A SUBMENU

Each menu block is limited to nine items. However, you can get around this restriction by using the SUBMENU command, which causes a menu item to display another set of choices.

The procedure is similar to that for defining main menu items. First, define the submenu in the [menu] block, using the command SUBMENU instead of MENUITEM. Then set up a menu block of MENUITEM commands for the submenu, as well as a menu block for each item in the submenu. When a user selects the block containing the submenu, the submenu is displayed automatically.

To understand how this works, you could define multiple startup menus for network users like this:

```
[menu]
...
submenu=Network, Network configuration
[Network]
menuitem=Lan1,Start LAN1
menuitem=Lan2,Start LAN2
[Lan1]
rem add lan1 commands here
[Lan2]
rem add lan2 commands here
```

The main menu display will include the selection **3. Network configuration.** If you select item 3, the submenu items will look like this:

```
1. Start LAN1
2. Start LAN2
```

THE CHOICE IS YOURS

If you have created multiple configurations in your CONFIG.SYS file, you can write a complementary set of menu items in the AUTOEXEC.BAT file. You can also use the new DOS 6 batch command CHOICE to allow users to select from a set of options in an AUTOEXEC.BAT file or other batch program.

CAPITALIZING ON STARTUP CHOICES IN AUTOEXEC.BAT

When a configuration is selected from the startup menu, DOS defines an environment variable named %CONFIG% and sets it to the name of the selected configuration block. You can pass this information to AUTOEXEC.BAT (or any other batch program) simply by branching to a label that has the same *name* as the *value* stored in the variable %CONFIG%.

See the GOTO entry in the Alphabetical Reference for information on using labels in batch programs.

To illustrate the power of this feature, the batch program shown in Figure 8.8 provides paths and loads programs appropriate to the configuration the user has selected. Note that the program names used in this example are fictitious, and you'll need to replace those names with actual commands. If you just want to experiment with the example, precede the sample commands with an ECHO command, as in ECHO PAINT. This way, DOS will just display a message on the screen, instead of trying to execute a nonexistent program.

MAKING CHOICES IN A BATCH PROGRAM

The command CHOICE lets you create and display a list of options, then it pauses execution of the batch program so that the user can choose one of them. After the user responds, program execution continues. In the sample batch program shown in Figure 8.9, the CHOICE command is followed by the /C switch, which lists the options the user can choose.

FIGURE 8.8:

A sample batch program that uses the %config% variable to determine which paths and programs to load

```
@echo off
goto %config%

:Windows
path c:\dos;c:\artist
paint
goto End

:DOS
path c:\dos;c:\spdsheet
spdsheet
goto End

:Network
path c:\dos;c:\net

:End
```

Other CHOICE switches allow display of the choices without a screen prompt (/N), determine how many seconds the options will be displayed before choosing a specified option automatically (/T:*c*,*nn*), and make the choice case-sensitive (/S).

Again, our example uses imaginary names for the SPDSHEET, DATABASE, and WORDPROC programs. You'll need to replace those names with actual program names or ECHO commands.

FIGURE 8.9:

A sample batch program that displays a menu and lets the user choose an option

```
@echo off
echo A Run Spreadsheet
echo B Run Database
echo C Run Word Processing
echo.
choice Whadd'ya want /c:abc
if errorlevel 3 goto WordProc
if errorlevel 2 goto Database
if errorlevel 1 goto Spreadsheet
goto End
:Spreadsheet
spdsheet
goto End

:Database
database
goto End

:WordProc
wordproc

:End
```

```
@echo off
goto %config%

:Windows
path c:\dos;c:\artist
paint
goto End

:DOS
path c:\dos;c:\spdsheet
spdsheet
goto End

:Network
path c:\dos;c:\net

:End
```

When the batch program is run, the screen display looks like this:

```
A Run Spreadsheet
B Run Database
C Run Word Processing
Whadd'ya want [A,B,C]?
```

If the user selects the third option (C), the IF ERRORLEVEL 3… command transfers control to the label **WordProc**. If the second option (B) is chosen, the IF ERRORLEVEL 2… command transfers control to the label **Database**. Finally, if the first option (A) is chosen, the IF ERRORLEVEL 1... command transfers control to the label **Spreadsheet**.

For more information on using IF ERRORLEVEL, please see the CHOICE and IF entries in the Alphabetical Reference.

SUMMARY

In this lesson you've learned to use the Editor to edit text files such as CONFIG.SYS, AUTOEXEC.BAT, and batch programs. You've also taken a closer look at the CONFIG.SYS and AUTOEXEC.BAT files, learned how to create powerful startup menus for multiple configurations, and discovered how to make choices in batch programs.

REFERENCE ENTRIES

To learn more about the topics covered in this lesson, see the entries for the CONFIG.SYS commands listed in Table 8.5 and the following entries in the Alphabetical Reference:

- CHOICE
- ECHO
- EDIT
- GOTO
- IF
- MemMaker
- PATH
- PROMPT
- SET

Transferring Files and Using a Laptop

INTRODUCING

Using Interlnk to transfer files without floppy disks

Conserving power on a laptop computer

In this lesson you will learn how to set up a direct connection between two computers using Interlnk and Intersvr. Doing so allows you to transfer files quickly from one computer to another without floppy disks and without expensive networking equipment.

You'll also learn about the POWER command, which can help conserve battery power on a laptop.

INTERLNK: THE COMPUTER CONNECTION

DOS 6 includes the Interlnk and Intersvr programs, which let you connect two computers and then use one of the computers to run programs and access data located on the other computer.

With Interlnk installed, the computer you use to type commands is called the *client*. The computer connected to the client is the *server*. The client can use the drives and printers of the server just as if they belonged to the client, and the server displays the status of the connection between the two computers.

Interlnk is especially useful for connecting a laptop client and a desktop server computer and transferring data from the laptop to the desktop. No longer must you connect those two computers via "SneakerNet"—that infamous procedure in which you copy data from one computer onto floppy disks, don your most comfortable sneakers, grab the floppies, dash to another computer, and feed it the floppy disks that you copied earlier.

UNDERSTANDING HARDWARE REQUIREMENTS

You don't need any fancy network cards or special hardware to use Interlnk. But the two computers must be connected from serial port to serial port or from parallel port to parallel port before you activate the Interlnk software. For a parallel connection, you need a bidirectional parallel cable. For a serial connection you need either a 3-wire serial cable or a 7-wire null-modem serial cable.

Be sure to connect the two computers before activating the Interlnk and Intersvr software. Otherwise, the software won't be able to recognize the connection.

You'll also need 16 KB of free memory on the client computer and 130 KB of free memory on the server. Moreover, both computers must be running MS-DOS 3.0 or later.

UNDERSTANDING SOFTWARE REQUIREMENTS

It's not necessary for both computers to be using DOS 6. However, at least the client must have INTERLNK.EXE on disk and at least the server computer must have a copy of INTERSVR.EXE on it (though there's no harm in having a copy of each program on both computers). Both INTERLNK.EXE and INTERSVR.EXE are copied to the \DOS directory when you install DOS 6.

MAKING THE CONNECTION

When the cable is in place, and each computer has the appropriate programs available, here's how you make the connection (note that Steps 1-4 only need to be performed once, not each time you wish to make a connection):

1. On the machine that will act as client, use Edit (described in Lesson 8) to open the C:\CONFIG.SYS file for editing (or A:\CONFIG.SYS if you're booting from a floppy).
2. Add the command **c:\dos\interlnk.exe** as the *last* command (on its own line) to CONFIG.SYS.
3. Save the changes to CONFIG.SYS and exit the Editor.
4. Reboot the client machine. You may notice a message indicating that no connection was made. Don't worry about that.
5. On the server machine, get to the DOS command prompt and enter the command **intersvr**.
6. On the client machine, enter the command **interlnk**.

You'll see a description of how the client will treat drives on the server, as in this example:

```
This Computer        Other Computer
   (Client)             (Server)
_______________      _______________
D:   equals          A:
E:   equals          B:
F:   equals          C: (212Mb) HARD DISK
LPT2: equals         LPT1:
```

This listing indicates that any reference to drive D on the current (client) computer really refers to drive A on the other (server) computer. Similarly, any reference to drive F that you make on this computer will actually be drive C on the other computer. So entering the command TREE F:\ would actually show you the directory tree of drive C on the server computer. The command COPY F:\MYDIREC*.* would copy all the files from C:\MYDIREC on the server computer to the current drive and directory of the client computer. A command like ECHO ^L >LPT2: (where you press Ctrl+L to type **^L**) would eject a page from the printer attached to LPT1 on the server computer.

In other words, you now have complete control over the server computer from your current client computer's keyboard. You can even go into the DOS Shell or Windows File Manager and copy and move files between computers simply by dragging. Just remember that all the drive letters on the server computer are "larger" now. For example, drive A on the server will be accessible from drive D (or whatever) on the client. Just look to the server's screen or type **interlnk** at the command prompt on the client computer when you need a reminder about which drive letter is which.

While Intersvr is running, the server can only display the status of the connection. You cannot type commands at the server keyboard.

COMMANDS TO AVOID DURING A LINK

The following DOS commands don't work with Interlnk: CHKDSK, DEFRAG, DISKCOMP, DISKCOPY, FDISK, FORMAT, MIRROR, SYS, UNDELETE, and UNFORMAT. You should also avoid task swapping in the Shell (and Windows) while you're in an Interlnk connection.

BREAKING THE CONNECTION

To break the Interlnk connection between computers, press Alt+F4 on the server's keyboard. To restart the server, type **intersvr** at the server's command prompt.

TROUBLESHOOTING INTERLNK

If you have a problem with Interlnk, you should first make sure that the computers are connected correctly and that you've started the server. If those areas check out, you should consider the potential trouble spots described below.

Only Three Drives Are Accessible on the Server

By default, Interlnk will allow the client computer to access three server drives. For example, if the server has two floppy drives (A: and B:) and two hard drives (C: and D:), you'll be able to access server drives A, B, and C—but not drive D—from the client computer. To access additional drives on the server, you must add the switch /DRIVES:*n* to the DEVICE= command in the client's CONFIG.SYS file (*n* is the number of server drives that can be accessed). The following command in CONFIG.SYS would allow you to access four server drives instead of the usual three:

```
device=c:\dos\interlnk.exe /drives:4
```

Remember that any time you change DEVICE commands or any other settings in your CONFIG.SYS file, you'll need to reboot to activate the new settings.

Not Enough Drive Names Are Available

If you still can't access all the server's drives, make sure that the LASTDRIVE= command in the client's CONFIG.SYS file is set high enough to accommodate all the drive names. For example, if each computer has four drives, A through D, you'll need to have eight drive names available on the client computer (A:, B:, C:, D:, E:, F:, G:, and H:). Thus, the appropriate command in the client's CONFIG.SYS file would be

```
lastdrive=h
```

If in doubt, err on the side of setting LASTDRIVE too high. For example, there's usually no harm in using the command LASTDRIVE=N rather than the command

LASTDRIVE=H in CONFIG.SYS. If you're *not* using a network, you can make your life extra easy—simply omit the LASTDRIVE command altogether and DOS will set the default LASTDRIVE value to the letter following the last one in use.

If the client computer is connected to a Novell network, you probably should not change the LASTDRIVE command and you should not delete it. See the next section for more information.

Interlnk Limitations with CD-ROMs and Networks

Interlnk has some limitations and potential pitfalls that you should know about. For one thing, Interlnk cannot access a CD-ROM or network drive, although third-party programs such as LapLink can.

Also, keep in mind that Interlnk works best when the client computer is *not* connected to a network. In particular, you should avoid using Interlnk when your client computer is attached to a network that relies on the LASTDRIVE= command for its drive assignments. On Novell networks, for example, network drive assignments start with the letter *after* the drive specified by LASTDRIVE. If you monkey with the LASTDRIVE= setting on a computer that's connected to a Novell network, you may discover that path names, batch programs, and other commands that rely on a specific drive letter may suddenly stop working. What's more, if you set the LASTDRIVE letter too high, you may be unable to access your network drives at all.

The easiest way to use Interlnk to communicate between a non-networked computer and a networked computer is to set up the non-networked computer as the *client* and the networked computer as the *server*. (If both computers are on the network, just use the usual network services to share files and directories.)

As an alternative, you can specify multiple startup configurations in your CONFIG.SYS file. Define one configuration that's just for use with Interlnk and another for use with your network (see Lesson 8).

Server Drives Are Empty

If you try to access a drive on the server computer and DOS reports that there is no disk in that drive, chances are you've just forgotten to run Intersvr. Go to the server computer's keyboard, enter the command **intersvr** to bring up the Intersvr screen. Then go back to the client computer's keyboard and try again.

For more information on the Interlnk and Intersvr commands and their optional switches, you can enter **help interlnk**, **help interlnk.exe**, *or* **help intersvr**.

Conserving Power on a Laptop

The DOS 6 command POWER can extend your laptop computer's battery life by 5% to 25%. The amount of extra life depends on how the computer manages power, with the greatest savings for computers that conform to the Advanced Power Management (APM) specification. Check your computer's documentation to see whether the specification applies.

To use POWER, open the CONFIG.SYS file through a text editor such as the DOS Editor and add the device driver POWER.EXE at the end of the file. For example, if the driver is stored on drive C in the \DOS directory, enter the command

```
device=c:\dos\power.exe
```

By default, DOS will try to load the driver into upper memory, if it's available. If you want to load the driver into conventional memory, use the switch /LOW, as in **device=c:\dos\power.exe /low**.

Now, save the changes to CONFIG.SYS, exit the editor, and restart your computer.

If you want to display the current power status of your computer, type the command **power** and press ↵.

You can control the power settings by adding options to the POWER command that you type at the command prompt or place in AUTOEXEC.BAT or to the line **device= c:\dos\power.exe** in CONFIG.SYS . Your options are as follows:

- To conserve power while programs and hardware are idle, use the parameter ADV and specify maximum (**power adv:max**), regular (**power adv:reg**), or minimum (**power adv:min**) power conservation.
- To use the hardware power management features of an APM computer, type **power std**. If you use the STD parameter on a non-APM computer, power management is turned off.
- To turn power management off, type **power off**.

SUMMARY

In this lesson you've learned to use Interlnk to connect two computers directly as client and server. You've also learned how to install and use the POWER program to optimize the battery life of your laptop.

REFERENCE ENTRIES

For more information, see the following entries in the Alphabetical Reference:

- DEVICE
- DEVICEHIGH
- INTERLNK
- INTERSVR
- LASTDRIVE
- POWER

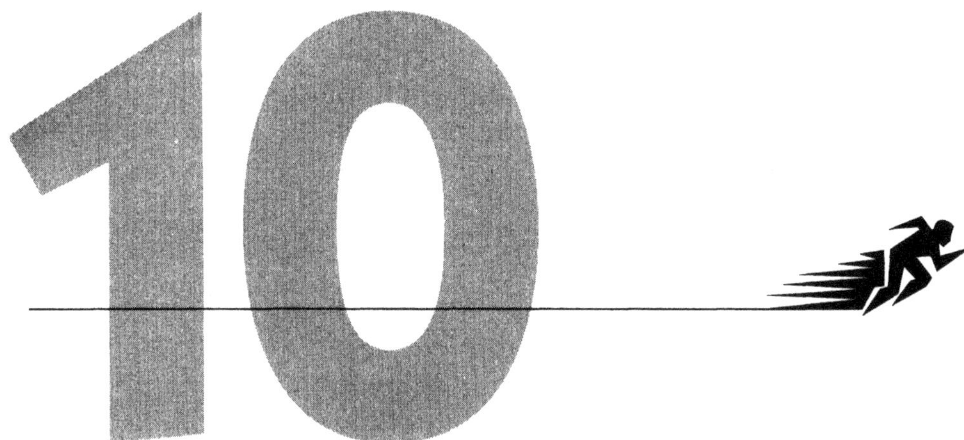

Staying out of Trouble

INTRODUCING

Troubleshooting DOS 6

Conquering DOS error messages

Seldom will a day go by when DOS doesn't register at least a minor complaint about your behavior or your computer's behavior. This lesson presents a concise troubleshooting guide to help you conquer cryptic messages and understand unexpected behavior from DOS. It also includes a handy alphabetical listing of common DOS error messages, what they mean, and what to do when they appear.

You can find additional troubleshooting information in the sources listed below.

- Appendix A offers solutions to some problems that can occur when installing DOS 6.
- The Microsoft *MS-DOS 6 User's Guide* provides in-depth coverage of troubleshooting techniques for many DOS commands and utilities. It also offers step-by-step first aid for systems that cannot start or restart properly.
- The DOS online Help (Lesson 3) shows how to type each command that can be used at the DOS command line, in the CONFIG.SYS file, and in batch programs. Be sure to check the <Notes> and <Examples> entries in Help for details that might explain how to solve problems you're having with a command.
- The documentation and online Help for application programs you run explain how to use the programs and discuss error messages displayed by those programs.

If you're still stumped, you might wish to contact a co-worker or computer consultant, attend meetings of computer user's groups, or call a technical support hotline for assistance. Most computer software and hardware manufacturers offer free or for-fee telephone assistance during normal business hours. Check your manuals for telephone numbers and hours of operation.

GETTING UNSTUCK: GENERAL GUIDELINES FOR SMOOTH COMPUTING

While it's true that many things can go wrong when you use a computer, most problems can be solved quickly and easily if you keep a cool head, a sharp eye, and try, try again.

A cool head will help you resist the urge to restart your computer (or throw it out the nearest window) if you're stuck and unsure of what to do next. Your sharp eyes can scrutinize error messages and study what you were doing before those error messages appeared on the screen. Once you've figured out the cause of the error and how to fix it, usually you can try again (especially if you've made a typing mistake). Chances are that your next attempt will succeed.

You may lose data if you restart the computer before exiting a program. Therefore, you should restart the computer only as a last resort, when all else fails.

AVOIDING TYPO TROUBLES

Typing mistakes are responsible for many of the error messages that DOS displays on your screen. For example, the message "Bad command or file name" is DOS's favorite answer to any command that it doesn't understand. Few users make it through a day without seeing that message at least once.

Another common mistake is forgetting to type a colon (:) after a drive letter, or typing a semicolon (;) instead. Remember that *path names*—that combination of drive letter, directories, and file name used throughout DOS and applications that you run under DOS—must be typed precisely, with a colon after the drive letter, backslashes (\ ) separating the directory and file names, a period before the file name extension, and no intervening spaces. For example, the following command will elicit the error message "Too many parameters - abc.exe":

```
dir c;abc.exe
```

What's wrong here? The problem is that I used a semicolon after the drive letter, instead of a colon. The correct form of the command is

```
dir c:abc.exe
```

Other common typing mistakes include confusing backslashes (\ ) with forward slashes (/), typing the letter *l* (el) instead of the number one (1), typing the letter *o* (oh) instead of zero (0), and so forth. If you make a typing mistake, simply retype the command correctly and things should proceed without a hitch.

LEARNING APPLICATION PROGRAMS

Whenever you're learning a new application program, you can avoid frustration and unnecessary problems by taking a few moments to master some basic tasks right off the bat.

Learn How to Get Help, Cancel Operations, and Exit

One of the most important skills for using any program is knowing how to get on-line help. In most programs, you can get help by pressing the F1 key, selecting a Help option from the menus, or choosing a Help button.

You should also know how to get out of trouble and into more familiar territory when you've chosen a command or option by accident. That is, you need to learn how to cancel commands and other operations. Techniques for canceling commands and operations differ from application to application. However, many programs use the Esc (Escape) key for this purpose. Others offer Cancel or Close buttons, while still others may be stopped by pressing Ctrl+C or Ctrl+Break.

Finally, you should learn the correct way to exit the program. As with canceling an operation, methods for exiting differ from application to application. You can exit most Windows programs by choosing File ➤ Exit from the menus.

WordPerfect for DOS uses some non-standard methods: To get help, press the F3 key; to cancel most operations, press F1; to exit, press F7 and answer the prompts.

Learn How to Use Menus and Make Selections

Once you've learned how to get help, cancel operations, and exit the program, you'll want to learn more about using menus and making selections in dialog boxes.

Many programs allow you to use the keyboard, the mouse, or both to select options from menus and dialog boxes. The mouse provides the easiest and most consistent method for making choices, for with it you can simply click on menus, options, buttons, and other selections.

When using the keyboard, often you can press the Alt key plus a colored or highlighted letter to open a menu or select a button from a dialog box. (Some programs use the F10 key to move the cursor into the menu bar.) Once a menu is opened (pulled down) you can type the highlighted letter to select an option.

Usually you can move from option to option in menus or dialog boxes by pressing the arrow keys (↑, ↓, ←, and →) or by pressing the Tab and Shift+Tab keys. After highlighting an option, typically you can press ↵ to select it.

Look for Screen Messages and Instructions

Many users, especially those who haven't hung around computers much, become so engrossed with what they're typing into the computer that they forget to watch the screen for helpful prompts and informative error messages. *Therefore, take some time to find out where error messages and prompts will appear, and look to the screen for messages and instructions.*

Messages usually appear near the bottom of the screen in a "status" area, but they also may appear in dialog boxes and prompts elsewhere on your screen.

PREPARING FOR OTHER PROBLEMS

We've now covered the most obvious methods for overcoming problems that you'll encounter in DOS or applications. Additional sources of trouble in DOS include incorrect settings in AUTOEXEC.BAT, CONFIG.SYS, or other startup files required by DOS and application programs; lost files; insufficient memory or disk space; and general mayhem caused by computer viruses. We'll take a look at these topics next.

SOLVING STARTUP WOES

If you're having problems starting your computer, especially after changing the CONFIG.SYS or AUTOEXEC.BAT startup files, you may need to bypass those files in order to start the machine successfully and identify and correct the cause of startup difficulties. DOS offers these two methods for bypassing startup files:

- To bypass the startup files completely, restart your computer with Ctrl+Alt+Del and press F5 when you see the message "Starting MS-DOS...." (Be sure to wait until this message appears, or you'll get a keyboard error; if a keyboard error does occur, press F1 to resume.)

- To execute CONFIG.SYS commands one by one and decide whether to execute the commands in AUTOEXEC.BAT, restart your computer and press F8 when you see the message "Starting MS-DOS...."

Applications that require settings in the CONFIG.SYS or AUTOEXEC.BAT files probably will not run properly (or at all) if you bypass CONFIG.SYS or AUTOEXEC.BAT. You should bypass these files only when you're trying to troubleshoot problems—not as a matter of course.

SOLVING CONFIG.SYS AND AUTOEXEC.BAT STARTUP PROBLEMS

If your computer is behaving strangely or having problems restarting, you may have a conflicting memory-resident program (TSR) or device driver in your CONFIG.SYS or AUTOEXEC.BAT file. Try bypassing the startup files completely (press F5 following the "Starting MS-DOS..." message). If the computer starts successfully, you can be reasonably sure that the culprit is lurking in one of those files.

Once you know that you can start your system *without* AUTOEXEC.BAT and CONFIG.SYS, the next step is to pin down which file and which commands are causing the problem.

Lesson 8 provides additional information on restarting your computer and configuring your startup files.

STEPPING THROUGH CONFIG.SYS

To determine whether the problem is in your CONFIG.SYS file, restart the computer and press F8 when you see the "Starting MS-DOS..." message. Then enable each command in CONFIG.SYS by pressing Y when prompted. When asked if you want to run AUTOEXEC.BAT, answer N. If your computer starts properly, your AUTOEXEC.BAT file probably is at fault and you can skip to the next section, "Stepping through AUTOEXEC.BAT."

You can create customized startup menus to provide alternate startup configurations that meet the needs of different computer users by specifying menu blocks in CONFIG.SYS. Lesson 8 explains how to create customized startup menus.

If your computer doesn't start, the problem is with CONFIG.SYS, and you should proceed as follows:

1. Restart your computer and press F8 when you see the "Starting MS-DOS..." message.
2. Answer Y when prompted to run the commands HIMEM.SYS, EMM386, DOS=HIGH, DOS=UMB, SHELL=, and any command that loads a device driver used in a disk-compression program (such as DoubleSpace) or that accesses your hard drive. Answer N when asked if you want to run any other commands.
3. Answer N when asked if you want to run AUTOEXEC.BAT.

If your computer stops running, EMM386 and HIMEM are probably in conflict (see your *MS-DOS 6 User's Guide* for detailed solutions). If your computer does not stop running, repeat Steps 1 through 3 exactly as above, except answer Y to run one of the remaining commands in CONFIG.SYS. Continue repeating these steps, answering Y to run a different command each time until you figure out exactly which command or commands prevent the computer from starting properly.

After identifying which CONFIG.SYS commands cause startup problems, back up CONFIG.SYS to a floppy disk, open the file in a text editor, and insert the command REM followed by a space in front of every problem command (this converts the command into a comment that isn't executed during startup). For instance, the following line in CONFIG.SYS will prevent DOS from running the mouse driver named GMOUSE:

```
REM device=c:\windows\gmouse.sys 2
```

Ultimately you should determine the proper settings for each command from the manufacturer or documentation and make the necessary corrections.

If your computer is equipped with an 80386 or higher microprocessor and extended memory, use MemMaker instead of manual methods to configure memory efficiently. This will reduce potential startup problems caused by faulty CONFIG.SYS and AUTOEXEC.BAT files.

Stepping through AUTOEXEC.BAT

If you suspect that AUTOEXEC.BAT is the source of your startup problems, open that file in a text editor and insert the command REM followed by a space in front of every command line except the @ECHO OFF, PROMPT, and PATH commands.

Next remove the REM command from the first line that you converted to a comment and restart your computer. If all works smoothly, remove the REM command from the next command and restart the computer again. Continue in this manner until you isolate the troublemaking command in AUTOEXEC.BAT. Once identified, the command can be corrected or removed.

KNOWING WHEN HIMEM.SYS IS MISSING OR NOT LOADED

When the HIMEM.SYS extended memory manager is loaded properly, you won't see any messages when you start your computer.

If a message informs you that the extended memory manager did not load properly or is not present, something is amiss. Most likely, the command **device=c:\dos\himem.sys** is not the first DEVICE command in CONFIG.SYS, and it should be.

Depending on the type of machine you have, you may need to add the /CPULOCK:ON and /MACHINE:N switches to the **device=c:\dos\himem.sys** *command line. See the MS-DOS 6 User's Guide or type* **help himem.sys** *for details.*

DODGING DOS SHELL MOUSE AND VIDEO PROBLEMS

When starting the DOS Shell, you may encounter the following problems:

- The graphical display is garbled or unreadable.
- The Shell may be unable to recognize your mouse.

GARBLED GRAPHICS

If the DOS Shell is unreadable when you start it, the video files that control your monitor may be missing or damaged. To solve this problem, you'll need to reinstall certain files from the DOS 6 setup disks. The *MS-DOS 6 User Guide* provides detailed instructions for reinstalling these files so that they work with various types of monitors.

MISSING MICE

When starting the DOS Shell, you may see a dialog box that lists the mouse driver version detected (or an *Unknown* version if DOS Shell isn't sure) and warns that your mouse isn't compatible with DOS 6. If you believe your mouse will work anyway, use the arrow keys or Tab to highlight the Use Mouse Anyway option and press ↵. If you know that your mouse won't work or you don't wish to use the mouse, highlight Disable Mouse and press ↵.

If you want the DOS Shell to offer the compatibility options again, you'll need to back up the file \DOS\DOSSHELL.INI for safety, open it in a text editor, remove the MOUSEINFO= line, save the file, exit the editor, and then restart the DOS Shell.

The mouse package or mouse driver startup message typically will list the version number of the driver. If you don't have a Microsoft Mouse and the mouse you do have is incompatible with the DOS Shell, ask the manufacturer for an updated driver program. The following mouse drivers are compatible with the DOS Shell:

TYPE OF MOUSE	COMPATIBLE VERSIONS
ATI	2.0 or later
Genius	9.06 or later
Hewlett-Packard	7.04 or later
IBM PS/2	7.04 of MOUSE.COM
Logitech	5.01 or later
Microsoft	7.04 of MOUSE.COM
Mouse Systems	7.01 or later

SINGING THOSE BACKUP AND LOST FILE BLUES

The time comes in every computer user's life that files must be restored from backups, or files that were deleted accidentally must be recovered. Perhaps you deleted an important data file that a program was expecting to use but can no longer find. Maybe you clobbered a drawing that you slaved over for hours and saved before you discovered the mistake. Or perchance your hard disk ran out of gas, crashed, and destroyed all of your data (this is rare, but it does happen). As you learned in Lesson 5, DOS 6 provides the MSBACKUP, BACKUP, RESTORE, and UNDELETE commands to help you recover from these situations.

You can only use RESTORE to restore files created with BACKUP. Only MSBACKUP, which is new in DOS 6, can be used to restore files backed up with MSBACKUP. Files saved with COPY or XCOPY can be copied from floppy disks to your hard disk using either COPY or XCOPY.

GETTING THE SQUEEZE ON DISK SPACE

Hard disks can fill up much faster than you might expect, especially if you've installed many Windows applications or stored a lot of bitmap (graphic) data. To solve this problem, back up your files and then try the following remedies in the order shown below:

- Clean up unnecessary files with the DEL or DELTREE commands (Lesson 4).
- Compress rarely used files (especially if they're bitmap files) with a third-party compression program such as PKZIP. Note that you'll need to expand the files (for instance, with PKUNZIP) before you can use them again.
- Increase the amount of disk space available with the DoubleSpace disk compression utility (Lesson 6). This utility compresses files when storing them to disk and decompresses them automatically when reading them from disk. Be forewarned—DoubleSpace is a one-way operation that *cannot* be undone without reformatting the disk and losing existing data.
- Buy a new disk with more space available.

MINIMIZING MEMORY MISERIES

If your system has an 80386 or higher microprocessor, you can use the DOS 6 MemMaker program to optimize computer memory automatically, with minimal tweaking on your part. Making manual changes to memory management commands in CONFIG.SYS and AUTOEXEC.BAT is a task best left to experts who thoroughly understand how DOS manages memory, since poorly configured memory may slow your system down, cause conflicts over memory areas, and lead to mysterious crashes on your computer.

A crash occurs when the computer freezes up and becomes completely unusable. Crashes can be caused by hardware problems, damaged files, viruses, power fluctuations, faulty software, and memory conflicts.

If a program consistently becomes erratic when loaded in the upper memory area, you may need to load it into conventional memory. If the erratic program is being loaded from CONFIG.SYS, change the DEVICEHIGH command that loads the program to a DEVICE command. If it is being loaded from AUTOEXEC.BAT, remove the LOADHIGH statement from the command. Then reboot the computer to have your changes take effect.

Occasionally a Windows program will freeze up, especially if you've been running it for a while. If you absolutely cannot operate the computer after trying all the normal methods to exit the program, your only alternative may be to restart the system. Usually a warm boot (Ctrl+Alt+Del) will do the trick, but you may have to resort to a cold boot, in which you turn the power off, wait for the disk drive to stop rotating, then turn the power on again.

Windows 3.1 will give you a chance to shut down just the frozen program or to restart the entire system after you press Ctrl+Alt+Del.

CONQUERING VIRAL DISEASES

If your computer suddenly starts making random sounds, greeting you with off-color screen messages, or experiencing damaged or lost files, it may have contracted a computer virus. Computer viruses are programs that stealthily replicate and spread throughout your system, sometimes rendering it useless. You can eradicate existing viruses and protect your computer against future invasions by using the Anti-Virus and VSafe programs that come with DOS 6, as described in Lesson 5.

DOS ERROR MESSAGES A TO Z

The remaining pages of this lesson list commonly encountered DOS error messages and how to solve them. The error messages are listed in alphabetical order, with the message shown in bold type, followed by a description of what could cause the error and how to solve the problem. This list of messages is by no means complete, but it should help you decipher the *most cryptic* error messages that DOS presents.

Abort, Ignore, Retry, Fail? or **Abort, Retry, Fail?** A disk or device error has occurred during a command or program. This message usually is preceded by a more detailed message indicating the nature of the problem. Type a single-character response as follows:

A	Abort and end the program or command.
I	Ignore the problem and continue. Selecting Ignore may result in some lost data. Ignore is not an option for floppy disk errors.
R	Retry the operation. Choose this option if you've fixed whatever problem caused the error (for example, you've correctly inserted a disk in a floppy drive or removed a write-protect tab from a disk) and want to try again.
F	Fail (end) the current operation and continue with the next one.

Access denied You've tried to replace a write-protected, read-only, or locked file. If necessary, use the ATTRIB command to change the file's attributes.

Attempt to remove current directory You've tried to use RM or RMDIR to remove a directory that's the current directory. Switch to the root directory (**cd **) and then try the RD or RMDIR command again. This time, however, you'll need to specify the full path of the directory you're trying to remove.

Bad command or file name The command you typed is not available because you misspelled it, it's not on disk, it's not in memory, or it's not available in the current path. You should correct the misspelling, supply a full path name (such as C:\MYPROGS\CALENDAR), switch to the directory containing the command file, or add the directory for the command to your PATH statement, as appropriate.

Bad command or parameters You've used incorrect syntax in the DEVICE or DEVICEHIGH line of CONFIG.SYS. Correct the problem in CONFIG.SYS and restart your system.

Bad or missing Command Interpreter DOS cannot find COMMAND.COM in the root directory, the file is invalid, or it has been moved from the directory it was in when you started DOS. Restart the system with a disk that contains a valid copy of COMMAND.COM, or copy the file from your backup DOS master disk (boot disk) to the disk used to start DOS.

This message also can appear if the SHELL command in CONFIG.SYS references a non-existent COMMAND.COM. Correct the problem in CONFIG.SYS and restart your computer.

Bad or missing *filename* You've specified a device incorrectly in the CONFIG.SYS file. Correct the error and restart your computer.

Convert lost chains to files (Y/N)? CHKDSK has found a problem with the file allocation table and wants permission to store the recovered information in files with the name FILE*nnnn*.CHK. Type Y (for Yes) to convert the information to files or N (for No) to free the lost data without storing it. Corrections are made only if you included the /F switch on the CHKDSK command line.

Data error reading drive *x*: DOS could not read the data from the disk, most likely due to a defective disk. Try typing **R** (for Retry) a few times when the "Abort, Retry, Fail?" message appears, or type **A** (for Abort). It's a good idea to make a new copy of this disk, because you may lose information if it's defective.

***xxxxxxxx* device driver cannot be initialized** See **Bad command or parameters** above.

Directory already exists You tried to create a directory that exists already, or the disk is full.

Disk error reading (or writing) drive *x*: See **Data error reading drive** *x* above.

Errors found, F parameter not specified
Corrections will not be written to disk The disk contains errors, but CHKDSK cannot correct them because you did not include the /F switch. Type the CHKDSK command again, this time with the /F switch.

File allocation table bad drive *x*: The disk may be defective. Run CHKDSK /F to check and repair the disk.

File creation error The file you're trying to create exists already; there is not enough space for the file; the root directory is full or out of files; or the file name is the same as a volume, directory, hidden file, or system file. After correcting the problem, try the operation again.

file* is cross linked on allocation unit *nn CHKDSK has found two files or directories that are recorded as using the same disk space. To correct this problem, copy the specified files or directories elsewhere and delete the originals. Some information may be lost. (See Lesson 5.)

General failure reading (or writing) drive *x*: Often occurs if you try to read to or write from a floppy disk that has not been formatted yet. Type **R** (for Retry) or **A** (for Abort) when the "Abort, Retry, Fail?" message appears. If necessary, use FORMAT to format the floppy disk.

Incorrect DOS Version The command cannot run on the version of DOS you are running at the moment. You may need to restart the computer, install versions of the command that match the DOS version, or make sure DOS is retrieving your command from the correct directory or search path.

Incorrect number of parameters You've specified too many or too few options on the command line.

Incorrect parameter You've specified an incorrect option on the command line.

Insufficient disk space The disk is full and does not contain enough room to perform the operation. You'll either need to free up space on this disk or retry the operation on another disk that has sufficient space.

Insufficient memory Your computer does not have enough memory to perform the operation. Remove memory-resident programs and try again, or try using MemMaker to configure memory more efficiently. If that doesn't work, you may need to install more memory on your computer.

Internal stack overflow
System halted The system tried to use more stacks than were available to handle hardware interrupts. Try restarting DOS, then edit CONFIG.SYS and allocate more stack resources. Type **help stacks** for more information.

Invalid drive specification You've specified an invalid drive name. Retype the command with the correct drive letter.

Invalid path, not directory, or directory not empty You've tried to use RM or RMDIR to remove a directory that is not empty, does not exist, or is a file.

Label not found Your batch program contains a GOTO command that has no corresponding label. Open the batch program with an editor, type the label correctly, and try again. See GOTO in the Alphabetical Reference or type **help goto** for more information.

No free file handles.
Cannot start COMMAND.COM, exiting DOS has run out of file handles. Restart DOS. If the message persists, increase the FILES= setting in CONFIG.SYS and restart your computer.

Non-DOS disk error reading (or writing) drive *x*: or Non-DOS diskette DOS cannot recognize the disk format because the disk is missing information or contains another operating system. Try running CHKDSK /F. If this fails, you may need to use FORMAT to reformat the disk (this will destroy files on the disk).

Non-System disk or disk error
Replace and press any key when ready You restarted your computer with a non-system disk in the floppy drive. Remove the floppy disk (or replace it with a DOS startup disk) and press any key to continue.

Not ready error reading (or writing) drive *x*: You've probably left the floppy disk drive door open or inserted the floppy disk upside down, backwards, or sideways. Correct the problem and type **R** (for Retry) when the "Abort, Retry, Fail?" message appears.

Out of environment space You've probably issued a SET command and DOS is out of environment space. Clear variables from the environment by typing the command **set *variable*=**. Alternatively, you can increase the environment space available by using the /E:*nnnnn* switch on the COMMAND or SHELL= line of CONFIG.SYS, then restart your computer.

Packed file corrupt All or a portion of a program has been loaded in the first 64 KB of conventional memory and cannot run successfully. Use the LOADFIX command to load the program above the first 64 KB of conventional memory.

Program is trying to modify system memory VSafe has detected that a program is trying to modify the system memory without using the standard DOS calls for memory-resident (TSR) programs. This could mean that a virus is trying to infect your system, although some network drivers can elicit this message from VSafe when they load. Run Anti-Virus if you suspect a virus invasion.

Program is trying to stay resident in memory You've selected the Resident option in VSafe, and VSafe has detected that another program is trying to load into memory. This could signal a possible virus infection. If you're suspicious, run Anti-Virus.

Program is trying to write to disk You've selected the General Write Protect option in VSafe and a program is trying to write to disk. This could signal a possible viral infection. Run Anti-Virus if you're suspicious.

Program too big to fit in memory See **Insufficient memory**.

Sector not found error reading (or writing) drive *x*: The disk probably has a bad spot that prevents DOS from finding the requested information. Copy all files from the disk onto a good disk, then use FORMAT to reformat the bad disk (or better yet, throw the bad disk away). Some data may be lost if the bad sector contained information. This can also occur if the floppy disk drive's heads need cleaning.

Sharing violation reading drive *x*: A program tried to access a file that another program is using. Type **A** (for Abort) or wait awhile and type **R** (for Retry).

Terminate batch job (Y/N)? You've pressed Ctrl+C or Ctrl+Break to interrupt a batch program. To stop the program, type Y (for Yes); to continue the program where it left off, type N (for No).

Too many parameters You've probably included a space in a file or path name or a semicolon after a drive letter. Retype the command correctly.

Unrecognized command in CONFIG.SYS There's an invalid command in CONFIG.SYS. Correct the error in CONFIG.SYS and restart your system.

Unrecoverable read (or write) error on drive *x*: DOS cannot read from or write to the disk because the floppy disk is inserted upside down, backwards, or sideways. Correct the problem and type **R** (for Retry).

WARNING: ALL DATA ON NON-REMOVABLE DISK DRIVE *x*: WILL BE LOST!
Proceed with Format (Y/N)? You are trying to format a hard disk. Type

N (for No) unless you are absolutely sure you want to reformat the hard disk and delete all of its data.

Verify Error Anti-Virus has discovered a change in an executable file, which may or may not be attributable to a virus. Anti-Virus presents several alternatives for handling the situation.

Virus Found Anti-Virus has found a virus. Your best bet is to eradicate the virus with the Clean button.

Write protect error writing drive *x*: You've tried to write to a floppy disk that is write-protected. Remove the write-protect tab from the disk and press **R** (for Retry) in response to the "Abort, Retry, Fail?" message.

SUMMARY

This lesson explained how to solve general problems with your DOS system and provided an alphabetical listing of the most cryptic messages that you're likely to encounter while using DOS.

REFERENCE ENTRIES

To learn more, see the lessons and Alphabetical Reference entries listed below.

- Lesson 1—restarting your system
- Lesson 2—starting and using the DOS Shell
- Lesson 3—using files and online Help
- Lesson 5 and the reference entries—using CHKDSK, MSBACKUP, Undelete, FORMAT, UNFORMAT, Anti-Virus, and VSafe
- Lesson 6 and the reference entries—using DoubleSpace (DBLSPACE) and Defragmenter (DEFRAG)
- Lesson 7 and the reference entries—using MemMaker
- Lesson 8—using the DOS Editor (EDIT) and customizing AUTOEXEC.BAT and CONFIG.SYS

PART II

ALPHABETICAL REFERENCE

ATTRIB

A

Lets you assign attributes to files in order to prevent accidental change or deletion, ensure backup, and hide (or display) files.

SYNTAX

attrib [+r|-r] [+a|-a] [+s|-s] [+h|-h] [[*drive:*][*path*]*filename*] [/s]

OPTIONS

r	determines the read/write status of the file; +r changes a file's attribute to read-only, –r changes a file's attribute to read/write
a	determines the archive status of the file; +a activates the archive status, –a deactivates the archive status
s	determines system status of the file; +s sets the system attribute, –s deactivates the system status
h	determines whether the file is hidden; +h sets the hidden attribute, –h deactivates the hidden status
[*drive*:][*path*]*filename*	drive, directory location, and name of the file; *filename* can contain wildcards (* and ?)
/s	makes the changes in the current directory and all of its subdirectories

EXAMPLES The command **attrib c:*.* /s > prn** prints the status of all files on drive C.

The command **attrib -r *.*** turns off the read-only attribute of all files on the current directory (so that those files could be changed or deleted).

NOTES You can also view and change file attributes in the DOS Shell. Select one or more files in the File List window, then choose File ➤ Change Attributes. In the Change Attributes dialog box, active attributes are indicated by a ➤ symbol. Clicking an attribute, or highlighting an attribute and pressing the spacebar, turns the attribute on or off.

See Also MSBACKUP, XCOPY

BUFFERS

BUFFERS, used only in CONFIG.SYS, sets the number of memory buffers available to programs that can take advantage of them. Each memory buffer holds one sector of data from the disk. This allows a program to make fewer disk accesses, and therefore run a little faster.

When you install a new program, that program typically will check the current BUFFERS setting. If it can use more buffers than you've allotted, the program will increase the BUFFERS setting automatically.

SYNTAX

buffers=*number* [,*sectors*]

OPTIONS

number	number of disk buffers specified, in the range of 1 to 99
sectors	maximum number of sectors that can be read or written in one disk transfer, in the range of 0 to 8

EXAMPLES The most common setting for buffers is **buffers=30,0.**

NOTES If you use a disk-caching program, such as SMARTDrive, you will need fewer buffers.

See Also FILES, SMARTDRV, Lesson 8

B

CALL

CALL is used within a batch program such as AUTOEXEC.BAT to execute another batch program (you cannot use CALL at the command prompt). When the called batch program finishes its job, the calling batch program continues with its next command.

If the batch program being called can accept command-line parameters, you can include them on the CALL command line. When calling another batch program, you must specify its location if it is not in the current directory or path.

SYNTAX

call [*drive*:][*path*]*filename* [*parameters*]

OPTIONS

[*drive*:][*path*]*filename*	location and name of the batch program that you want to run; the batch program file must be saved with a .BAT extension
parameters	list of parameters that the called batch program can accept

EXAMPLES Suppose you have a batch program named MACROS.BAT on your C:\DOS directory. That batch program contains commands to create several favorite DOSKEY macros.

To have DOS run that batch program automatically, load those macros each time you start your computer, and return control to AUTOEXEC.BAT, you would add the command **call c:\dos\macros.bat** to your AUTOEXEC.BAT file.

See Also DOSKEY, EDIT, GOTO, Lesson 8

CHDIR OR CD

CHDIR (or its abbreviated form, CD) displays the name of the current directory and lets you switch to a different directory. Include the \ in the directory name unless you're moving directly down the directory tree or you're using the .. shortcut to move up one level.

Including the drive name in the CHDIR command does *not* switch you to that drive. It just sets the current directory on that drive.

SYNTAX

chdir [*drive*:][*path*]

OPTIONS

[*drive*:][*path*]	drive, directory (and, optionally, subdirectory) to switch to; you can use .. in the *path* to move up one directory level

EXAMPLES The command **cd** displays the name of the current directory. Type **cd** to move to the root directory of the current drive. The shortcut command **cd..** moves you up one directory level.

The command **cd \wp** switches you to the directory named WP. To move to the subdirectory named \WP\DOCS from anywhere on the hard drive, type **cd \wp\docs** and press ↵. If you were already in the \WP directory, you could type **cd docs** to move down one level (to the \WP\DOCS directory).

NOTES

- Use the command **tree ** or **tree \ >prn** to view or print a list of all the directories on the current drive.
- Include the command PROMPT PG in your AUTOEXEC.BAT file to display the name of the current directory at the command prompt at all times.

- The DOS Shell offers the easiest techniques for viewing and switching directories.

See Also MKDIR, PROMPT, RMDIR, TREE, Lesson 4

CHKDSK

Checks the status of a disk and optionally fixes any minor errors on the disk. CHKDSK also informs you of total and available memory (RAM).

SYNTAX

chkdsk [*drive*:][[*path*]*filename*] [/f] [/v]

OPTIONS

[*drive*:][*path*]*filename*	specifies the drive, directory location, and name of the file or files to check; *filename* can include wildcards (* and ?)
/f	fixes errors on the disk
/v	displays the drive, path, and file name for all files on the disk as the disk is checked

EXAMPLES The command **chkdsk** produces a CHKDSK status report for the current drive.

The command **chkdsk /f** checks all the files on the current drive and allows you to convert any lost clusters (small errors on the disk) to files named FILE0000.CHK, FILE0001.CHK, and so forth. You can erase those files if you wish.

NOTES

- Never run CHKDSK /F when Windows or any other program is running.

- If CHKDSK finds errors, and you did not use the /F switch, you'll see the message "Corrections will not be written to disk." You can enter the command **chkdsk /f** to correct those errors.

See Also DBLSPACE, DEFRAG, Lessons 5 and 6

CHOICE

Temporarily stops a batch program, displays a prompt on the screen, and waits for the user to respond to that prompt. Once the user responds to the prompt, the batch program resumes.

You can define any characters as a list of acceptable responses from the user. The user's response, however, is always converted to a number and placed in the DOS ERRORLEVEL parameter. The number stored in ERRORLEVEL is determined by the position of the acceptable choice in the list.

Suppose, for example, that the acceptable choices are A, B, and C. If the user chooses the first one (A), ERRORLEVEL will receive a value of 1. If the user chooses the second option (B in this example), ERRORLEVEL will receive a value of 2 (and so forth).

You can use a series of IF commands in the batch program to respond to the user's selection. Have each IF command check for a specific ERRORLEVEL value, then branch to some label using a GOTO command, as in Figure 1 below. Always list the IF ERRORLEVEL commands in descending order. For instance, if the batch program presents four options, have the batch program check for ERRORLEVEL 4 first, then ERRORLEVEL 3, then ERRORLEVEL 2, and finally, ERRORLEVEL 1.

SYNTAX

choice [*text*] [/c:*keys*] [/n] [/s] [/tc,*nn*]

OPTIONS

/c:*keys*	specifies each letter or number that will be accepted as a valid response; if omitted, the acceptable choices will be Y and N
/n	prevents display of acceptable choices
/s	if specified, acceptable keys will be case-sensitive; omitting this switch makes the choice case-insensitive
/tc,*nn*	*nn* specifies the amount of time (in seconds) to wait for a response; if no choice is made during that time, the key specified by *c* will be selected automatically
text	the prompt that you want to appear on the screen; if omitted, only the acceptable keys will be displayed on the screen

EXAMPLES The command **Choice Continue** (with a blank space after "Continue") displays the message "Continue [Y,N]?" If the user types Y, ERRORLEVEL will equal 1. If the user types N, ERRORLEVEL will equal 2.

The following command displays the message "What'll it be?" and waits for the user to press 1, 2, 3, or 4.

```
CHOICE What'll it be? /c:1234 /n
```

Figure 1 shows a practical example of the CHOICE command used in a batch program. The ECHO commands display a series of options, and then the CHOICE command waits for a response.

The /T4,10 switch in Figure 1 tells the batch program "If the user does not respond within ten seconds, assume he or she selected the fourth option."

NOTES

- The CHOICE command is useful only in batch programs, although you can try it out at the command prompt.
- If the user presses a key not specified in the /C switch, CHOICE will sound a beep and continue displaying the prompt.

FIGURE 1:

A sample batch program, named MAINMENU.BAT, that presents a menu of options, then runs the appropriate program

```
@ECHO OFF
REM ************************************ MainMenu.bat
REM Provide a "shell" for running programs.
:ShowMenu
CLS
ECHO ======================================================
ECHO.
ECHO           What do you want to do?
ECHO.
ECHO           1. Use WordPerfect
ECHO           2. Use Quattro Pro
ECHO           3. Use dBASE IV
ECHO           4. Go to DOS Command Prompt
ECHO.
ECHO ======================================================
ECHO.
CHOICE What'll it be? /c:1234 /t4,10
IF ERRORLEVEL 4 GOTO toDOS
IF ERRORLEVEL 3 GOTO dBASE
IF ERRORLEVEL 2 GOTO Qpro
IF ERRORLEVEL 1 GOTO WordPerf
GOTO ShowMenu
REM ********************** Run WordPerfect
:WordPerf
CD C:\WP51
WP
CD \
GOTO ShowMenu
REM ********************** Run Quattro Pro
:Qpro
CD C:\Qpro
Q
CD \
GOTO ShowMenu
REM ********************** Run dBASE IV
:dBASE
CD C:\DBASE
DBASE
CD \
GOTO ShowMenu
REM ********************** Return to the DOS Prompt
:toDOS
CD \
ECHO.
ECHO Type MAINMENU to use the menu again.
PAUSE
CLS
PROMPT $p$g
```

- If the user presses Ctrl+C or Ctrl+Break, ERRORLEVEL will be set to 0.
- If CHOICE detects an error, ERRORLEVEL will be set to 255.

If you want the batch program MAINMENU.BAT or a similar batch program of your own creation to take over after the user starts the computer, run it from AUTOEXEC.BAT. For instance, if MAINMENU.BAT is stored on C:\DOS, make C:\DOS\MAINMENU the last command in AUTOEXEC.BAT.

See Also CLS, ECHO, IF, GOTO, PAUSE, REM, Lessons 3 and 8

CLS

Clears the screen, leaving only a new prompt. You can use CLS at the command prompt or in a batch program. It has no effect on memory or disk storage.

SYNTAX

```
cls
```

COMMAND

COMMAND.COM is the DOS *command interpreter*, the program DOS uses to process commands that you enter at the command prompt. You can use COMMAND.COM to change the size of your DOS *environment* (see the entry for SHELL) or to start a new temporary DOS session.

SYNTAX

command [[*drive*:]*path*] [/c *command*] [/e:*size*] [/k *filename*] [/p]

OPTIONS

[*drive*:]*path*	drive and directory location of COMMAND.COM
/c *command*	specifies a series of DOS commands that are to be executed immediately
/e:*size*	lets you set the size of the DOS environment, within the range of 160 to 32,768 bytes; default is 256 bytes (see SHELL)

/k *filename*	runs the specified program (or batch program); not recommended for use on the SHELL command line in your CONFIG.SYS file
/p	disables the EXIT command so that the copy of the command processor remains in memory for the current session (that is, until you turn off the computer or reboot); use only on the SHELL command line in your CONFIG.SYS file

NOTES

- The location of COMMAND.COM is usually recorded in the COMSPEC (%COMSPEC%) environment variable. To check this, type **set** at the DOS command prompt.
- Lesson 8 shows how to display a DOS command prompt that reminds you how to return to Windows after you've exited to DOS temporarily.

See Also PROMPT, SET, SHELL, Lessons 1 and 8

COPY

Lets you make copies of files. You can copy files from one disk to another, from one directory to another directory, or from one file name to another file name in the same directory. You can also use COPY to copy files from one device to another. For example, you can "copy" a text file from disk to your printer. Hence, the command **copy letter.txt prn** prints the contents of the LETTER.TXT file.

The file being copied is the *source* file and is listed first in the COPY command. The copied file is the *destination* or *target* file and is listed second in the COPY command. You always copy *from* someplace *to* some other place.

If you use only one file name (or file specification) in the COPY command, the current directory is the target. For example, the command **copy a:*.*** copies all the files from the root directory of drive A to the current directory.

Keep in mind that COPY overwrites any file of the same name automatically and without warning. You might find it safer (and easier) to copy files using the DOS Shell.

SYNTAX

copy [*drive1*:][*path1*]*filename1* [*drive2*:][*path2*][*filename2*]

OPTIONS

[*drive1*:][*path1*]*filename1*	drive, directory location, and file name of the existing (source) file or files you want to copy; *filename1* can include wildcards (* and ?)
[*drive2*:][*path2*]*filename2*	target drive, directory location, and file name for the copied file or files; *filename2* can include wildcards (* and ?); if *filename2* is omitted, the target files will have the same name as the source files

EXAMPLES Type **copy *.* a:** to copy all files from the current directory to the root directory of drive A.

To make an extra copy, named JAN1993.BAK, of the file JAN1993.WK3, type

```
copy jan1993.wk3 jan1993.bak
```

The next command copies the file named DAD.LET from the \WP51 directory on drive C to the disk in drive A:

```
copy c:\wp51\dad.let a:
```

NOTES

- Lesson 4 explains how to use the DOS Shell to copy files.
- You cannot copy files to a write-protected disk.
- Unlike DISKCOPY, which copies all files plus the volume label and system tracks (if any), the COPY command copies only the files you specify.

- COPY will quit if the destination drive runs out of space.
- Many applications need to be *installed* on the hard disk—not just copied—with a special install or setup program that comes with the application.

See Also DISKCOPY, MOVE, MSBACKUP, RENAME, REPLACE, XCOPY, Lesson 4

C

DATE

Displays the current system date (the date your computer thinks is correct) and allows you to change the date. All programs that allow you to access the system date use the date defined by the DATE command.

SYNTAX

date [*current date*]

OPTIONS

current date	an optional date, entered in the format *mm-dd-yy* (for example, *1-11-93* for January 11, 1993)

EXAMPLES To check the current system date, type **date** and press ↵. Press ↵ when prompted for a new date, or type in a new date and press ↵.

The command **date 01-30-93** changes the current date to January 30, 1993. (You could also specify the date as **01/30/93**, and you can omit leading zeros, as in **1-30-93**.)

See Also TIME

DBLSPACE

DoubleSpace (invoked with the command DBLSPACE) is a new DOS 6 utility that compresses hard disk drives and configures drives that were previously compressed with DoubleSpace.

The uncompressed portion of the drive is called the *host*. Each compressed portion of the host drive is called a *compressed volume file* (CVF). After compressing a drive, you can refer to it in DOS commands by its drive letter, just as you refer to uncompressed drives.

To use DoubleSpace interactively and select options from menus, type **dblspace** and press ↵. This is the easiest way to use DoubleSpace. To exit DoubleSpace, select Drive ➤ Exit. Please refer to Lesson 6 for more details on using DoubleSpace interactively.

If you include switches or parameters on the DoubleSpace command line, you'll be able to bypass the menus and carry out tasks directly. The switches and parameters used depend on the task you're trying to perform. Type **help dblspace** or **dblspace /?** at the command prompt to see the available options.

The first time you start DoubleSpace, the program will set up your system for disk compression and compress the drive of your choice. After initial setup, you can use DoubleSpace to maintain your compressed drive and to compress additional drives.

Warning: Once you compress a drive, you cannot uncompress it, although you *can* reduce the size of the compressed volume.

See Also CHKDSK, DEFRAG, FORMAT, UNDELETE, Lesson 6

D

DEFRAG

The MS-DOS Defragmenter (DEFRAG) reorganizes the files on your disk to optimize disk performance. As programs read from and write to your hard disk, information can become fragmented. The information is valid, but it takes much longer for your computer to read and write fragmented files than it does to read and write unfragmented files.

To run Defragmenter interactively, type **defrag** and press ↵. You can then press Esc and select options from the Optimize menu. To exit the program, select Optimize ➤ Exit or press Alt+X.

Lesson 6 explains how to run Defragmenter interactively. For information on options available from the command line, type **help defrag** or **defrag /?**.

See Also CHKDSK, DBLSPACE, Lesson 6

DEL OR ERASE

The DEL command (or its alternative, ERASE) erases one or more files from the disk. The UNDELETE command can recover a file that you remove with DEL—but you must use UNDELETE *immediately*.

SYNTAX

```
del [drive:][path]filename [/p]
```

OPTIONS

[*drive*:][*path*]*filename*	drive, directory location, and name of the file (or group of files) to delete; *filename* can include wildcards (* and ?)
/p	DOS asks for permission before deleting each file (I strongly recommend using this switch!)

EXAMPLES To delete a file named MYFILE.BAK from the current drive and directory, type **del myfile.bak**.

To delete all files with the .BAK extension from the current drive and directory, type **del *.bak**. To delete files that have the .BAK extension from a directory named \WP\WPFILES, type

```
del c:\wp\wpfiles\*.bak /p
```

NOTES Lesson 4 explains how to delete files from the DOS Shell.

See Also DELTREE, UNDELETE, Lesson 4

DELTREE

Deletes a directory and all of its files and subdirectories, including hidden files, system files, and read-only files. Be careful with DELTREE, as it can be very destructive and you may not be able to undo your deletions.

SYNTAX

deltree [/y] [*drive*:]*path*

OPTIONS

/y	deletes the directory and its files *without* prompting for confirmation (watch out, this is dangerous!)
[*drive*:]*path*	drive and location of the directory to delete; subdirectories of *path* will also be deleted

D

EXAMPLES To delete the directory named \JUNK and all of its files and subdirectories on drive D, type **deltree d:\junk**.

NOTES

- For safety, do not use the /Y option.
- Before using DELTREE, type **dir [*drive*:]*path* /s /p** to verify that you don't need any of the files in the *path* directory or its subdirectories. If necessary, use MSBACKUP, COPY, MOVE, or XCOPY to prevent data loss.
- You can use wildcards in the path, but be extremely careful because wildcards can match file names as well as multiple directory names. Use DIR first to check for potential data loss.

See Also CHDIR, DEL, DIR, RMDIR, TREE, UNDELETE, UNFORMAT, Lesson 4

DEVICE

DEVICE, used only in CONFIG.SYS, installs drivers for optional devices, such as a mouse, RAM disk, and extended memory.

DOS offers several of its own device drivers, including ANSI.SYS, DISPLAY.SYS, DRIVER.SYS, EGA.SYS, PRINTER.SYS, RAMDRIVE.SYS, HIMEM.SYS, and SMARTDRV.SYS. Your computer and any devices that you add will provide their own device drivers, which must be loaded by an appropriate DEVICE command in CONFIG.SYS.

SYNTAX

device=[*drive*:][*path*]*filename* [*options*]

OPTIONS

[*drive*:][*path*]*filename*	drive, directory location, and complete file name and extension of the device driver file
options	represents additional parameters and switches supported by the device driver

EXAMPLES To load the device driver C:\DOS\ANSI.SYS into memory, add **device=c:\dos\ansi.sys** to your CONFIG.SYS file. ANSI.SYS supports escape sequences that customize your screen and keyboard.

NOTES Use the DEVICEHIGH command to load a driver into upper memory.

See Also DEVICEHIGH, Lessons 7, 8, and 9

DEVICEHIGH

DEVICEHIGH, used only in the CONFIG.SYS file, loads device drivers such as RAMDRIVE.SYS and ANSI.SYS into reserved (upper) memory on 80286, 80386, and 80486 systems. This frees more of your conventional memory for additional application programs.

If there isn't enough free upper memory for your driver, it will be loaded into conventional memory, just as if you had used the DEVICE command.

Before you can use this command, you must activate an upper memory block manager. With an 80386 or 80486 computer, you can use the HIMEM, DOS=, and EMM386 commands (in that order) to activate upper memory blocks.

SYNTAX

devicehigh [*drive*:][*path*]*filename* [*parameters*]

OPTIONS

[*drive*:][*path*]*filename*	drive, directory location, and file name of device driver
parameters	command line information required by the device driver

Note that DEVICEHIGH provides other options to define exactly which region of upper memory is assigned to the drivers. However, it's easier and safer to let the new DOS 6 utility MemMaker analyze your system memory and assign the correct values automatically (see Lesson 7).

See Also DEVICE, EMM386, LOADHIGH, MEM, MEMMAKER, Lessons 7, 8, and 9

DIR

Displays the names of files on any disk drive or directory. The default display includes each file name and extension, the size of each file (in bytes), and the date and time of the most recent change to each file.

You can use the DIRCMD environment variable to specify default switches for the DIR command. All you need to do is add the command SET DIRCMD=*switches* to your AUTOEXEC.BAT file (where *switches* are any of the available switches for the DIR command).

SYNTAX

dir [*drive*:][*path*][*filename*] [/a[*attributes*]] [/b] [/l][/o[*order*]] [/p] [/s] [/w]

OPTIONS

[*drive*:][*path*]*filename*	drive, directory location, and file name to display; *filename* can include wildcards (* and ?)
/a[*attributes*]	displays only names with the specified attribute(s). When you use /A without the *attributes* value, the list includes all files, even system and hidden files. The *attributes* can be any combination of the following values (do not separate values with spaces):

–	reverses the action of the *attributes* value that follows
a	displays names of files that will be archived during the next backup
d	displays directory names
h	displays hidden file names
r	displays read-only file names
s	displays system file names

/b	lists only the names of files and directories; the list shows one name per line (useful if you wish to redirect the output to a file and then edit the file)
/l	displays all names in lowercase letters

/o[*order*]		specifies the order of the file and directory names. When you use the /O switch without *order*, directories are listed before files, and names are sorted alphabetically. The *order* can be any combination of the following values (do not separate values with spaces):
	–	reverses the sort *order* value that follows
	n	sorts alphabetically by name
	e	sorts alphabetically by extension
	d	sorts by date and time, earliest first
	s	sorts by size, smallest first
	g	sorts with directories grouped before files
/p		pauses after each screenful of information
/s		displays the list of file and directory names in all subdirectories
/w		displays the list in a wide format that includes the file name, extensions, and directory names only

EXAMPLES To display all of the file names, sizes, dates, and times on the current disk drive and directory, type **dir** and press ↵.

To create a text file named DBFILES.TXT, which contains a vertical list of files in the \DBMS directory on drive C that have the extension .DAT, type

```
dir c:\dbms\*.dat /b > dbfiles.txt
```

To display all the directories and files (including system files and hidden files) in the current directory, sorted in alphabetical order, type **dir /a /o**.

The command below locates all files that were created or changed on January 30, 1993:

```
dir /s | find "01-30-93"
```

See Also ATTRIB, FIND, MSBACKUP, SET, Lessons 2, 3, 4, and 8

DISKCOPY

Makes an exact duplicate of all files in all directories of a floppy disk, using either one or two floppy disk drives. If the target is not formatted, DISKCOPY will format the disk automatically.

SYNTAX

diskcopy [*source*: [*target*:]] [/1] [/v]

OPTIONS

source:	drive containing the disk to be copied; if omitted, the current drive is assumed
target:	drive that is to receive the copy; if omitted, the current drive is assumed and you'll be prompted to switch disks as needed
/1	copies only the first side of a disk
/v	verifies that the copy is correct; this slows the copy process

EXAMPLES To copy the files on the floppy disk in drive A to another disk of the same size in drive B, type **diskcopy a: b:**.

Type **diskcopy a: a:** to copy a floppy disk in drive A to another floppy disk. The screen will prompt you to remove and insert the source and target disks as necessary.

NOTES DISKCOPY cannot be used to copy a hard disk to another hard disk, a hard disk to a floppy disk, or to copy floppy disks that are different sizes; for instance, you cannot use it to copy a 3 ½-inch disk to a 5 ¼-inch disk, or vice versa.

See Also COPY, XCOPY

DOSHELP

Use the DOSHELP command to display a brief explanation of DOS commands. The information displayed is less comprehensive than the information available with the HELP command.

SYNTAX

```
doshelp [command]
```

or

```
command /?
```

OPTIONS

command any DOS command; if you omit *command*, DOSHELP will present a brief summary of all the DOS commands

EXAMPLES To display a brief summary of the DIR command, type **doshelp dir** or **dir /?** and press ↵.

See Also HELP, Lesson 3

DOSKEY

DOSKEY is a command-line editor/macro generator that lets you recall, edit, and reuse previously executed commands. DOSKEY also enables you to create and run *macros*, which act like small, fast batch programs.

DOSKEY provides a remarkable array of convenient command-line tools. In fact, unless you use the DOS Shell exclusively, you probably should add the DOSKEY command to your AUTOEXEC.BAT file so that its features will always be available. With DOSKEY you can

- Issue more than one command on a single line
- Display and reuse previously executed commands
- Edit previously executed commands
- Save and store a list of commands
- Create, use, and save macros

SYNTAX

doskey [/bufsize=*size*] [/macros] [/history] [*macro*=[*commands*]]

OPTIONS

macro=commands	creates a macro (named *macro*) that carries out one or more DOS commands
/bufsize=*size*	determines the size of the buffer (in bytes) that stores the macros you create; default is 512 bytes
/history (or /h)	displays all command lines stored in memory
/macros (or /m)	displays all current macros

EXAMPLES To display a list of all the commands stored in the DOSKEY buffer, type **doskey /h.**

You can create the macro below to pause after displaying each screenful of information. Your new macro will always execute when you type the command **type**.

```
doskey type=type $1 $b more
```

To list all of your current macros in a file named MACROS.TXT, type

```
doskey /m > macros.txt.
```

NOTES Macros are stored in memory and, therefore, are lost when you turn off your computer. However, if you store DOSKEY commands that create macros in a batch program and then execute that batch program from AUTOEXEC.BAT, your computer will load your macros at the start of each session, thus creating your own "permanent" extensions to DOS.

Normally, macros that have the same names as DOS commands will be used instead of the DOS command. To use the DOS command, type a space and then type the command.

The following keystrokes can be used to recall a DOS command after loading DOSKEY into memory:

↑	recalls the command used before the command displayed currently
↓	recalls the command used after the command displayed currently
PgUp	recalls the oldest command used in the current session
PgDn	recalls the most recent command used in the current session

After loading DOSKEY, you can use any of the following keystrokes to edit commands on the command line:

←	moves the cursor back one character
→	moves the cursor forward one character
Ctrl+←	moves the cursor back one word
Ctrl+→	moves the cursor forward one word
Home	moves the cursor to the beginning of the line
End	moves the cursor to the end of the line
Esc	clears the command from the display
F1	copies one character from the template to the command line (the template stores the last command you typed)
F2	searches forward in the template for the character you type, copying all characters from the template up to, but not including, the character you typed
F3	copies the remainder of the template to the command line

F4	deletes characters from the cursor position up to, but not including, the next character you type
F5	copies the current command into the template and clears the command line
F6	places an end-of-file character (Ctrl+Z) into the command line
F7	displays all commands stored in memory, along with their associated command numbers
F8	cycles through stored commands that start with the characters you specified before pressing F8
F9	prompts for a command number and displays the associated command
Alt+F7	deletes all commands stored in memory
Alt+F10	deletes all macro definitions

The following characters are valid in DOSKEY macros:

$g	the output redirection symbol (>)
gg	the append symbol (>>)
$l	the input redirection symbol (<)
$b	the pipe symbol (|)
$t	used between commands to specify multiple commands on a macro line
$1 through $9	replaceable parameters (equivalent to %1 through %9 in batch programs)
$*	replaced with everything you type on the command line following the macro name
$$	the dollar sign character

See Also Lessons 1 and 3

DOSSHELL

Lets you perform all of the essential DOS commands—copying files, creating directories, listing file names, and so on—from an easy-to-use graphical interface that includes pull-down menus, dialog boxes, an extensive context-sensitive help system, movable icons, mouse support, and enhanced DOS commands.

You can perform many operations from the Shell that are not available from the command line, including task switching, associating data files with executable files, moving or copying files by dragging file icons to other locations, viewing files in text or hexadecimal format, and creating groups of related programs.

To start the DOS Shell, type **dosshell** and press ↵ at the command prompt. See Lessons 2 and 4 for details on using the Shell. Type **help dosshell** or **dosshell /?** for a list of video display options that you can include on the DOSSHELL command line.

NOTES

- The DOS 6 installation program creates an initialization file named \DOS\DOSSHELL.INI that configures the Shell to your particular computer and devices.
- On a hard disk system, the directory that contains DOSSHELL files must be listed in the current PATH setting.

See Also Lessons 2 and 4

ECHO

Indicates whether the command echoing feature is on or off and whether to display or hide messages on the screen. Echo is used most often in batch programs.

SYNTAX

```
echo [on|off|message]
```

OPTIONS

on	turns command echoing on
off	turns command echoing off
message	the text you want to display on the screen

EXAMPLES The following batch program types a two-line message that is preceded and followed by a blank line (echo.):

```
@echo off
echo.
echo This batch program counts the number of occurrences
echo of a text string in the specified file.
echo.
```

NOTES

- ECHO *message* is most useful when echo is turned off.
- It is common to place @ECHO OFF as the first line in a batch program. This turns echoing off until DOS encounters an ECHO ON command. The @ symbol prevents the ECHO OFF command from echoing and is used only in batch programs.
- To echo a blank line, use the command **echo.** (do not type a space before the period).
- To display the current status of command echoing, type **echo** by itself.
- You cannot use ECHO to display a pipe (|) or redirection character (< or > or >>).

See Also CHOICE, PAUSE, REM, Lesson 8

E

EDIT

EDIT is a full-screen text editor with menus, mouse support, cut-and-paste options, and a search-and-replace feature. This program lets you create and edit ASCII files much more easily than you could with the archaic EDLIN line editor. As a bonus, EDIT's full-screen display lets you browse through text files.

As with most Microsoft products, EDIT includes a context-sensitive help system that provides instant online help. EDIT lets you use two sets of keyboard commands for most actions—a Microsoft set and a WordStar-compatible set.

See Lesson 8 for information on using the Editor. Type **help edit** or **edit /?** for a list of video display options that you can include on the EDIT command line.

SYNTAX

edit [[*drive*:][*path*]*filename*]

OPTIONS

[*drive*:][*path*]*filename*	drive, directory location, and name of the file to edit

EXAMPLES You can bring a copy of the CONFIG.SYS file into the Editor and make changes to it by typing **edit c:\config.sys**.

NOTES

- The EDIT and QBASIC programming environments share common code in DOS 6, and they use the QBASIC.INI initialization file. Any color or configuration changes made to EDIT take effect automatically when you start QBASIC, and vice versa.
- QBASIC.EXE must be available in the search path, current directory, or the same directory as EDIT.COM; otherwise EDIT will not run.

See Also Lesson 8

EMM386

The EMM386 program is a memory manager that can be used only by computers with 80386 or 80486 microprocessors. From the CONFIG.SYS file, it lets DOS

- Simulate expanded memory in extended memory. (Use EMM386 if your computer has only extended memory available, but your applications need to use expanded memory.)
- Access your system's upper memory. (Use EMM386 if you want to store device drivers and TSRs there rather than in conventional memory.)

Before you can use EMM386 from the command line, you must install the driver (with the appropriate options) in your CONFIG.SYS file. Used from the command line, EMM386 performs these functions:

- Displays the status of the EMM386 driver
- Enables or disables expanded memory
- Enables and disables support for the Weitek math coprocessor

For a much easier way to set up memory, use MemMaker, a new DOS 6 utility that configures memory automatically by analyzing your system and choosing optimal settings. If you need details on using EMM386 from CONFIG.SYS or the command line, type **help EMM386** or **EMM386 /?** at the DOS prompt.

See Also DEVICE, DEVICEHIGH, LOADHIGH, MEMMAKER, Lesson 7

ERASE

Allows you to erase files. See DEL.

E

EXIT

Quits the command interpreter program (COMMAND.COM). When you return temporarily to the DOS command prompt from the Shell, Windows, or another program, or you use the COMMAND command, you're actually starting a new instance of the command interpreter. When you're finished performing tasks in the new command interpreter, you should type **exit** to return to the previous program. Be sure to return to the original program and exit that program properly *before* turning off your computer.

SYNTAX

exit

See Also COMMAND, SHELL, Lesson 2

EXPAND

Lets you retrieve DOS 6 files that are compressed on the installation or update disks. EXPAND can be used with network drives.

Compressed source files have an extension that ends with an underscore character. For example, .EX_ is the compressed file extension for .EXE files, which will be executable after expansion.

To locate the compressed file you need to expand, use a text editor to open the file named PACKING.LST on the DOS installation or update disk (PACKING.LST is not compressed).

SYNTAX

expand [*drive*:][*path*]*filename* [[*drive*:][*path*]*filename*[...]] [*destination*]

OPTIONS

[*drive*:][*path*]*filename*	name of the drive, directory, and file or files to be expanded
destination	location and/or name of the expanded file or files

EXAMPLES To expand the compressed file EMM386.EX_ on drive A and place the expanded file named EMM386.EXE in the \DOS directory on drive C, type

```
expand a:\emm386.ex_ c:\dos\emm386.exe
```

NOTES

- The *destination* can consist of a drive letter and colon, a directory name, a file name, or a combination of these elements. However, you cannot specify a file name for the destination unless you also specify a single compressed file for *filename*.
- If you simply type **expand** (without parameters), you'll be prompted for the location and name of the compressed file and the expanded destination file.

See Also Appendix A

FC

Compares two files and displays the differences between them. You can perform an ASCII (text) comparison or a binary comparison.

SYNTAX

To perform an ASCII comparison, use this syntax:

fc [/a] [/c] [/n] [t] [/w] [*drive1*:][*path1*:]*filename1* [*drive2*:][*path2*][*filename2*]

To perform a binary comparison, use this syntax:

fc /b [*drive1*:][*path1*][*filename1* [*drive2*:][*path2*]*filename2*

OPTIONS

[*drive1*:][*path1*]*filename1*	drive, directory location, and file name of the first file to be compared; the file name can include wildcards (* and ?)
[*drive2*:][*path2*]*filename2*	drive, directory location, and file name of the second file to be compared; the file name can include wildcards (* and ?)
/a	displays only the first and last line in each set of differences
/b	compares files byte by byte, without resynchronizing after a mismatch
/c	ignores the case of letters
/n	displays line numbers during an ASCII comparison
/t	does not expand tabs to spaces; by default, each tab is converted to spaces, with stops at each eighth character position
/w	compresses tabs and spaces during the comparison, treating consecutive spaces or tabs as a single space; ignores tabs and spaces at the beginning and end of a line

EXAMPLES

Suppose the file *test1* contains these lines:

```
1
2
3
4
5
6
7
8
9
```

And the file *test2* contains these lines:

```
1
2
4
5
7
8
9
```

After typing the command **fc test1 test2**, you would see these results:

```
Comparing files TEST1 and TEST2
**** TEST1
2
3
4
**** TEST2
2
4
****
**** TEST1
5
6
7
```

```
**** TEST2
5
7
****
```

This report illustrates the differences between the two files: *test1* includes the numbers 3 and 6, but *test2* does not.

The command **fc thismnth.rpt lastmnth.rpt > prn** compares THISMNTH.RPT and LASTMNTH.RPT in ASCII format and redirects the output to the printer.

NOTES Type **help fc** for information on other options and for details on how FC displays differences between binary files.

FILES

FILES, used only in CONFIG.SYS, specifies the maximum number of file handles that DOS can manage simultaneously. By default, DOS allows eight active file handles. Five of these file handles are used by the standard input and output devices: the screen, keyboard, printer, communications devices, and the DOS error handle. This leaves three file handles available for open disk files.

Most modern programs, particularly database management and multisheet spreadsheet programs, can handle more than three open files simultaneously. Therefore, to use those programs without getting an error message, you probably need to use a FILES command to manage more than eight file handles. Few programs require that you set FILES to a number greater than 50.

Most installation programs update the FILES command automatically, so you'll rarely need to update it yourself.

SYNTAX

files=*max*

OPTIONS

max	maximum number of files that can be open simultaneously, in the range of 8 to 255

See Also Lesson 8

FIND

Searches for a specific string of text in a file or files and displays any lines of text that contain that string.

SYNTAX

find [/v] [/c] [/n] [/i] "*string*" [[*drive*:][*path*]*filename*[...]]

OPTIONS

string	the characters you're looking for; the string must be enclosed in quotation marks
[*drive*:][*path*]*filename*	drive, directory, and name of the file you want to search; *filename* cannot contain wildcards (* and ?), but you can list several file names on the command line
/v	displays all lines that *do not* contain the specified string
/c	displays only a count of lines that contain the specified string; if used with /V, this switch counts only lines that *do not* contain the string
/n	precedes each displayed line with its actual line number in the file you're searching

/i	makes the search case-insensitive; that is, uppercase and lowercase letters are treated the same

EXAMPLES The command below finds all lines in the files STARTREK.DOC and SPOCK.DOC that contain the words “final frontier” on a single line:

```
find "final frontier" startrek.doc spock.doc
```

If the string you’re searching for includes quotation marks, you must enclose the entire string in quotation marks as usual, and then use two quotation marks for each quotation mark in the string. The example below performs a case-insensitive search for the string *with a “need to know”* in a file named SECRET.DOC:

```
find /i "with a ""need to know""" secret.doc
```

FIND does not recognize wildcards in file names. If you want to search for the same string in groups of files based on file names, use FIND in a FOR command. For example, the command below will perform a case-insensitive search for “hanley” in all files that have a .TXT extension.

```
for %c in (*.txt) do find /i "hanley" %c
```

To send the output of the previous command to a text file named MATCHED, type

```
for %c in (*.txt) do find /i "hanley" %c >> matched
```

FIND can also be used as a filter, in which case you would omit the file name and use the pipe (|) to send the output of a command to FIND. Suppose you want to find all files on drive C that were created or modified on January 30, 1993. The command below will do the trick:

```
dir c:\ /s | find "01-30-93"
```

NOTES

- Unless you use the /I switch, FIND searches for the exact uppercase and lowercase letters you specify in the string.
- FIND does not recognize carriage returns. For instance, if you’re searching for “bad politicians”, FIND will report a match only if those two words appear on the same line.

F

- FIND works best with text (ASCII) files. Many word processors use a special format for document files that you create, and FIND may fail to recognize the text in such files. Therefore, to search for text in a file that you created in a word processing program, you're better off using the tools that the word processing program provides for that purpose.

See Also DIR, EDIT, FOR, Lessons 3 and 8

FOR

FOR is used at the command prompt or in batch programs to execute a command repeatedly for each file in a set of files.

SYNTAX

for %[%]*letter* in (*set*) do *command* [*parameters*]

OPTIONS

%%*letter* or %*letter*	a one-letter variable whose value is replaced with the value of each text string in the *set* until the *command* has processed all items in the set; use %%*letter* in batch programs and %*letter* when typing FOR commands at the DOS prompt
set	a list of file names or text strings to be processed by the command and its parameters
command	the command you want to carry out on each item in the set
parameters	parameters or switches required for the *command*

EXAMPLES When executed in a batch program, the following FOR command displays the value of each item in the set:

```
for %%f in (*.exe *.com apples oranges) do echo %%f
```

In place of the ECHO command above, you could use COPY, DEL, or other commands to build powerful batch programs or command lines that perform the same operation on many files with unrelated names. For instance, the batch program command below copies each file in the set from the current directory to drive A:

```
for %%f in (*.exe *.com apples oranges) do copy %%f a:
```

To try these examples from the command prompt, simply omit one percent sign (%) when specifying the variable name, for example,

```
for %f in (*.exe *.com apples oranges) do echo %f
```

NOTES

- Each time the FOR loop is executed, the variable assumes either the next value in the list of items or the next file name in the list produced by the file name wildcard.
- You must include the IN and DO keywords.

FORMAT

Prepares blank (empty and unformatted) disks for use with your computer. The FORMAT command normally performs a "safe format" on hard disks and floppy disks because it deletes only the file allocation tables (FAT) and directory information, without destroying data. However, data will be destroyed if you use the /U switch or any other switch that changes the initial storage capacity of the disk. If you do mistakenly format your hard drive or a floppy disk that contains information, you can use the UNFORMAT command to restore the original FAT and recover most of your files (again, assuming data wasn't destroyed).

SYNTAX

format *drive*: [/f:*size*] [/s] [/q] [/u] [/1] [/8]

OPTIONS

drive:	name of the drive containing the disk to be formatted
/f:*size*	specifies the amount of storage in kilobytes; valid sizes include 160, 180, 320, 360, 720, 1.2, 1.44, and 2.88; if the /F switch is omitted, the floppy disk will be formatted at the capacity of the disk drive
/s	makes the formatted disk a system disk that can be used to boot the computer
/q	performs a "quick" format on already formatted disks; this switch cancels screening for bad sectors and simply deletes the FAT tables and directory information
/u	cancels the "safe format" and performs an unconditional format on your disk
/4	formats a 5¼-inch 360 KB floppy disk in a high-density drive
/8	formats eight sectors per track

EXAMPLES To format a floppy disk in drive A, type **format a:** at the command prompt. To make the disk in drive A bootable, so that you can use it to start your computer, type **format a: /s** at the command prompt.

To format a 720 KB 3½-inch disk in drive B, which is a 1.44 MB 3½-inch drive, type **format b: /f:720** at the command prompt.

NOTES

- After formatting the disk, FORMAT will ask if you want to add a volume label. Type up to 11 characters and press ↵, or simply press ↵ without typing any characters to leave the label blank. The label appears when you use the DIR, CHKDSK, and VOL commands. You can use the LABEL command to change or add the label.
- You cannot format the following types of disks: a floppy disk that has a write-protect tab on it; any "virtual" disk, such as a RAM disk; a network or Interlnk disk; or a disk affected by the SUBST command.

- After the formatting procedure is completed, FORMAT displays the number of bytes available on the disk. Any flaws on the disk are marked as bad sectors, which are not usable. The total amount of available disk space is equal to the total space minus the bad sectors.
- You cannot format a 1.2 MB disk in a low-capacity (360 KB) drive, although you can format a 360 KB disk in a high-capacity drive for later use in a 360 KB drive. Similarly, you cannot format a 3½-inch 1.44 MB disk in a 720 KB drive.
- Do not format a floppy disk at a size higher than it was designed for; for instance, do not format a 720 KB disk at 1.44 MB.

See Also LABEL, SYS, UNFORMAT, VOL, Lessons 4 and 5

F

GOTO

In a batch program, execution normally proceeds in order from the first command to the last. You can use the GOTO command to execute a specified line other than the next one. (GOTO is ignored when you type it at the command prompt.)

SYNTAX

goto *label*

OPTIONS

label	the label that precedes the line in the batch program where execution should resume

EXAMPLES

See IF for examples that use the GOTO command.

NOTES

- The label can include spaces but no other separators. However, only the first eight characters are significant. Hence, the labels **labelnum1** and **labelnum2** are considered the same.
- The label in the batch program must be preceded by a colon (:).
- GOTO is often used with the IF command.

See Also

IF, Lesson 8

HELP

Provides a reminder of the syntax and options of DOS commands. The DOS 6 Help topics include command syntax, notes about the command, and examples of its use. If you're using the DOS Shell, you can get help by selecting the Help pull-down menu or pressing F1.

SYNTAX

help [*command*]

OPTIONS

command the command you need help with

EXAMPLES Type **help** and press ↵ to display an index of help topics.

Type **help dir** for help with the DIR command.

NOTES After getting into the Help system, you can press F1 to find out more about how to use the MS-DOS Help system.

See Also DOSHELP, Lesson 3

IF

You can use IF in a batch program to perform conditional processing. IF commands take the general form

```
if condition command
```

where *condition* is a condition to test for and *command* is a command to carry out if the test succeeds. You can precede the *condition* with NOT to carry out the *command* if the condition fails.

SYNTAX

```
if [not] errorlevel number command
if [not] string1==string2 command
if [not] exist filename command
```

OPTIONS

not	carries out the command if the condition is false
command	the command to execute if the condition is met; often, this command is GOTO
ERRORLEVEL *number*	true if the previous command returned an exit code that is greater than or equal to *number*; always test for exit codes in descending order
string1==string2	true if the two strings are the same; *string1* and *string2* can be literal text (without quotation marks) or batch variables (%0 through %9)
EXIST *filename*	true if the file name exists; *filename* can include wildcards (* and ?)

EXAMPLES The following example branches execution to the label named **SkipCopy** if the files named in the first parameter of the batch program exist:

```
if exist %1 goto SkipCopy
```

The next example displays either the message "The parameter is" followed by the name of the parameter that you typed on the batch program command line or the words "The parameter is missing."

```
@echo off
if %1.==. goto Missing
echo The parameter is %1
goto Done
:Missing
echo The parameter is missing
:Done
```

The batch program below displays "Why aren't you happy?" if the user types N in response to the prompt "Are you happy [Y,N]?", displayed by the CHOICE command.

```
@echo off
choice Are you happy /c:yn
if errorlevel 2 echo Why aren't you happy?
```

NOTES To test for the existence of a directory, add the device name NUL to the end of the path. For example, the command

```
if exist c:\dos\games\nul goto GameTime
```

branches to the label **GameTime** if the directory C:\DOS\GAMES exists.

See Also CHOICE, GOTO, Lesson 8

INCLUDE

Allows you to include the contents of one configuration block in another when you define multiple startup configurations in CONFIG.SYS.

SYNTAX

include=*blockname*

OPTIONS

blockname	specifies the name of the configuration block to include; block names are enclosed in square brackets in the CONFIG.SYS file (e.g., **[full_config]**)

EXAMPLES To include a block of commands common to two configurations (**windows** and **network**) in a block named **full_config**, type

```
[full_config]
include=windows
include=network
```

See Also MENUCOLOR, MENUDEFAULT, MENUITEM, NUMLOCK, SUBMENU, Lesson 8

INTERLNK

Interlnk connects two computers via parallel or serial ports and enables the computers to share disks and printer ports. This is particularly useful for connecting a laptop computer to a desktop computer and sharing files.

Before using Interlnk, you must install the INTERLNK.EXE driver in your CONFIG.SYS file with the DEVICE or DEVICEHIGH command. The INTERLNK.EXE driver redirects commands on Interlnk drives and printer ports to drives and printer ports on the Interlnk server. Lesson 9 explains how to use Interlnk and its related command Intersvr. For additional information, type **help interlnk** or **help interlnk.exe** at the command prompt.

See Also INTERSVR, Lesson 9

I

INTERSVR

Starts an Interlnk server, which lets you share drives and printers between two computers. See Lesson 9 for details on using INTERSVR and its related command, INTERLNK. You can also type **help intersvr** for information on available command-line options.

See Also INTERLNK, Lesson 9

LABEL

Allows you to create, change, or delete the volume label, or name, of a disk. The volume label is part of the directory listing and is purely informational. If you type the LABEL command without any options, you'll be prompted to enter a label for the current drive.

SYNTAX

label [*drive*:][*label*]

OPTIONS

drive:	the drive letter of the disk you want to name
label	the new volume label (up to 11 characters)

EXAMPLES You could use the command **label a: budget 1993** to label a floppy disk in drive A that contains budget information for 1993.

NOTES

- If you omit the drive letter, DOS will label the current drive.
- If you omit the label, DOS will prompt you to enter a new label. Type the new label and press ↵, or just press ↵ if you want to delete the label.
- The volume label can contain up to 11 characters, including spaces. Lowercase letters are converted to uppercase automatically. Consecutive spaces may be interpreted as a single space. Labels cannot include tabs or any of the following characters:

  * ? / \ | . , ; : + = [ ] ( ) & ^ < > "

- LABEL does not work on a drive created with the command SUBST.
- Use VOL (or CHKDSK or DIR) to display a volume label.

See Also CHKDSK, DIR, FORMAT, VOL, Lesson 5

LASTDRIVE

Used only in the CONFIG.SYS file, LASTDRIVE specifies the last valid drive letter that DOS can recognize.

SYNTAX

lastdrive=*d*

OPTIONS

d drive letter, in the range A through Z

EXAMPLES The command **lastdrive=F** allows DOS to access up to six drives, named A, B, C, D, E, and F.

NOTES

- If you do not use the LASTDRIVE command, the default last drive letter is the one following the last drive in use. Hence, if you're using drives A and C, the default value is D. Do not specify more drives than are necessary, since DOS allocates memory space for each valid drive letter.
- Novell networks (and possibly others) use the LASTDRIVE= setting to determine the next drive letter available for use as a network drive. See Lesson 9 and your network documentation before changing the LASTDRIVE setting on a computer that's attached to a network.

See Also Lessons 1, 8, and 9

LOADFIX

Loads and runs a program above the first 64 KB of conventional memory. DOS 6 uses a memory-management scheme that releases much of the conventional memory that earlier versions of DOS used for themselves. Some programs may have trouble running if loaded into this now-free area of memory. When this happens, the error message "Packed file corrupt" appears.

To get around this, use the LOADFIX command to run the program in more "traditional" areas of memory above 64 KB.

SYNTAX

loadfix [*drive*:][*path*]*filename* [*parameters*]

OPTIONS

[*drive*:][*path*]*filename*	drive, directory location, and file name of the program to run
parameters	parameters used by the file being run

EXAMPLES If you receive the message "Packed file corrupt" after running the program TICTAC, type the following command to fix the problem:

```
loadfix c:\games\tictac.com
```

See Also SETVER

LOADHIGH OR LH

Lets you free as much conventional memory as possible for your application programs. Before using LOADHIGH, you must run an upper memory block manager (UMB) program by adding appropriate options to your CONFIG.SYS file. LOADHIGH (or its equivalent LH) can be used either at the command prompt or in the AUTOEXEC.BAT file. LOADHIGH is probably most effective as a command in your AUTOEXEC.BAT file.

For an easier way to configure memory, use the DOS 6 MemMaker program, which adds or updates all the required AUTOEXEC.BAT and CONFIG.SYS commands (including LOADHIGH) automatically. Lesson 7 explains how to use MemMaker.

See Also MEMMAKER, SETVER, Lesson 7

MEM

Displays all currently used and unused conventional memory (RAM) and extended or expanded memory, if it's available. MEM is discussed fully in Lesson 7.

See Also CHKDSK, DIR, MEMMAKER, Lesson 7

MEMMAKER

MemMaker optimizes memory usage and frees conventional memory on an 80386 or 80486 computer with extended memory. The program automatically modifies your CONFIG.SYS and AUTOEXEC.BAT files, so that your memory-resident programs (TSRs) and device drivers use less conventional memory.

MemMaker provides a much better alternative to typing complex memory-management commands such as DEVICE, DEVICEHIGH, LOADHIGH, and EMM386 into your CONFIG.SYS and AUTOEXEC.BAT files. See Lesson 7 for complete instructions on using this program.

See Also DEVICEHIGH, LOADHIGH, MEM, Lessons 7 and 8

MENUCOLOR

You can use MENUCOLOR within a menu block of the CONFIG.SYS file to set text and background colors for a startup menu that has multiple configurations.

SYNTAX

menucolor=*text* [,*background*]

OPTIONS

text the number of the text color you want to set (0 to 15)

background the number of the background color you want to set (0 to 15)

EXAMPLES To set the text color to bright white (15) and the background color to royal blue (1), type **menucolor=15,1** into CONFIG.SYS.

NOTES

- Be sure to specify different values for the text and background colors; otherwise, the text will be unreadable.
- Valid color settings are 0=black; 1=blue; 2=green; 3=cyan; 4=red; 5=magenta; 6=brown; 7=white; 8=gray; 9=bright blue; 10=bright green; 11=bright cyan; 12=bright red; 13=bright magenta; 14=yellow; 15=bright white.

See Also INCLUDE, MENUDEFAULT, MENUITEM, NUMLOCK, SUBMENU, Lesson 8

MENUDEFAULT

Allows you to specify a default menu item on the multiple configurations startup menu defined in CONFIG.SYS. You also can specify a timeout value.

SYNTAX

menudefault=*blockname*[,*timeout*]

OPTIONS

blockname	specifies the block name of the default menu item
timeout	determines the number of seconds (0 to 90) that DOS waits before starting your computer with the default menu item; if *timeout* is omitted, DOS will not continue until you select an item and press ↵

EXAMPLES The command **menudefault=network,20** specifies *network* as the default configuration menu item and sets a timeout value of 20 seconds. DOS will start the computer with the default configuration if no item is selected within 20 seconds.

See Also INCLUDE, MENUCOLOR, MENUITEM, NUMLOCK, SUBMENU, Lesson 8

MENUITEM

You can use the MENUITEM command in your CONFIG.SYS file to define up to nine menu items on the multiple configuration startup menu.

SYNTAX

menuitem=[*blockname*][,*text*]

OPTIONS

blockname	specifies the name of the associated configuration block
text	specifies the text to display on the menu; if omitted, the block name is used

EXAMPLES When typed into the CONFIG.SYS file, the command below defines an item that will appear on the menu. *Network* specifies the name of the associated configuration block and "Start the network" specifies the text to display on the menu.

```
menuitem=network,Start the network
```

NOTES

- A *menu block* is a set of menu-definition commands that begins with a block name, enclosed in square brackets. A menu block must contain at least one MENUITEM or SUBMENU command.
- Use the SUBMENU command if you need to define more than nine menu items.

See Also INCLUDE, MENUCOLOR, MENUDEFAULT, NUMLOCK, SUBMENU, Lesson 8

M

MKDIR OR MD

MKDIR (or its abbreviated form, MD) allows you to create a new directory or subdirectory on a disk. The directory you create can be either one level beneath the root (such as \UTILS), or a child directory of one or more other directories (such as \UTILS\DATA). A single directory name can consist of one to eight characters and can include a three-letter extension preceded by a period (exactly the same format as a file name). An entire path name, consisting of several subdirectory names (such as WP\BOOKS\CHAPTERS), can contain up to 63 characters.

SYNTAX

mkdir [*drive*:]*path*

OPTIONS

[*drive*:]*path*	drive and directory location for the new directory that you want to create

EXAMPLES To create a directory named WP one level beneath the root directory, type **md \wp** or **md wp** at the command prompt.

Type **md \wp\wpdocs** to create a subdirectory named WPDOCS beneath the \WP directory. If you were already in the \WP directory, you could type this command as **md wpdocs**.

See Also CHDIR, DELTREE, MOVE, RMDIR, Lesson 4

MODE

Configures system devices and displays their status. The syntax depends on the task you're trying to perform. To display all mode settings, type **mode** without any options.

SYNTAX

mode [*options*]

OPTIONS

To display the status of one or all devices:

mode [*device*] [/status]

device	name of the device to display status for
/status	includes redirected parallel printers

To configure a printer connected to the parallel printer port:

mode lpt*n* [cols=*c*] [lines=*l*] [retry=*r*]

n	parallel port number (1 to 3); PRN and LPT1 are equivalent
c	number of characters per line (80 or 132)
l	vertical lines per inch (6 or 8)

r — retry action to take if a timeout occurs (press Ctrl+C or Ctrl+Break to break out of a timeout loop); values are **b** (return "busy" from status check of a busy port); **e** (return error); **p** (continue retrying); **r** (return "ready"); **n** (take no retry action, the default); do not use the retry option on a network

To configure a serial communications port:

mode com*n* [baud=*b*] [parity=*p*] [data=*d*] [stop=*s*] [retry=*r*]

n — serial port number (1 to 4)

b — first two digits of the transmission rate in bits per second (for example, use 96 for 9600 baud)

p — method used for parity checking; values are **n** (none), **e** (even, the default), **o** (odd), **m** (mark), **s** (space)

d — number of data bits in each character (5 to 8; default is 7)

s — number of stop bits that define the end of a character (1, 1.5, or 2); default is 1 for baud rates other than 110

r — retry action to take if a timeout occurs; same values as for MODE LPT*n* above

To redirect output from a parallel port to a serial port:

mode lpt*n*=com*m*

n — parallel port number (1 to 3)

m — serial port number (1 to 4)

To change the rate at which DOS repeats a key when you hold it down:

mode con [rate=*r* delay=*d*]

r — character repeat rate; values can be from 1 to 32 (1 is about two characters per second; 32 is about 30 characters per second); default is 20 for IBM AT-compatible keyboards and 21 for IBM PS/2 *d* delay before character begins repeating; values can be 1, 2, 3, or 4 (representing 0.25, .50, .75, and 1 second, respectively); default is 2

EXAMPLES Type **mode con rate=32 delay=1** to set the keyboard repeat rate to its maximum speed.

Type **mode lpt1 retry=p** to have DOS 6 continue trying to send output to the parallel printer LPT1 even after an error occurs.

See Also PRINT

MORE

Use the MORE command to make a display pause automatically at the end of each screenful. MORE is useful in your DOSKEY macros to create pausing "DOS commands" (see DOSKEY for an example). When MORE is activated, scrolling pauses automatically after every 24 lines of text and the prompt **—More—** appears at the bottom of the screen. Press any key to continue to the next screen. MORE acts as a filter, and it must have information piped or redirected into it.

SYNTAX

```
more
```

EXAMPLES Type **more < read.me** to display a file named READ.ME one screenful at a time. The command **type read.me | more** accomplishes the same result by using MORE as a filter to the TYPE command.

See Also DOSKEY, TYPE, Lesson 3

MOVE

Moves one or more files to another drive or directory location and allows you to rename directories.

Be careful when using this command: If the destination files exist already, they will be overwritten by the source files.

SYNTAX

```
move [drive:][path]filename [[drive:][path]filename[...]] destination
```

OPTIONS

drive:[path]filename	drive, directory location, and file name of the file or files you want to move, or the directory you want to rename; *filename* can include wildcards (* and ?)
destination	drive and directory location for the new file or renamed directory; if you're moving one file only, you can also include a file name

EXAMPLES Suppose you accidentally created a directory named ORKDIR on drive C and want to rename it WORKDIR. If drive C is not the current drive, type this command:

```
move c:\orkdir c:\workdir
```

If drive C is the current drive, you can omit the drive letter in the command above, like this:

```
move \orkdir \workdir
```

The following command moves the files ICECUBE.TXT and SNOWMAN.DAT from the current directory to the C:\COOLDATA directory:

```
move icecube.txt snowman.dat c:\cooldata
```

The next command moves all batch program files from the current directory to the directory \BAT\SAVEPGMS on drive D:

```
move *.bat d:\bat\savepgms
```

The command below moves all batch programs from \BAT\SAVEPGMS on drive D to drive A:

```
move d:\bat\savepgms\*.bat a:
```

NOTES

- Moving a single file to the same drive and directory location simply renames the file as if you had used the RENAME command.
- You cannot move a directory to a different drive or to a different level in the file hierarchy. For example, **move c:\mydir c:\yourdir\mydir** is not valid if \MYDIR is a directory on drive C.

See Also CHDIR, COPY, MKDIR, RENAME, REPLACE, RMDIR, XCOPY, Lesson 4

MSAV

Protects your system from viruses by scanning the computer's memory and disk drives. MSAV scans for viruses, displaying information about each virus found and cleaning the viruses from your computer.

The Anti-Virus program is available for both DOS and Windows. Lesson 5 provides information on using both versions of Anti-Virus.

SYNTAX

msav [*drive*:] [/s | /c] [/r] [/a | /l] [/p] [/f] [/video]

OPTIONS

drive:	drive to check for viruses
/s	scans but does not remove any viruses
/c	scans the specified disks and removes any viruses
/r	creates a report file (\MSAV.RPT) on the drive you scanned; the report lists information about viruses checked for, found, and removed
/a	scans all drives except drive A and drive B
/l	scans all non-network drives
/p	displays a command-line interface instead of the graphical interface
/f	turns off file name display during scans
/video	displays a list of video display modes and mouse parameters that you can type as switches on the MSAV command line

EXAMPLES To start the Microsoft Anti-Virus program from the command prompt, type **msav**.

To scan and remove any viruses found from drive D and create a report in the file D:\MSAV.RPT, type **msav d: /c /r**.

See Also VSAFE, Lesson 5

MSBACKUP

MSBACKUP is a fully-interactive DOS 6 utility program that allows you to back up or restore files from one disk to another. When you type the MSBACKUP command, the program takes over (press F1 any time you need help). Lesson 5 explains how to back up and restore files with MSBACKUP for DOS and MSBACKUP for Windows.

SYNTAX

msbackup [*setupfile*] [/bw | /lcd | /mda]

OPTIONS

setupfile	specifies the setup file name; if *setupfile* is omitted, MSBACKUP uses DEFAULT.SET
/bw	displays MSBACKUP screens in black-and-white
/lcd	starts MSBACKUP in a video mode that's compatible with laptop displays
/mda	displays MSBACKUP on a monochrome display adapter

EXAMPLES To start MSBACKUP and use the default setup file, type **msbackup**. See Lesson 5 for additional examples.

NOTES

- MSBACKUP is the successor to BACKUP and RESTORE, which were used in previous versions of DOS. Unlike BACKUP and RESTORE, MSBACKUP is completely interactive and can restore files to any drive or directory.
- You should start MSBACKUP only from the hard disk.
- You cannot use MSBACKUP to restore backup data created by BACKUP. Conversely, you cannot use RESTORE to restore backup data created by MSBACKUP. Please refer to the online help for information on using BACKUP and RESTORE.

See Also Lesson 5

MSD

The MSD (Microsoft System Diagnostics) command displays detailed technical information about your computer, including the microprocessor manufacturer and model, memory configuration, video adapter and other adapters, network, operating system version, mouse, disk drives, ports, IRQ status, and memory map. You can examine the information interactively on the screen or have DOS create a printed report.

SYNTAX

msd [/b] [/i] [[/f | /p | /s] *filename*]

OPTIONS

/b	displays in black-and-white instead of color; ignored when used with /F, /P, or /S
/i	bypasses the initial hardware detection (useful if MSD is not running properly); ignored when used with /F, /P, or /S
/f *filename*	prompts for customer information (name, address, and phone), and then writes a complete report to the specified file name
/p *filename*	writes a complete report to the specified file name
/s *filename*	writes a summary report to the specified file; you can omit a file name to display the summary on the screen

EXAMPLES

Type **msd** to start the MSD program and use it interactively.

To prompt for customer information and write a report to the file named C:\DOS\DIAGREPT, type **msd /f c:\dos\diagrept**.

NUMLOCK

Use NUMLOCK in a menu block of your CONFIG.SYS file to specify whether the Num Lock numeric keypad feature is set on or off.

SYNTAX

```
numlock=[on | off]
```

OPTIONS

on	sets the Num Lock keypad feature on
off	sets the Num Lock keypad feature off

See Also INCLUDE, MENUCOLOR, MENUDEFAULT, MENUITEM, SUBMENU, Lesson 8

PATH

Sets up a series of disk drives and directories that DOS will search for program files. The PATH command allows you to access external DOS programs (such as ATTRIB, CHKDSK, FIND, and PRINT), batch programs, and application programs from any drive and subdirectory.

Whenever you attempt to run a DOS command, application program, or batch program, DOS searches memory, then the current drive and directory, for the appropriate file. If the file cannot be found, DOS checks the PATH setting and searches the specified directories and subdirectories in the order in which they are listed. As soon as the file is located, DOS loads it into memory and the program is executed. Because PATH is such an important and frequently used command, it is nearly always included in the AUTOEXEC.BAT file.

SYNTAX

path [[*drive*:]*path* [;...]]

OPTIONS

[*drive*:]*path*	name of the drive, directory, and any subdirectories to search
;	when used alone, clears the path so that DOS searches the current directory only; multiple drive and directory specifications must be separated by semicolons, with no blank spaces

EXAMPLES The command below looks for programs in the following directories on drive C: the root directory, then the \DOS directory, then the \UTILS directory, and finally the \WP directory.

```
path c:\;c:\dos;c:\utils;c:\wp
```

To view the current PATH setting, type **path.** Type **path ;** to cancel a previously defined path.

NOTES

- The current PATH setting is always stored in the %PATH% DOS environment variable. A batch program can access this variable and you can display it by typing **set** at the command prompt.
- The PATH command only searches for executable program files that have the extensions .COM, .EXE, or .BAT (in that order).

See Also SET Lessons 1, 3, and 8

PAUSE

Temporarily halts a batch program and presents the message "Press any key to continue...." When you press a key, processing continues normally at the next line in the batch program. However, if you press Ctrl+Break or Ctrl+C, the batch program will ask if you want to terminate the program; type **Y** to terminate or **N** to continue, and press ↵.

SYNTAX

```
pause
```

EXAMPLES The following batch program displays the message "Place a diskette in drive A:." Then PAUSE suspends command execution and waits for a keypress.

```
echo Place a diskette in drive A:.
pause
```

NOTES

- The PAUSE command can be useful in a DOSKEY macro.
- The CHOICE command provides a more flexible alternative to PAUSE.

See Also CHOICE, DOSKEY, ECHO, Lesson 8

POWER

You can use the POWER command to conserve battery power on your laptop computer when your applications and devices are idle. Before using the POWER command, you must use the DEVICE= command in CONFIG.SYS to install the POWER.EXE driver. See Lesson 9 for complete information.

See Also DEVICE, Lesson 9

PRINT

Lets you print text files "in the background," allowing you to use your computer for other DOS commands while the printer is active. PRINT allows you to specify several files to be printed, and then it places all the files in a queue. When one file finishes printing, the next file in the queue begins printing automatically.

PRINT can be used only to print ASCII text files. It cannot print files created by spreadsheet, database management, or word processing programs, unless those files have already been converted to ASCII text format. PRINT cannot print executable program files, such as those with the extensions .BIN, .COM, or .EXE.

SYNTAX

print [/d:*device*] [/t] [[*drive*:[*path*]*filename*[...]] [/c] [/p]

OPTIONS

[*drive*:][*path*]*filename*	drive, directory location, and name of the file or files to be printed
/d:*device*	loads a portion of PRINT into memory; *device* can be any valid DOS device name, such as LPT1, LPT2, LPT3, PRN, COM1, COM2, COM3, COM4, or AUX; this switch must precede any file name on the line

/t	terminates the entire print queue, including the current file
/c	removes preceding files from the print queue
/p	adds preceding file names to the print queue

EXAMPLES To display the names of files currently in the queue in the order in which they will be printed, type **print**. If PRINT is not loaded yet, this command will prompt for a device and then load PRINT.

To remove the file CHAP2.DOC from the print queue and insert the file CHAP2.TXT into the queue, type

```
print chap2.doc /c chap2.txt /p
```

To stop all background printing and empty the queue, type **print /t**.

NOTES

- The PRINT command must be loaded into memory before you send files to be printed and before you use the File ➤ Print option from the DOS Shell.
- You cannot specify the /D option again after PRINT is loaded into memory, unless you reboot your computer first.

See Also MODE, TYPE, Lesson 2

PROMPT

Changes the system prompt and activates ANSI features. Initially, DOS displays the command prompt as the current drive followed by a greater than sign (C>). You can change the prompt to include any text by typing the text after the PROMPT command. In addition, you can use the codes listed under Options to display special information and characters.

Note in the table that the $_ code, which displays a carriage return/line feed combination, actually breaks the prompt into two lines. The $H character is a backspace that erases the preceding character. For example, $t displays the system time in the format 12:29:03.25. However, thhh erases the last three characters and displays 12:29:03 instead.

SYNTAX

prompt [*codes*]

OPTIONS

Prompt Code	Displays
$$	$ symbol
$_	carriage return/line feed
$b	| character
$d	current date
$e	Escape character
$g	> symbol
$h	backspace
$l	< symbol
$n	current drive
$p	current drive and directory path
$q	= symbol
$t	current time
$v	version of DOS in use

EXAMPLES The following command changes the system prompt to display **Current location - C:\DOS ->** when you enter the command from the DOS directory of your hard disk:

```
prompt Current location - $p -$g
```

To change the system prompt to display **Say the magic word >**, type

```
prompt Say the magic word $g
```

The command **prompt $d thhh** displays a prompt containing the current date and the current time, in the format **Mon 1-13-1993 22:29:56** (erasing the hundredths of a second).

NOTES

- The $e character can be used with display control codes offered by ANSI.SYS to control the screen colors and to customize function keys. These codes work only if your CONFIG.SYS file contains the command DEVICE=ANSI.SYS.
- To have DOS display a different command prompt when you exit temporarily from Windows to the DOS prompt, change the environment variable named WINPMT. See Lesson 8 for examples.

See Also COMMAND, DATE, DEVICE, TIME, Lessons 1, 2, and 8

RAMDRIVE

The RAMDRIVE.SYS device driver allows you to use your computer's memory (RAM) to simulate a hard disk drive. RAM disks are much faster than hard disk drives and can be used as you would use any normal drive. However, a RAM disk exists only in memory and its data is lost when you turn off or restart your computer. For this reason, RAM disks are most useful for storing temporary files created by database programs and other disk-intensive programs or for storing copies of frequently used programs. Do not use the RAM disk to store data files, since those files will be lost if the system fails.

SYNTAX

device=[*drive*:][*path*]ramdrive.sys [*disksize* [*sectorsize* [*entries*]]] [/e | /a]

OPTIONS

[*drive*:][*path*]	drive and directory location of RAMDRIVE.SYS
disksize	kilobytes of memory, in the range 4 to 32767, to use for the RAM disk; default is 64 (64 KB)
sectorsize	disk sector size in bytes (valid sizes are 128, 256, or 512); the default size of 512 is recommended. If you specify *sectorsize*, you must also specify *disksize*.
entries	the number of files and directories allowed in the RAM disk's root directory, in the range 2 to 1024; default is 64. If you specify *entries*, you must also specify *disksize* and *sectorsize*.
/e	creates the RAM disk in extended memory; requires that you first load an extended-memory manager, such as HIMEM.SYS
/a	creates the RAM disk in expanded memory; requires that you first load an expanded-memory manager, such as EMM386, 386MAX, CEMM, or QEMM

EXAMPLES To create a 512 KB RAM disk in extended memory, add the following line to CONFIG.SYS (below the DEVICE=HIMEM.SYS command):

```
device=c:\dos\ramdrive.sys 512 /e
```

The drive letter of your RAM disk will be one letter higher than that of your last physical drive. (If the last physical drive is D, the RAM disk will be drive E.)

If you want to run a program from a RAM disk, first copy the program's executable files to the RAM disk (for example, type **copy c:\games\gamestuf.exe e:**). You can make the RAM disk your current drive or add it to your search PATH, then start the program from the RAM disk. Because you'll need to copy the program files to the RAM disk each time you start the computer, it's easiest to place the COPY commands in your AUTOEXEC.BAT file.

NOTES

- SMARTDrive may be a faster alternative to RAMDrive. However, if you frequently run programs that use many small temporary files, RAMDrive might be faster than SMARTDrive.
- If you omit the /A and /E switches, RAMDrive will use conventional memory. You should avoid running RAMDrive in conventional memory, especially if you have an 80386 or 80486 computer and a hard disk.
- After installing RAMDRIVE.SYS on an 80386 or 80486 system, you can use MemMaker to change the DEVICE= command in CONFIG.SYS to a more efficient DEVICEHIGH= command.
- For best performance with programs that use temporary files, set temporary environment variables to a subdirectory on the RAM disk (for example, **set temp=e:\tempfile**). Many programs, including Windows, use the variable TEMP for temporary files; however, TMP, DBTMP, and other variables may also be used (see your program's documentation for details). If you use Windows and have set the TEMP variable to use a RAM disk, the RAM disk should be at least 2 MB to allow adequate space for temporary print files.

See Also DEVICE, DEVICEHIGH, MEMMAKER, PATH, SET, SMARTDRV, Lessons 6, 7, and 8

REM

REM is generally used to write remarks (notes to yourself) within a batch program to remind you of what various commands do. If ECHO is on, any text to the right of the command will appear on the screen while the batch program is running. If ECHO is off, the text will not be displayed while the batch program is running.

REM is also useful in CONFIG.SYS files for canceling commands temporarily. For example, if you occasionally need to use a one-megabyte RAM disk, but you don't want to tie up your extended memory all the time, you can include the following command in your CONFIG.SYS file:

```
rem device=c:\dos\ramdrive.sys 1024 512 /e
```

This keeps the command in the file but makes it a nonexecuting line. To activate your RAM drive later, delete the REM command and the space after it from the DEVICE= line and reboot your computer.

SYNTAX

rem [*comment*]

OPTIONS

comment	any text; omit the comment if you want a blank line to appear

EXAMPLES Place the following lines at the beginning of a batch program to remind yourself what the program does:

```
rem Program written 3-31-93 to perform
rem automatic hard disk backups.
```

See Also ECHO, Lesson 8

R

RENAME OR REN

RENAME (or its abbreviated form, REN) allows you to change the name of a file or group of files. It has no effect on the contents of the file. RENAME cannot be used to change the drive or directory location of a file (use the MOVE command for this purpose).

If you try to rename a file to a name that exists on the specified drive or directory, or you try to rename a file that does not exist, DOS will return the error message "Duplicate file name or file not found."

SYNTAX

rename [*drive*:][*path*]*oldname newname*

OPTIONS

[*drive*:][*path*]*oldname*	drive, directory location, and name of the file you want to rename; *oldname* can include wildcards (* and ?)
newname	new name for the file; *newname* can include wildcards

EXAMPLES To rename a file named MY_FILE.LST to OUR_FILE.LST in the current directory, type

```
ren my_file.lst our_file.lst
```

To change the extension of all files in the current directory from .DOC to .WP, type **ren *.doc *.wp**.

NOTES

- You can rename files easily from the DOS Shell (see Lesson 4).
- Use the COPY command to copy a file or files to a different directory, renaming them at the same time.
- Use MOVE to rename directories or move files to another directory.

See Also COPY, MOVE, REPLACE, XCOPY, Lesson 4

REPLACE

Replaces files in the destination directory with same-named files in the source directory. You can also use REPLACE to add unique file names to the destination directory.

SYNTAX

replace [*drive1*:][*path1*]*filename* [*drive2*:][*path2*] [/a] [/p] [/r] [/w] [/s] [/u]

OPTIONS

[*drive1*:][*path1*]*filename*	drive, directory location, and names of source files; *filename* can include wildcards (* and ?)
[*drive2*:][*path2*]	destination drive and directory where files will be replaced; if omitted, the current drive and directory are assumed
/a	adds new files to the destination directory, instead of replacing existing files; cannot be used with /S or /U
/p	prompts for confirmation before replacing or adding files
/r	also replaces read-only files; if you omit this option, read-only files in the destination directory will abort the replacement operation
/w	waits for you to insert a floppy disk before searching for source files

/s	replaces matching files in the destination directory and its subdirectories; cannot be used with /A; does not search subdirectories of *path1*
/u	updates files on the destination directory only if they are older than the source files; cannot be used with /A

EXAMPLES To add new games from the floppy disk in drive A to a directory named C:\FUN that already contains some games, type

```
replace a:*.* c:\fun /a
```

Suppose you receive some driver programs on a floppy disk and need to update the existing versions in the \DRIVERS directory of drive C. The following command replaces the drivers on the hard disk with the same-named files on the floppy disk only if the floppy disk files are newer, and prompts you for confirmation:

```
replace a:*.* c:\drivers /u /p
```

NOTES You cannot use REPLACE to update hidden files or system files (for example, IO.SYS and MSDOS.SYS).

See Also ATTRIB, COPY, MOVE, MSBACKUP, XCOPY, Lesson 4

RMDIR OR RD

RMDIR (or its abbreviated form, RD) lets you remove a directory from a disk. You cannot remove the root directory, the current directory, or a directory that contains files or directories.

Another (somewhat more dangerous) command, named DELTREE, allows you to delete directories and subdirectories in a single step, whether or not they are empty.

SYNTAX

rmdir [*drive*:]*path*

OPTIONS

[*drive*:]*path*	drive and directory location of the directory you want to remove

EXAMPLES Assuming that you've removed all files from a directory named C:\TEST, and that C:\TEST does not contain any subdirectories, you can remove that directory as follows. Type **cd c:** and press ↵ to switch to the root directory of drive C. Now, type **rd c:\test** and press ↵ to remove C:\TEST.

See Lesson 4 for additional examples.

See Also CHDIR, DELTREE, MKDIR, Lesson 4

R

SET

Lets you set, remove, or display environment variables associated with programs, batch programs, and DOS operations. The environment is an area in memory reserved for storing certain settings, such as the drive and directory location of the command processor (COMMAND.COM), any customized DOS command prompts in use, and the current search path.

Parameters defined in the environment can be accessed from within batch programs. To do so, use a variable name surrounded by percent signs (no blank spaces) as follows:

%COMPSEC%	returns the location of the command processor
%PATH%	returns the path used to search for program files
%PROMPT%	returns the current customized prompt setting
%WINPMT%	returns the current customized prompt setting that is used when you exit temporarily from Windows to DOS

You can also use SET to store your own information in the environment. (This is sometimes handy with batch programs.)

SYNTAX

set [*variable*=[*setting*]]

OPTIONS

variable	a variable name
setting	the value you want to store in that variable; if it's omitted, the variable is cleared from the environment

EXAMPLES

To store the name *Alec* in a variable named *kidname*, type

```
set kidname=Alec
```

To clear the kidname variable from the environment, and free up environment space, type

```
set kidname=
```

Type **set** to view the current status of the environment.

NOTES By default, DOS sets aside 256 bytes for the environment. You can use the SHELL= command to increase the size of the environment; however, you should do so early in your CONFIG.SYS file because as soon as DOS loads a memory-resident program, you will no longer be able to expand the size of the environment.

See Also COMMAND, PATH, PROMPT, SHELL, Lessons 4 and 8

SETVER

Lets you trick software into believing it is running under a previous version of DOS, for example DOS 3.3 or DOS 4.01.

SETVER must be initialized in the CONFIG.SYS file, using either the DEVICE= or DEVICEHIGH= command, before you can use it at the command prompt or in AUTOEXEC.BAT. If SETVER is not initialized, an attempt to use it at the command prompt will seem successful at first, but will be followed by a note reminding you that SETVER is currently inactive. When you install DOS 6, the Setup program adds the SETVER command to CONFIG.SYS automatically.

SYNTAX

If SETVER is installed in the CONFIG.SYS file, you can use this syntax at the command prompt to view the current version table:

setver [*drive*:][*path*]

Use the following syntax to add a program to the version table:

setver [*drive*:][*path*] *filename n.nn*

Use this syntax to delete a program from the current version table:

setver [*drive*:][*path*] *filename* /delete [/quiet]

OPTIONS

[*drive*:][*path*]	drive and directory location of the SETVER.EXE file (if not in the current path)
filename	the file name of the program that you want to add to or delete from the version table
n.nn	the DOS version number that you want the program to "think" it's running under
/delete	(or /D) deletes the named program from the version table
/quiet	suppresses the information message when used with /DELETE

EXAMPLES The command **device=c:\dos\setver.exe** in the CONFIG.SYS file loads SETVER into conventional memory during startup.

To print the current version table, type **setver > prn**.

The command **setver game.exe 3.30** adds a program named GAME.EXE to the SETVER table and assigns version 3.30 of DOS to that program. If you get an updated version of your GAME.EXE program that runs successfully under DOS 6, you should use the command **setver game.exe /d** to remove the program from the SETVER table.

NOTES As convenient as it might be, SETVER is not foolproof. You might have problems with the old software anyway; for example it could inexplicably lock up, or it could consistently lose data files. Therefore, before you use SETVER, always be sure to back up the specified program, its auxiliary files, and any data files you've created to this point.

See Also DEVICE, DEVICEHIGH, LOADFIX, MEMMAKER, Lessons 7 and 8

SHARE

Starts the program that oversees file sharing and locking on your disks and network drives. Typically, you'll need to install SHARE in a network or multitasking environment in which programs share files.

SYNTAX

share [/f:*space*] [/l:*locks*]

OPTIONS

/f:*space*	specifies the amount of space (in bytes) to set aside for file-sharing information; default is 2048
/l:*locks*	defines the number of files that can be locked at once; default is 20

EXAMPLES Type **share** at the command prompt to load SHARE with default settings.

SHELL

Installs the DOS command processor, which takes commands from the *command prompt* and executes them. The default DOS command processor is COMMAND.COM. SHELL, used only in the CONFIG.SYS file, has three main purposes:

- To specify the location of the command processor (usually COMMAND.COM)
- To specify an alternate command processor (perhaps one you created)
- To increase the size of the environment where SET variables are stored

The SHELL command does not support any switches of its own. However, you can use whatever parameters and switches the command processor normally recognizes to the right of the command processor's file name.

S

SYNTAX

shell=[[*drive*:]*path*]*filename* [*options*]

OPTIONS

[[*drive*:]*path*]*filename*	drive, directory location, and file name of the command processor
options	options provided by the command processor

EXAMPLES The following command, placed in the CONFIG.SYS file, specifies that the command processor to be used is COMMAND.COM, which is located in the C:\DOS directory. Note that the parameter and switch at the end of the command, C:\DOS and /P, are part of COMMAND.COM, not the SHELL command. C:\DOS sets the COMSPEC environment variable to C:\DOS, and /P makes the command processor permanent so that another command processor cannot be executed during the current session.

```
shell=c:\dos\command.com c:\dos /p
```

Suppose that you want to increase the size of the DOS environment from 256 bytes to 512 bytes because there isn't enough room for all your SET variables. You could change the previous example to look like this:

```
shell=c:\dos\command.com c:\dos /e:512 /p
```

NOTES

- When using a custom command processor, you must use the SHELL command to indicate the processor's location and file name.
- The minimum size of the environment is 160 bytes, the maximum size is 32,768 bytes, and the default is 256 bytes.

See Also COMMAND, EXIT, SET, Lessons 2 and 8

SHIFT

Shifts the position of each replaceable parameter in a batch program by copying each parameter to the previous one. The value of %1 is copied to %0, the value of %2 is copied to %1, and so forth. This is useful when writing batch programs that perform the same operation on any number of parameters, and allows you to create batch programs that can accept more than nine parameters. You cannot shift parameters back; however, you can use the SET command to preserve the value of any parameter before shifting.

SYNTAX

```
shift
```

EXAMPLES The following batch program, named COPYANY.BAT, copies any number of files to the directory specified as the first parameter on the batch program command line:

```
@echo off
rem copyany dir file1 file2 ...
set toDir=%1
:GetNext
shift
if %1.==. goto Done
copy %1 %toDir%
goto GetNext
:Done
```

After creating COPYANY.BAT, you could use it to copy any number of files to the directory A:\BAKUPS, like this:

```
copyany a:\bakups *.txt apple prune x y z d e f
```

See Also SET, Lesson 8

S

SMARTDRV

SMARTDrive speeds up disk operations by storing recently accessed information in extended memory so that your program can use the data directly from memory rather than accessing the disk again. Reading from memory is almost instantaneous; reading from a disk (especially a floppy disk) is much slower. Windows and many other programs run much faster with SMARTDrive installed.

You can install SMARTDrive by placing the SMARTDRV command in AUTOEXEC.BAT or by typing it at the command prompt. Alternatively, you can install SMARTDrive via the DEVICE= command in CONFIG.SYS to implement double-buffering.

Lesson 7 explains how to use SMARTDrive to speed up your system. If you'd like more information on available options, type **help smartdrv**. For information about double-buffering, type **help smartdrv.exe**.

See Also DEVICE, Lesson 7

SORT

Sorts lines of text that are input from a command, device, or file, and outputs the sorted text to a file or device. You can use SORT as a command or as a filter for other commands.

SORT provides only a rudimentary sorting capability. For more realistic sorts (and sorts within sorts) you need a more powerful program, such as a database management system, a spreadsheet, or a word processor.

SYNTAX

sort [/r] [/+n] < [*drive1:*][*path1*]*filename1* [> [*drive2:*][*path2*] filename2]

or

[*command* |] sort [/r] [+n] [> [*drive2:*][*path2*]*filename2*]

OPTIONS

[drive1:][path1]filename1	drive, directory location, and name of file with data to be sorted
[drive2:][path2]filename2	drive, directory location, and name of file where sorted data is to be stored
command	command whose output is data to be sorted
/r	sorts in reverse order (Z–A and 9–0)
/+n	sorts the file by the specified column number

EXAMPLES The command **setver | sort** displays the DOS version table sorted alphabetically by file name.

The command **sort ascii.txt** sorts the rows of an ASCII text file named ASCII.TXT into alphabetical or numerical format.

The following example uses input redirection (<) and output redirection (>) to sort the file NAMES.TXT to a new file named NEWNAMES.TXT:

```
sort < names.txt > newnames.txt
```

NOTES

- SORT performs its sort in a "literal" manner, without processing the information first. For example, when sorting dates, SORT considers 12/31/90 to be later than 1/1/93 because 12 is larger than 1 (it does not take the year into consideration). When sorting times, 5:00 P.M. is considered earlier than 8:00 A.M., because 5 is smaller than 8.
- To sort directory listings, use either the SORT command (for example, DIR | SORT) or the /O option of the DIR command (for example, DIR /ON).

See Also DIR, Lesson 3

SUBMENU

Defines an item on the startup menu that, when selected, displays another set of choices. Use this command only within a menu block in your CONFIG.SYS file.

SYNTAX

submenu=*blockname* [,*menutext*]

OPTIONS

blockname	the name of the associated menu block
menutext	the text to display for this menu item; if *menutext* is omitted, the block name is used

See Also INCLUDE, MENUCOLOR, MENUDEFAULT, MENUITEM, NUMLOCK, Lesson 8

SYS

Makes a bootable DOS system disk. If your system does not have a hard disk, drive A must contain a bootable floppy disk when you turn on the computer (otherwise, the error message "Non-system disk" will appear). You can use the SYS command to make a bootable disk from a floppy disk that is already formatted and contains files. To make a system disk from an unformatted floppy disk, use the FORMAT command with the /S option.

You must consider the following rules before using SYS:

- SYS does not work on drives that have been redirected by using SUBSTR or INTERLNK.
- The floppy disk to which you are copying the system tracks must be formatted. The disk also must have sufficient space to store the system tracks (otherwise, DOS will display the error message "No room for system on destination disk").

The SYS command copies COMMAND.COM and the hidden files necessary to start the computer. However, SYS does not copy your CONFIG.SYS or AUTOEXEC.BAT files, so the new bootable disk might not behave exactly as your original startup disk, unless you copy CONFIG.SYS and AUTOEXEC.BAT to the new startup disk yourself.

The SETUP /F /M command, described in the appendix, provides another way to create a startup disk.

SYNTAX

sys [*drive1*:][*path*] *drive2*:

OPTIONS

[*drive1*:][*path*]	source drive and directory location of the system files; if omitted, the system files will be copied from the root directory of the current drive
drive2:	drive to which system files are to be copied

EXAMPLES To make a bootable copy of your system disk, start your computer as usual, then put a formatted floppy disk in drive A and type **sys a:** at the command prompt.

See Also FORMAT, Appendix

S

TIME

Lets you view or change the system time. The time can be expressed in the familiar A.M. and P.M. format, where **12a** is 12 midnight, **12p** is 12 noon, and **11p** is 11 P.M. Alternatively, you can express time on a 24-hour clock, where 0 is midnight, 12 is 12:00 noon, 13 is 1:00 in the afternoon, and 23 is 11:00 P.M. The current system time and date are recorded when you save or change files.

SYNTAX

time *[hh[:mm[:ss[.hn]]]]* [a | p]

OPTIONS

hh	hour, in values from 0 through 23
mm	minutes, in values from 0 through 59
ss	seconds, in values from 0 through 59
hn	hundredths of a second, in values from 0 through 99
a | p	specifies A.M. or P.M.; if omitted, you must express the time using a 24-hour format

EXAMPLES To display the current system time on your computer, type **time** and press ↵. Press ↵ again to leave the time unchanged, or type the new time and press ↵.

To enter the current time as 1:50 in the afternoon, type **time 1:50p**.

See Also DATE

TREE

Shows a graphical display of the names of all directories on a disk. If you include the /F option, TREE will also show the names of all files on each directory and subdirectory.

SYNTAX

tree [*drive*:][*path*] [/f] [/a]

OPTIONS

[*drive*:][*path*]	drive and location of the directory structure you want to display; if omitted, TREE will use the current drive and directory
/f	displays each directory's files
/a	displays the directory with text characters rather than graphics; this is useful when redirecting the output to a printer that doesn't interpret graphic characters properly

EXAMPLES To view the names of all directories on the current drive and directory, type **tree**. To list all the directories and their files on drive A, pausing after each screenful, type **tree a:\ /f | more**.

To print a copy of the full directory tree on the current drive, type **tree \ > prn**. To print a list of all files in all directories using a text display, type **tree \ /f /a > prn**.

See Also CHDIR, DIR, MKDIR, MORE, Lessons 2 and 4

TYPE

Provides a quick and easy way to look at the contents of a file. If the file that you display contains ASCII text characters only, the output will be quite readable. However, if you use TYPE to display a program, spreadsheet, database, or some word processing files, the display will consist of strange graphics characters and the computer might even beep occasionally.

To interrupt the TYPE command, press Ctrl+Break (or Ctrl+C).

To view a file from the DOS Shell, select the file in the File Display window. Then select File ➤ View File Contents or press F9.

T

SYNTAX

type [*drive:*][*path*]*filename*

OPTIONS

[*drive:*][*path*]*filename*	drive, directory location, and name of the file you want to view

EXAMPLES To view the contents of a file named READ.ME on the current drive and directory, type

type read.me

See Also DOSKEY, EDIT, MORE, PRINT, Lesson 3

U

UNDELETE

Allows you to restore files that were erased with the DEL or ERASE commands. UNDELETE provides three levels of protection against deletion: Delete Sentry (highest level), Delete Tracker (medium level), and MS-DOS (lowest level). The MS-DOS level of tracking is provided automatically when you turn on your computer and does not require you to load the memory-resident portion of UNDELETE.

DOS 6 provides a version of UNDELETE for Windows that will be available if you chose to install it during setup. Please see Lesson 5 for details on using UNDELETE for DOS and UNDELETE for Windows. For additional information on UNDELETE's command-line options, type **help undelete** or **undelete /?**.

See Also DEL, DELTREE, RMDIR, UNFORMAT, Lessons 4 and 5

UNFORMAT

Restores a local disk erased with the FORMAT command. When DOS reformats a hard disk, it doesn't actually delete the data on that hard disk (unless you specified the /U switch); it simply clears the root directory and deletes the file allocation tables (FATs).

SYNTAX

```
unformat drive: [/l] [/test] [/p]
```

OPTIONS

drive:	the drive from which you want to recover directories and files
/l	lists all files and subdirectories found; if /L is omitted, only fragmented subdirectories and files will be listed
/p	sends output messages to LPT1 printer port

/test	shows how information would be recreated, but does not unformat the disk (don't be alarmed by the CAUTION messages; this switch performs a simulation only)

EXAMPLES The command **unformat a:** restores an accidentally formatted floppy disk in drive A.

To see whether files might be deleted or truncated while UNFORMAT is restoring drive D, but without actually unformatting the drive, type

```
unformat d: /l /test
```

See Also DELTREE, FORMAT, UNDELETE, Lesson 5

VER

Displays the number of the version of DOS that's currently running on your computer.

SYNTAX

ver

VOL

Displays a volume (disk) label assigned with the FORMAT or LABEL command. The label appears whenever you use the DIR, LABEL, TREE, or CHKDSK commands.

To view this information from the DOS Shell, select Options ➤ Show Information. The disk's volume label (if there is one) is shown as the Disk Name.

SYNTAX

vol [*drive*:]

OPTIONS

drive: the drive whose label you want to see; if omitted, the current drive is assumed

EXAMPLES To see if the disk in drive A has been assigned a label, type **vol a:**. If the disk has no label assigned, DOS will display the message "Volume in drive A has no label." If a label is assigned to the disk, DOS will display the message "Volume in drive A is *name*," in which *name* is the volume label.

See Also FORMAT, LABEL

VSAFE

VSafe is a memory-resident program that continuously monitors your computer for viruses and displays a warning message when it detects a virus or a change to certain system files and programs. VSafe is discussed in Lesson 5. For information on command-line options, type **help vsafe** or **vsafe /?**.

See Also MSAV, Lesson 5

XCOPY

XCOPY is an extended version of the COPY command that can copy files (except hidden and system files) from subdirectories beneath the current directory, creating subdirectories on the destination disk as needed. It also allows you to copy files that have been changed since the last XCOPY command or since a particular date.

SYNTAX

xcopy [*drive1*:][*path1*]*source* [[*drive2*:][*path2*]*destination*] [/a | /m] [/d:*date*] [/p] [/s [/e]] [/v] [/w]

OPTIONS

[*drive1*:][*path1*]*source*	drive, directory location, and name of the source file or files; *source* can include wildcards (* and ?) and must include either a drive or a path
[*drive2*:][*path2*]*destination*	drive, directory location, and name of the destination file or files; *destination* can include wildcards (* and ?)
/a	copies files that have archive attributes set, without changing the attributes
/m	copies files that have archive attributes set and turns the attributes off
/d:*date*	copies source files modified on or after the specified date
/p	prompts for confirmation before creating each destination file
/s	copies all source directories and subdirectories that aren't empty
/e	copies all source subdirectories, including empty ones (you must use /S with /E)

/v	verifies each file as it is written to the destination file
/w	waits for you to press a key before copying

EXAMPLES To copy the current directory (but not its subdirectories) from drive A to the \MISC directory on drive C, type **xcopy a: c:\misc**.

To copy all of your spreadsheet files with the extension .WK? from all directories on hard disk drive C to the floppy disk in drive A, type the commands below (you can omit the first command if the current drive is C).

```
c:
cd \
xcopy *.wk? a:\ /s
```

Because the /S option is used and the copy was initiated from the root directory, all files with the .WK? extension will be copied. New directories will be created on drive A as needed.

To copy all files with the extension .DBF from the \DBASE directory and its subdirectories on drive C to drive A only if those files were created or modified on or after December 1, 1993, type

```
xcopy c:\dbase\*.dbf a:\ /s /d:12-1-93
```

NOTES

- If the destination does not contain an existing directory and does not end with a backslash (\ ), XCOPY will ask if the target location is a file (F) or directory (D). Press **F** to copy the source files to a file or **D** to copy the source files to a directory.
- Unlike DISKCOPY, XCOPY can copy to disks of any size or capacity and from hard disks to floppy disks, and vice versa. However, XCOPY does not copy hidden files or system files.

See Also ATTRIB, COPY, DISKCOPY, MSBACKUP, Lesson 4

INSTALLING DOS 6

Upgrading to DOS 6 from a previous version of DOS really is a breeze. In this appendix you'll learn how to use the SETUP program that comes with your DOS package to install DOS 6. You'll also learn how to use the EXPAND command to decompress and copy selected DOS system files to your computer.

Because most newly purchased IBM-compatible personal computers already have some version of DOS installed on them, I won't explain how to install DOS on a computer that has never run DOS before or how to upgrade from OS/2 to DOS 6. Please refer to the Microsoft MS-*DOS 6 User's Guide* if you need help completing those tasks.

GETTING READY

DOS 6 weighs in at a hefty 4 megabytes (approximately 4,200,000 bytes). Therefore, the hard disk on which you install DOS 6 must have at least that amount of free space. You can use the CHKDSK command to find out how much space is available. If you need to make room for DOS 6, back up your files and then delete the ones you don't want.

If you plan to install all the optional versions of Undelete, Backup, and Anti-Virus, you'll need about 6 MB of free disk space.

HEADING OFF POTENTIAL PROBLEMS AT THE PASS

Chances are excellent that your upgrade to DOS 6 will be as smooth as ice cream on a summer day. However, it might be worthwhile to preview situations that can prevent SETUP from completing its job. If your system falls into the categories listed below, please refer to the *MS-DOS 6 User's Guide* for special procedures to follow before you upgrade to DOS 6.

- You are running a disk compression program.
- You have a hard disk that is incompatible with SETUP, is supported by a device driver, or is malfunctioning. The following partitions and devices require special handling: Priam or Everex partitions, SyQuest removable hard disks, Vfeature Deluxe partitions, Novell partitions, UNIX or XENIX partitions, Bernoulli drives or caches, Disk Manager partitions, and SpeedStor Bootall partitions.

- Your hard disk has too many primary partitions or has incompatible primary DOS partitions.
- Your computer uses a password protection program.

PREPARING FOR SETUP

Before you upgrade to DOS 6, you must prepare one or two Uninstall disks, disable some memory-resident programs, and disable automatic message services. These three tasks are discussed below.

Preparing Uninstall Disks

SETUP creates an Uninstall floppy disk to safeguard the files on your computer while you're installing DOS 6. You can use this disk later if you need to undo the DOS 6 installation and return to a previous version of DOS.

Your Uninstall disk must be usable in floppy drive A, and it shouldn't contain any files that you want to keep. The disk can be newly formatted or unformatted. SETUP will format the disk and erase any existing files automatically.

If you're using a 360 KB disk, you'll need two Uninstall disks. Label the disks **DOS 6 Uninstall 1** and **DOS 6 Uninstall 2**, and include the current date on each label. If you're using disks with capacity greater than 360 KB, you'll need only one Uninstall disk. Label this disk with the title **DOS 6 Uninstall** and the current date.

Disabling Memory-Resident Programs

Some memory-resident programs can prevent SETUP from working properly. These include the deletion protection program DELWATCH, third-party anti-virus programs, such as VSafe (VSAFE.COM), and disk-caching programs other than SMARTDrive. You should disable commands that start those programs. To do this, open AUTOEXEC.BAT and CONFIG.SYS in a text editor, such as EDIT or EDLIN. Then convert startup commands for the memory-resident programs to comments.

You do not need to disable the command for SMARTDrive (SMARTDRV.EXE).

To convert a command to a comment so that DOS will ignore it during startup, type **rem** followed by a space at the beginning of the line. For instance, the line **rem c:\cpav\vsafe.com** would prevent DOS from starting the Central Point Software anti-virus program VSafe.

After disabling the commands in CONFIG.SYS and AUTOEXEC.BAT and saving your changes, press Ctrl+Alt+Del to restart your computer.

Disabling Automatic Messages

You should turn off any automatic message services before you upgrade to DOS 6. Message services include network pop-up menus or announcements that appear when electronic mail arrives or printing completes. Please see the documentation for your message service for instructions on disabling messages.

Running Setup

With the three preparation steps completed, you're ready to install DOS 6. The SETUP screens will prompt you through the entire process, so read each screen carefully. You'll have many chances to abandon the setup if any problems occur or you change your mind.

If DOS 6 is installed already and you just want to add the optional Backup, Undelete, or Anti-Virus programs, skip to the section "Installing the Optional Programs," later in this appendix.

Now, start your computer, grab your DOS 6 setup disks, and complete the steps below.

1. Insert Setup Disk 1 in floppy drive A or B.

2. If you inserted the disk in drive A, type the command **a:** and press ↵ (the Enter key) to switch to drive A. If you inserted the disk in drive B, type **b:** and press ↵.
3. Type **setup** and press ↵.
4. SETUP will check your system configuration and make sure there's enough free space on your hard disk. If it finds any problems, SETUP will display an error message and further instructions.

If you've installed DOS 6 at least once before, SETUP may ask you to delete the file BEFSETUP.MSD. Press **Y** *to continue.*

5. If the preliminaries went well, a Welcome screen will appear. Press ↵ to proceed with the setup, or press F1 to get help before continuing. If you want to exit SETUP immediately, press F3 twice.
6. SETUP will check your system settings for the DOS type, MS-DOS path, and the screen display. If all settings are correct, simply press ↵. To change a setting, press ↑ or ↓ to highlight the setting you want, and press ↵. Now follow the screen instructions to select alternatives. You can change the DOS type to MS-DOS (the default), COMPAQ, ZENITH, or OTHER. You can change the MS-DOS path to install DOS on a directory other than C:\DOS. You can also choose to use a different screen display with DOS.
7. SETUP will let you decide which version of Backup, Undelete, and Anti-Virus to install. For each program, you can choose *MS-DOS only*, *Windows only*, *Windows and MS-DOS*, or *None*. The default setting is MS-DOS only. To change a setting, use the ↑ and ↓ keys to highlight the setting you want to change, and press ↵. Next, use the arrow keys to highlight the new setting and press ↵.

In Step 7 you can choose Windows settings only if Windows is currently installed on your system.

8. If you chose one of the Windows installations in Step 7, SETUP will ask you to verify the path for Microsoft Windows and press ↵.

9. To begin installing, press **Y**. To cancel the installation, press F3 twice.
10. Follow the screen prompts and insert new disks as needed.
11. After SETUP copies the DOS files, it will prompt you to remove all disks from the floppy drives and press ↵.
12. Finally, SETUP will prompt you to restart the computer by pressing ↵ again.

If you see the message "Insert disk with batch file," simply insert Setup Disk 1 in the floppy drive and press any key to continue.

INSTALLING THE OPTIONAL PROGRAMS

Backup, Undelete, and Anti-Virus are optional programs that come with DOS 6. You can install them for use with the DOS command prompt, Windows, or both DOS and Windows. Table A.1 shows the amount of disk space you'll need to install each optional program.

TABLE A.1: Disk Space Requirements for the Optional DOS 6 Programs

	ANTI-VIRUS	BACKUP	UNDELETE
Windows Only	786,432	884,736	278,528
DOS Only	360,448	901,120	32,768
Windows & DOS	1,032,192	1,785,856	278,528

Typically, you'll install the optional programs when you upgrade to DOS 6. However, you can install them later if you wish. This would be useful if you installed Windows after you installed DOS 6, and now you want to add the Windows versions of these optional programs. Perhaps you installed the Windows versions initially and now want to run the programs from the DOS command prompt. Or maybe you just didn't have enough hard disk space available when you first installed DOS 6.

You can install the optional programs for Windows only if Windows is installed.

To run SETUP just to install the optional programs, complete the first two steps listed in "Running Setup," above. When you get to Step 3, type the command **setup /e** and press ↵. Now complete Steps 4 through 10.

CREATING A DOS 6 STARTUP DISK

A *startup disk* is useful for booting a computer that doesn't have hard disks, or as a safety valve in case you cannot start your system from the hard disk. To make a startup disk, grab a fresh floppy disk (formatted or unformatted) that will work in drive A. Label the disk **DOS 6 STARTUP** and include the current date. Now, complete the first two steps of the setup procedure (see "Running Setup," above). When you get to Step 3, type the command **setup /f /m** and press ↵. Follow the screen prompts to complete the remaining steps.

SETUP erases existing files from the disk before it copies the DOS 6 startup files. Therefore, be sure that your startup disk doesn't contain files that you want to keep.

SUMMARY OF OPTIONAL SETUP SWITCHES

You've already learned how to perform special setup tasks by adding switches to the SETUP command line. Table A.2 summarizes all the optional switches that you can use with SETUP.

TABLE A.2: Summary of Switches for Setup

SWITCH	MEANING
/b	Displays Setup screens in monochrome instead of color
/e	Installs the Windows and DOS optional programs Undelete, Backup, and Anti-Virus
/f	Installs a minimal DOS 6 system on a floppy disk (especially useful with the /M switch)
/h	Uses default Setup options
/i	Turns off hardware detection (useful if your monitor cannot display the Setup screens properly)
/m	Installs a minimal DOS 6 system (especially useful with the /F switch)
/q	Copies DOS files to the hard disk but does not restart the system with the DOS 6 operating system
/u	Installs DOS even if Setup detects disk partitions that might be incompatible with DOS 6. DO NOT use this switch without contacting Microsoft Product Support first.

RESTORING YOUR PREVIOUS VERSION OF DOS

When you installed DOS 6, SETUP created a directory named \OLD_DOS.1 on your hard disk and copied the old DOS files to that directory. It also copied your AUTOEXEC.BAT file, your CONFIG.SYS file, and information about the old version of DOS, to the Uninstall disk. (If you install DOS 6 again, the old DOS directory will be named \OLD_DOS.2, then \OLD_DOS.3, and so forth.)

If you have problems with DOS 6 after setup, you can use the Uninstall disk to restore the old version of DOS. However, you can't restore the previous version of DOS if you do any of the following after installing DOS 6:

- Repartition or reformat your hard disk
- Delete or move the IO.SYS and MSDOS.SYS hidden system files
- Delete the \OLD_DOS.X directory
- Install DoubleSpace or another disk-compression program

See the MS-DOS 6 User's Guide for recommendations on how to proceed if your system uses compressed disks.

If you need to restore the old version of DOS, proceed as follows:

1. Insert the Uninstall disk in drive A.
2. Restart the computer by pressing Ctrl+Alt+Del.
3. Follow the instructions on your screen.

Always use your most recent Uninstall disk to restore the prior version of DOS. Otherwise, you may have problems.

If you receive some error messages when you run Windows after uninstalling DOS 6, don't worry. Simply follow the screen instructions. Windows should work correctly in the future.

DELETING OLD DOS FILES

You can recover disk space occupied by the old version of DOS. If you're *absolutely sure* that you'll never need to restore the old version of DOS, type **deloldos** at the command prompt and press ↵. When prompted, you can press **Y** to delete the old DOS files and the \OLD_DOS.X directory. If you press any other key, you'll exit without deleting any files.

The DELOLDOS command deletes itself automatically after it removes the old DOS files.

EXPANDING A DOS FILE FROM THE SETUP DISKS

DOS 6 system files are stored in a compressed form on the installation disks to reduce the number of disks required. Compressed files are completely useless unless they're expanded first.

The SETUP program expanded the system files automatically when you installed DOS 6. Fortunately, you don't have to go through the entire SETUP procedure to copy just a few files from the installation disks. Instead, you can use the EXPAND command to copy compressed files to a usable form. This can be handy if you've erased a DOS 6 file from your hard disk accidentally, or you need to copy compressed files that you didn't install originally.

The format of DoubleSpace compressed files is completely different from that of compressed files on the DOS installation disks.

FINDING A COMPRESSED FILE ON YOUR INSTALLATION DISKS

Compressed files have extensions that end with an underscore character, as in XCOPY.EX_ (the compressed version of XCOPY.EXE) or DOSSHELL.CO_ (the compressed version of DOSSHELL.COM). To learn which disk contains the compressed file you want, insert the DOS 6 Setup Disk 1 in a floppy drive. Then use the EDIT command to open the file PACKING.LST, which isn't compressed.

For example, type **edit a:packing.lst** if your setup disk is in floppy drive A. Scroll through the file until you find the compressed file name, its corresponding expanded file name, and the disk number you're looking for. Exit the Editor (select File then Exit from the menus), insert the correct disk in the floppy drive, then use EXPAND to copy the file in expanded form.

The packing list file is quite long. To print it for easy reference, type **edit a:packing.list** *and press ↵. Then open the File menu, select Print, and press ↵. Finally, select File ➤ Exit. Lesson 8 provides a quick tour through the Editor.*

COPYING A COMPRESSED FILE IN EXECUTABLE FORM

You can copy the file DOSSHELL.CO_, for example, from the disk in drive A to the \DOS directory on drive C with the command below:

```
expand a:\dosshell.co_ c:\dos\dosshell.com
```

To have EXPAND prompt for all the information it needs, simply type **expand** and press ↵. EXPAND will ask you to enter the path and name of the compressed file. Then it will ask for the path and name for the expanded file.

INDEX

Note: Boldfaced page numbers indicate definitions of terms and principal discussions of primary topics and subtopics. Italic page numbers indicate illustrations.

NUMBERS AND SYMBOLS

A

B

C

D

E

F

N

R

S

T

U

V

W

X

9 781583 482148

www.ingramcontent.com/pod-product-compliance
Lightning Source LLC
Chambersburg PA
CBHW062100050326
40690CB00016B/3156
* 9 7 8 1 5 8 3 4 8 2 1 4 8 *